A
HISTORY LOVER'S GUIDE
TO
LOUISIANA

A
HISTORY LOVER'S
GUIDE
TO
LOUISIANA

by Mary Ann Wells

QRP BOOKS

Baton Rouge / Brandon

Copyright 1990 by
Quail Ridge Press, Inc.

All Rights Reserved

Manufactured in the United States of America
Designed by Barney McKee
Library of Congress Catalog Card Number: 90-8100

Library of Congress Cataloging-in-Publication Data

Wells, Mary Ann, 1944-
   A history lover's guide to Louisiana / by Mary Ann Wells.
       p.   cm.
  ISBN 0-937552-37-2 : $12.95
   1. Louisiana—Description and travel—1981Guide-books.
2. Historic sites—Louisiana—Guide-books. 3. Automobiles—Road
guides—Louisiana. 4. Louisiana—History, Local. I. Title.
F367.3.W45 1990
917.6304'63—dc20   90-8100

Contents

Introduction

History lovers want more than good food, comfortable lodgings and entertainment when they travel. They want to visit places where the ordinary world of other times can be experienced, places that reflect a true picture of the past. They want spiritual fulfillment as well as destinations where momentous events transpired.

Louisiana offers history lovers opportunities for travel adventures as well as the spriritual fulfillment that all too often is elusive. Louisiana allows travelers to dip into cultures, traditions and customs that bring the dimensions of her past into focus.

The state abounds with historic sites, gracious antebellum homes, and exotic memories of the past. Many volumes would be necessary to contain them all. This book contains stories and practical traveling information that can guide readers to many specific sites as well as serve as a basic orientation for other journeys history lovers may wish to map out on their own.

My own journeys in Louisiana have been ones of adventure and discovery. Perhaps one of the most fascinating people with whom I became better acquainted along the way was Jean Laffite. Though his last name is commonly spelled Lafitte, he spelled it Laffite. In *A History Lover's Guide to Louisiana* his name is spelled Laffite when referring to the man and Lafitte when referring to the places and institutions named for him that have chosen that spelling.

For travelers who prefer mild weather, the best time to visit Louisiana may be from October through April. Summers are hot and steamy. They come early and stay late. There are some winter days that require an overcoat but "cold spells" seldom last for more than a few days at a stretch. Umbrellas may prove useful most of the year. History lovers always need to wear their walking shoes. To be comfortable while traveling in Louisiana, cotton clothing, worn in layers during the winter, is probably the best bet.

Louisiana is a very relaxed and casual place. Visitors should not be surprised if various enterprises don't open or close on a precise schedule. Travelers should call or write to verify hours and admission fee policies for any given day at special attractions.

One of the best sources for general information on traveling in the state is the Louisiana Office of Tourism, Box 94291, Baton Rouge, LA 70804-9291. Telephone 800-334-8626 or in Louisiana 504-342-8119.

Mary Ann Wells

1

The *Coureurs de Bois* Trail
East/Central Louisiana Highways

I am running through the woods, a child of my own times, wrapped in the cocoon of my automobile, racing down the levees, through the pine forests, across the bayous, escaping the crowds and the shopping malls, distancing myself from the constraints of cities and towns. I am a spiritual descendant of the *coureurs de bois*, the French Canadian woods runners, who ventured out into the great unknown of America called Louisiana in the 17th century.

The *coureurs de bois* were the first Europeans to savour Louisiana's freedom, the first white men to touch the essence of her being. Heart spoke to heart. A love affair began. The *coureurs de bois* ventured deeper and deeper into the wilderness. They neglected their European upbringing, set up housekeeping with mother nature, became children of the forests.

Now on Louisiana's highways I am hot on their trail. My car windows are down. I smell freedom in the air. I hear it in the wind. I catch a fleeting glimpse of it darting through the thick woods and skirting around the edges of the towns.

I have my priorities—traveling to places where a sense of the past, of momentous events, great tragedy and everyday life can be found in quantities sufficient to offer a feeling of spiritual fulfillment. Mystery and romance come as a bonus. And though my route detours through towns and cities occasionally, I still find most places of my search, of my liking, wrapped in a thin blanket of tranquility, the same blanket of tranquility, perhaps slightly thicker at the time, that warmed the souls of the *coureurs de bois*.

My journeys along the *coureurs de bois* trails often begin at Vidalia and the Mississippi River bridge.

The tantalizing visions fading and expanding in the rearview mirror always lure me to the river bank. One of the best viewing spots of the mythical river city of Natchez is at the north end of Riverside Street in the vicinity of the West Bank Eatery. Sandbars come and go, the river swallowing up and spitting out at whim. In other times, when dueling was illegal in Mississippi and Vidalia was out of the immediate reach of the Louisiana law, hot-tempered Natchez planters and easily-insulted gentry sought satisfaction on Vidalia's sandbars. Perhaps the most well-remembered confrontation here was between Jim Bowie of Opelousas and Samuel Wells of Natchez on one side and Thomas Maddox and his cohorts on the other. The face-off took place near the foot of the north bridge on September 19, 1827. Tempers cooled, and the duel was called off. Bowie and Wells later said they didn't remember what prompted the challenge in the first place, but before they could get off the sandbar a melee erupted into one of the bloodiest free-for-alls ever recorded in the area. Bowie was shot and stabbed so many times (according to a newspaper account of the event) that a man of lesser legendary dimensions would surely not have survived.

Vidalia's flat, black fields were the source of many Natchez fortunes. The planters preferred the high bluffs on the east side of the river for their homes because the west side flooded regularly.

Winter comes to Vidalia with almost immediate promises of spring, quickly offering swollen buds and tender sprouts. I am here in winter, but already the first green blades are poking through the brown grass. Herds of cattle graze on the levee mowing the winter rye. A cold front pushes down hard, reaching too far south, sprinkling dry, sugar-like snow across the flat fields. I'm as nervous as the birds scurrying along the roadside. What are we supposed to do in the snow?

Drive on.

US 84 and US 65 come across the river at Vidalia and head out across the flatness to Ferriday where US 65 and LA 15 veer north. I veer with them. The powdery snow blows from the west. Ferriday once boasted of favorite sons, Jerry Lee Lewis and Howard K. Smith, on a billboard. The sign is gone now. But everyone remembers Jerry Lee and his cousins, Mickey Gilley and Jimmy Swaggart. They were hometown boys, too.

At Clayton, US 65 goes northeast and LA 15 goes northwest. I go with LA 15, headed across the Tensas towards Sicily Island. The snow melts as soon as it hits my windshield. The highway is a solid channel between the winter mush of the cotton fields. The only bright colors in the winter world are the red, yellow and blue cotton wagons with lint still clinging to their mesh sides. A grove of oaks—grey, leafless trees keeping each other company in their close circle— stand on the high spot of a field. Clumps of mistletoe hang from the oaks' bare branches. Limestone outcrops form a ridge. I ride through the landscape searching for the places where the ghosts

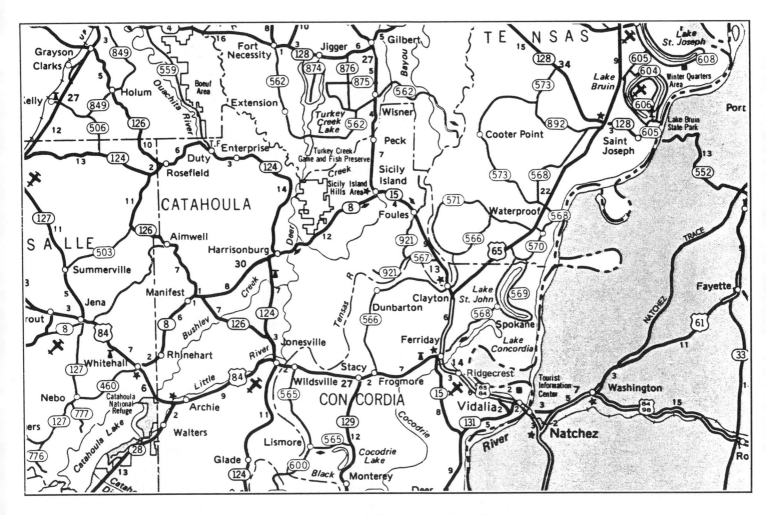

of the woods runners linger, but they don't linger anywhere long.

I listen to the legend of Sicily Island. Supposedly, an early European arrival said the place looked like his homeland, Sicily, and the name stuck. Back in 1870 an attempt by a group of Russian Jews to colonize the area failed due to their lack of expertise as farmers. Some historians believe one of the most decisive battles of the Natchez Indian Uprising (1729-32) took place here at Battleground Plantation, LA 15 north, in 1729.

Ancient Indian mounds from the Marksville, Coles Creek and Mississippian periods—a time span from before the birth of Christ to A.D. 1600—dot the area.

LA 8 goes west from Sicily Island, and I follow past a field of millet stubble, a swamp, a deer stand. I am moving through, by, and around images. A drawbridge spans the Ouachita (wash-i-taw) at Harrisonburg. Houseboats are moored on the river. I stop at the Catahoula Parish courthouse and read the historic markers. "Fort Beauregard—one-half mile west was one of four forts built by Confederates in May 1863 to prevent the ascent of Federal gunboats on the Ouachita River. It was abandoned in 1863 but was reoccupied in 1864.''

A museum in the courthouse displays Civil War relics and recalls the days during the war when Federal gunboats shelled the town and the Confederates abandoned Fort Beauregard. Also on display are prehistoric Native American artifacts found in the area. An ancient mound along LA 8 at LA 124 is said to have been both a religious and commercial center in prehistoric times. The Harrisonburg Methodist Church, on LA 8, is still full of bullet holes, souvenirs of the Civil War.

A ridge rises behind the town. LA 8 curls around the base of the ridge. Houses hide up on the pine rock rises. Huckleberry bushes cluster in the underbrush. The patchwork road, abstracts of asphalt fitted together to make a pavement, is the main stream for dozens of tributary logging trails. In cleared spots white frame farmhouses are encircled with deeply recessed porches.

Just beyond Rhinehart, LA 8 rejoins US 84, heading northwest. The snow is memory. Louisiana Colonial Trail markers remind travelers that early settlers and emigrants from the southeastern states trekked through the wilderness along this route.

Plum thickets nestle at the base of the hills of Jena, a town with fast food fill-up stations lined up along the highway eagerly greeting travelers. Just off US 84 in the turn-of-the-century village of Good Pine, which snuggles so close to the boundaries of Jena you don't know when you've left one and entered the other, is the La Salle Parish Museum. (The La Salle Parish Water Tower on the north side of US 84 is across the highway from the village.) A Victorian cottage with a wraparound porch, the museum, circa 1906, was originally built to serve as headquarters for the Good Pine Lumber Company. The setting in a real-life village lends the museum a quiet charm.

The pine hills could have inspired the Irish-named town of Tullos, about halfway between Jena and Winnfield, but local legends claim the town was named for Joe Tullos, and there is a monument to that gentleman near the New Union Baptist Church. The area abounds in legends. La Salle is said to have smoked the peace pipe with a Choctaw chief here, while other legends claim the ''Natchez Treasure'' is buried somewhere in the area. The Natchez Treasure, according to old-timers, is believed to contain ''sacks of gold, diamond-studded jewelry and lumps of silver the size of cannon balls.''

The forests are deep and thick for a space, then clear-cut on up US 84 along the way to Winnfield, a town where legendary politicians

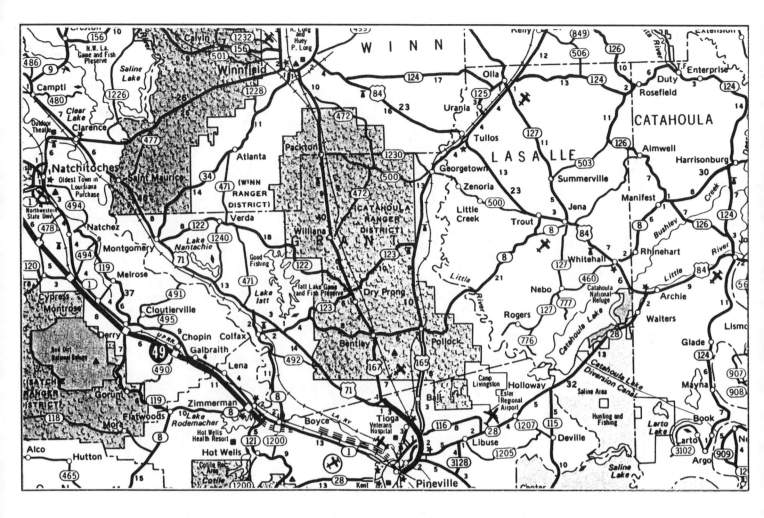

were born. Earl K. Long Memorial Square, Elm Street, is the site of
the Long home, the birthplace of Huey and Earl. Though the house
is gone, the straight, clean street climbing up a short hill retains the
aura of an earlier age. A statue of Earl, who served three terms as
governor, dominates the park-like square. Flowering quince, bridal
wreath, cedars, oaks and pines shelter walkways and picnic areas.
US 84 twists and turns through town with ample signs directing
travelers to the Earl K. Long State Commemorative Area.

    A few miles short of Natchitoches (nakatosh) at Clarence, US 84
crosses US 71. About seven miles north on US 71 is Campti, a rural
village unanxious for the hurry and bother of modern cities. The
Great Raft, the mammoth log jam that once blocked passage on the
Red River for over 160 miles, reached here on its southern end.
Back down US 71 the highway runs through the thick green woods
and empty spaces to Pineville and LA 28. LA 28, northeast, cuts out
through the forest, then across the low places where the highway
becomes a levee between the swampy reaches of Catahoula Lake.
Fishermen stake out their territories along the water. Boats slip down

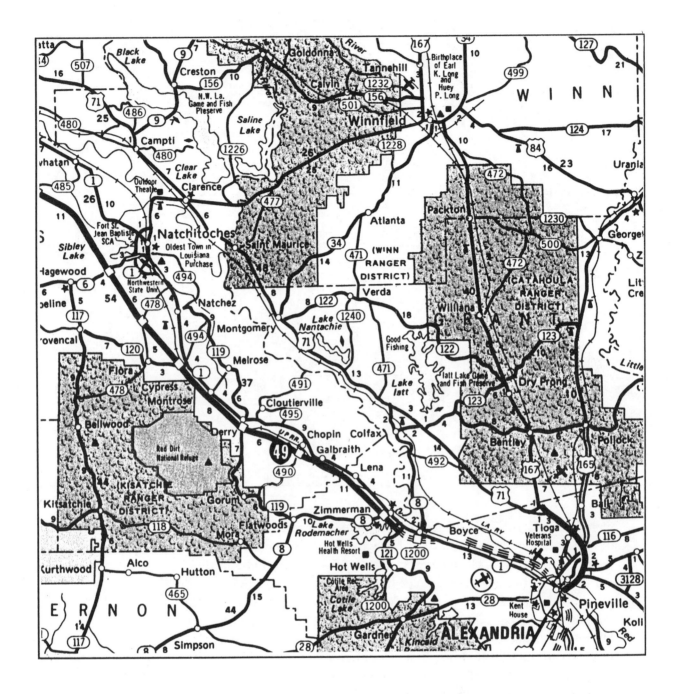

the levee to the lake's edge. Cows graze in palmetto groves. Over 5,000 acres here are included in the Catahoula National Wildlife Refuge, an area set aside for migrating waterfowl and native wildlife. White-tailed deer and bobcats freely roam the refuge. LA 28 joins US 84 between Walters and Archie.

Going east, US 84 parallels the Little River all the way to Jonesville. The town is believed to be the site of the Indian village of Anilco referred to in the De Soto expedition's records. Historic markers at the intersection of US 84 and LA 124 tell of the passing of the expedition through the area in 1540s as well as the story of the

Natchitoches/Natchez Trail, one of the old Spanish trails which became a favorite route westward for early European settlers. Near the town, four rivers converge. Little River, the Tensas, and the Ouachita flow into the Black at almost the same point.

Traveling backwards over the Nolan Trace, the El Camino Real, the San Antonio Road, and the old Spanish trails, memories of the swarms of westward bound adventurers come at me head-on. Remember Philip Nolan? Edward Everett Hale called him ''The Man Without a Country'' in his famous short story. The story has become so well-known that there is a tendency to forget that it is fiction, and that the real-life Philip Nolan's adventurers far out-dazzle those of his make-believe namesake. A romantic Irishman, a friend of the notorious American General James Wilkinson, a correspondent of Thomas Jefferson, and a map-maker, Nolan often followed the trail that now bears his name, back and forth to Natchez where he sold strings of wild horses he had captured in Texas. Some say he was a smuggler, others that he was an agent for the Spanish or the Americans—maybe both—no one is quite sure. He died in a shoot-out with the Mexican militia in Texas when he was leading an advance troop of a shadowy invasion force. Nolan disappeared into the mysteries which had engulfed much of his life.

Nolan may have passed the Frogmore Indian Mound on his numer-

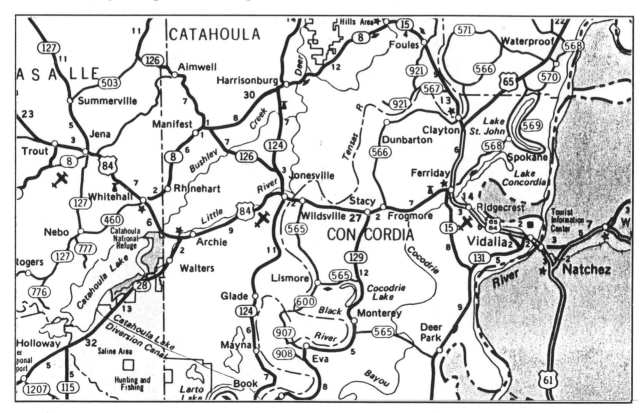

ous journeys back and forth to Texas. It still stands proud, straight and tall at a curve on US 84, right next door to the Frogmore Plantation, circa 1843. Back in Vidalia US 84 heads straight towards the high bluffs of Natchez across the river. But the *coureurs de bois* never felt compelled to end their wanderings, why should we?

From Vidalia, US 65 goes to Waterproof, a town that is said to have been relocated four times because of floods and caved-in river banks. Finally it found a home on a knoll out of the flood waters. The original town site is now across the river in Mississippi. Nearby, Myrtle Grove Plantation, just off US 65 on LA 570, was built in 1810 in prefabricated sections at Louisville, Kentucky, and transported downriver on barges.

Continuing on US 65, up to Newellton, travelers can make the loop around Lake St. Joseph on LA 608, and visit Winter Quarters State Commemorative Area. The house here began as a three-room hunting lodge constructed in 1803 on a Spanish land grant to Job Routh. Routh's daughter later added several more rooms and a

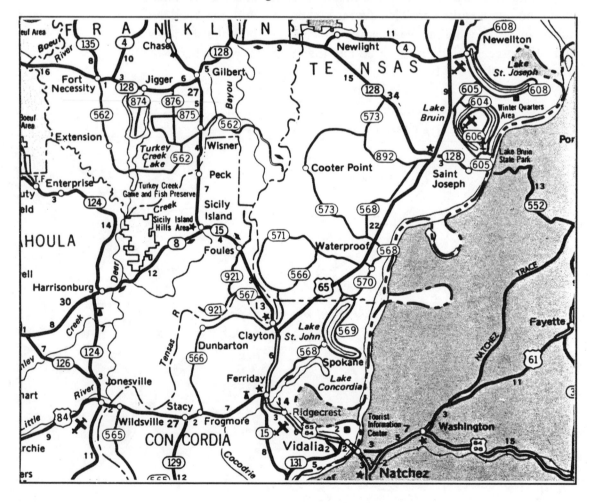

gallery. In 1850, Dr. Haller Nutt, a physician and planter who built
the famouns octagon house, Longwood, at Natchez, Mississippi,
bought Winter Quarters and made the additions that give it the look it
retains to this day. According to legends passed on at the plantation,
over 2,000 acres here were tended by 300 slaves at one time. The
plantation was a complex of boat docks, milk houses, cotton gins, a
sawmill, a machine shop, a hospital, a smokehouse and the other
usual plantation buildings. Dr. Nutt's wife, Julia, loved Winter
Quarters so much that she went to extraordinary lengths to preserve
the place when General U. S. Grant's troops were torching the surrounding Confederate countryside. She traveled through hostile lines
to reach General grant at his Milliken's Bend Camp. Mrs. Nutt,
whose husband was a legitimate Union sympathizer, offered to feed
and quarter troops and officers in exchange for the general sparing
her home. Supposedly, General Grant gave his word to bond the
bargain. But in the end, his troops chose to give a narrow interpretation to the agreement. They spared the house but burned all the
support buildings, then confiscated all the livestock and provisions on
the place.

Winter Quarters, now a museum, houses many mementoes of the
antebellum and Civil War era. One of the most interesting souvenirs
of those times is a book written by Dr. Nutt entitled *Book of Receipts,
Prescriptions, Useful Rules, Etc., for Plantation and other Purposes.*
Medical treatments for people and animals, advice on measuring the
height of trees, computing the volume of a cistern, making white-
wash that will last a century, eliminating cockroaches and how to
cure an egg-sucking dog are some of the issues addressed in the
book. Reprints are on sale at the museum.

A few weeks later, I come back to Vidalia, to the river bank and
take LA 131 to LA 15 and follow it, and the Mississippi, southward.
The road hugs the twists, turns and curves of the snaky old river.
Flocks of red-winged blackbirds rise from the grassy fields of spring
time. The deserted road wanders through the lush green grass
sprinkled with wildflowers: purple vetch, red clover, daises and wild
mustard. Cows, slightly resembling their Brahman ancestors, graze
on the levee. Occasionally horses peek over the edge. Blue herons
rise over the road. Black dirt, wet muck, gumbo mud is attacked by
discs and plows. Cattle egrets, their white wings tucked close to their
sides, follow the tractor trails, dining on the newly uncovered delica-
cies.

The road wanders on, down and around and over the Old River
control structures. The Black Hawk Plantation advertises its boundaries. The road occasionally crawls up on top of the levee. The river

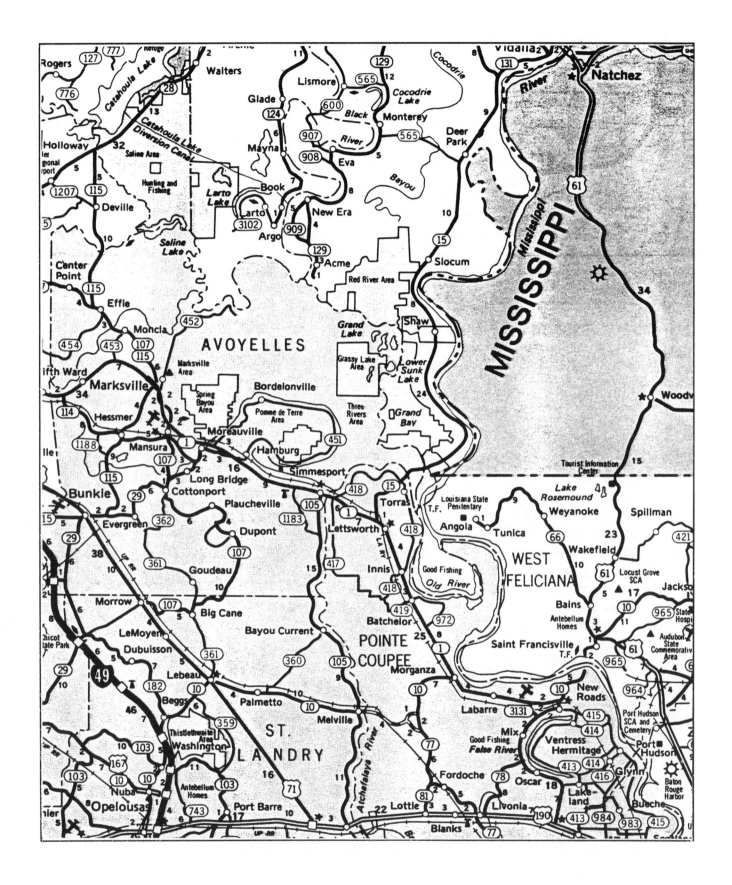

is beyond the bottomland willows. Down in Pointe Coupee Parish, LA 15 runs into LA 1 where wild spider lilies grow in the ditches, crowding along the edges of the roadway with blue-eyed grass and red irises. Pirogues are pulled up under cypress trees along slivers of bayous.

Here, in these vast tracts of near-wilderness where the roads are generally neglected by travelers, you can see the shadow of the *coureurs de bois*, however fleetingly. I head across the Atchafalaya at Simmesport. The bridge is so steep that from a distance I think it is a drawbridge in the up position. I take LA 105 south. Life along the road is so rural and uncomplicated that people on porches wave at my passing car. I wave back. I pass a man walking down the road with a crab net and crocker sack over his shoulder. A ball cap is pulled low over his forehead. He scans the ditches along the road looking for crawfish.

Here's a swamp. There's a marsh. I take LA 360 to LA 10, I intend to go west. Inadvertently, I go east. I end up in Melville brought up short by the Atchafalaya. The ferry's not running today. Folks who want to cross are advised to go south to Krotz Springs. There was a German prisoner-of-war camp here at Melville during World War II. But that's only a memory now, more distant, more alien than the *coureurs de bois*.

It is early morning. The fog is rolling towards me. Ghostly eyes of on-coming car lights never completely materialize. We are alone, my car and me, in the woods.

Vidalia is located on US 65 and 84 about 175 miles upriver from New Orleans.

These journeys along Louisiana's east central highways are best undertaken with well-stocked picnic baskets.

Ample overnight accommodations are available in Alexandria, a few are also available at Vidalia, but are scarce elsewhere. Fast food establishments along the way have the added attraction of restrooms.

For more information contact: Lousisiana Colonial Trails, P. O. Box 8076, Alexandria, LA 71306. Telephone 318-487-5454.

Winter Quarters State Commemorative Area, Route 1, Box 91, Newellton, LA 71357. Telephone 318-467-5439. An admission fee is charged.

Vidalia Chamber of Commerce, P.O. Box 267, Vidalia, Louisiana 71373. Telephone 318-336-7310.

2

Poverty Point

This is the world of the unknown, the place of the ancients, once the home of a people now lost in time. This is a place where the vast empty delta fields hug the bayou banks, holding tightly to a sacred trust. Here six ridges curved into semicircles, laid out in neat rows, stretching up to three-fourths of a mile in length are crowned with a giant effigy bird mound at the top center. Across the fields, forming a rear guard to the city of ridges, a conical mound sits atop a crematorium, a place where the ashes of the unknown people have become one with the earth.

According to a spokesman for the Poverty Point Commemorative Area, "The age, size and character of the structures place them among the most significant finds in America today. The site dates from between 700 and 1700 B.C."

Poverty Point.

Poverty Point Mound.

When Moses was leading the Israelites out of Egyptian bondage, the two main streets of this Louisiana city were aligned with the winter and summer solstices, artisans were creating exquisite crafts and merchants were offering goods for sale from all across the continent.

We are aliens here, traveling across time from cultural dimensions that tend to blind us to ancient reality. These silent fields, so long empty, don't even have a ghost of a memory to whisper in our ear, to remind us of what has gone before. The birds sing. We imagine that their song has not changed. The insects talk to the wind, calling to their kinsmen. In the distance automobile engines buzz and hum, moving across the delta of ancient history. Can we imagine a Native American world dated 1700 B.C.? Our intentions are honorable. We want to understand, but our notion of our own superiority gets in the way. Perhaps this is a place for us to contemplate our own destiny.

We have no name to call the ancient people. No word of theirs we can read, no mark we can decipher to know the name of their city. The earth has reclaimed their material goods and gives up clues of their culture reluctantly. Even the descendants of the people have disappeared, their identity dissolved, their culture absorbed by other peoples and cultures.

The site was discovered many years ago, and named by a plantation owner of European descent who was struggling to farm the area. In antebellum days a mound and a ridge at the site were used as cemeteries because they rose out of the reaches of flood waters. One mound is a burial site for members of a white family; a portion of one of the ridges was a slave cemetery. Not until a visiting scientist photographed Poverty Point from the air in the 1950s was its complexity learned. Up until then it was believed that effigy mounds had not been built this far south.

Scholars say new evidence points to the fact that these unknown people had established a viable culture and city that may be called ''a prehistoric New York City or London.'' Here in northeastern Louisiana prehistoric is defined as the period before A.D. 1680.

A red jasper owl was the city's mascot and symbol. Delicately carved and marked on the bottom with the individual artists' ''signatures,'' many of the owls survive and are among the most numerous of the artifacts extracted from the earth at the site.

Oak trees shroud the bird effigy mound. Walkways wind up a wing tip to the head and then down the spine and tail. The ridges are not always discernible to the naked eye.

This is still a land of secrets, in a deceptively familiar landscape, a place anthropologists and archaeologists are trying to decipher and interpret. The state of Louisiana operates the site. A museum on the grounds regularly shows a movie about the site and exhibits artifacts found here. Included in the exhibitions are fertility effigies, earth

Poverty Point Excavations.

goddesses, clay figurines, red jasper owls, tools and cooking implements. There are ongoing demonstrations of tool making by park personnel. Outside the museum a scale model of the ancient city in a garden setting can be viewed from an observation tower. From here the layout of the ancient city can be more easily grasped. The lookout tower also gives visitors an opportunity to peruse the countryside. The thick jungle-like growth in the woods and brush alongside the bayou hint of the elements the ancients conquered. Usually from April to October, trams ferry visitors around the 400-acre site on an accompanied tour. Throughout the year visitors may walk on a 2.6 mile trail over the ridges to the heart of the old complex, the effigy mound.

According to archaeologists working at Poverty Point, the bird symbol was an important part of religious ceremonies, and the alignment of streets with the solstices is the "earliest one of this nature we have discovered in America." They go on to say, as cultures are measured the one here was very successful, yet it eventually gave way to others more adapted to survival in later times.

The experts tell us the ancient inhabitants built this complex array of earthen mounds and ridges overlooking the Mississippi River flood plain in a very deliberate fashion. They estimate some five million man hours were necessary to build the massive earthworks, a mammoth engineering feat. The central construction consists of the six rows of concentric ridges, which at one time were five to ten feet high. The rows join with four main aisles to suggest an octagonal shape. The ridges probably served as foundations for dwellings. Bayou Maçon, which flows past the site, has eroded some of the original complex and is even now nibbling at the backside of the museum complex. The Arkansas River flowed through the Bayou Maçon channel 20,000 years ago. A thousand years after the inhabitants of Poverty Point disappeared into other cultures and nations, a group called the Coles Creek Indians built six mounds just to the south of the site.

Tail of Bird Effigy Mound.

Four mounds of the Poverty Point period are dramatically visible. The Poverty Point Mound, the bird-shaped effigy, measures about 700 by 800 feet at its base and rises about 70 feet. Motley Mound is located due north of the central village and is similar in size and shape, although the bird form lacks a tail. North of the Poverty Point Mound is a 20-foot-high conical mound called Mound "B." (This is the mound believed to be built over a crematory.) The fourth earthen mound, called Lower Jackson Mound, lies about a mile due south of Poverty Point Mound and is similar in shape and size to Mound "B." Neither Motley Mound nor Lower Jackson Mound are on the park site, but both are visible from the highway (LA 577) that passes through the commemorative area.

In more modern times, steamboats plied up the bayou to pick up cotton at the town of Floyd, three miles north of Poverty Point. Because of the naturally gentle slope, the ancient town site became a commonly used ford in historic times.

In an eclectic mixture of times and people, the museum also chronicles the activities of Jesse James and his cohorts in this area. Jesse and the Younger brothers hung out in and around Epps and Carroll Parish during the period after the Civil War. Some folks say Jesse owned a home at Floyd. He did have a sister who lived near Delhi, and the area is rich with stories and folklore which can be attributed to his stay in the area.

Poverty Point State Commemorative Area is located in West Carroll Parish, northeast of Monroe on LA 577. From I-20 take the Delhi exit on LA 17 for about 16 miles to Epps, then right on LA 134 for about five miles to LA 577 and the commemorative area. There are restrooms and picnic areas at the site. An admission fee is charged.

Fast food is available at Delhi and Epps. Overnight accommodations and restaurants are available at Monroe.

For more information contact: Poverty Point State Commemorative Area, Box 208-A, Epps, Louisiana 71237. Telephone 318-926-5492.

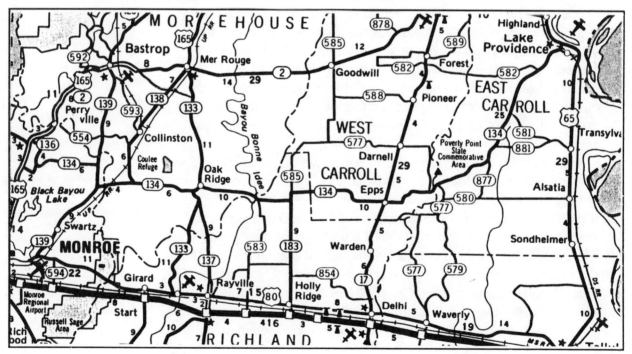

3

Monroe

The Mississippi Delta stretches westward to Monroe and the banks of the Ouachita, then disappears as the west side of the river rises into red hills and piney woods.

The area's first contact with Europeans is shrouded in legends, probabilities, maybes and could have beens.

One enduring story says the Pargoud Indian Mound is the burial place of Wichita, daughter of Ucita. Wichita died of a broken heart after being deserted by a member of the Narváez Expedition which was lost along the Gulf Coast in 1528. She had married the Spaniard after saving his life. Even though the legend is skimpy on details it does name the Spaniard, Juan Ortega. (In Florida there are similar legends of a Juan Ortiz who came to the west coast of Florida looking for the lost Narváez Expedition, was captured by the Indians, saved from execution by an Indian maiden, married and then deserted her. This Juan Ortiz was rescued by the De Soto Expedition in 1539, became an interpreter for De Soto and died in 1542, probably somewhere in southern Arkansas, while traveling with the expedition.)

Other stories say that De Soto may have passed through the area descending the Ouachita to the junction with the Tensas in 1542; Tonti may have passed through looking for La Salle in 1689; Bienville and St. Denis probably visited the area in 1700. White colonists of European ancestry were on the Ouachita in the first half of the 18th century. All in all, the careful qualifications add credibility to the local historians' stories.

Jean Baptiste Filhiol (Don Juan Bautista Fihiol) became the founding father of modern Monroe when in 1785 he established Fort Miro along the banks of the Ouachita. Up until then the area had been known as Prairie des Canots and had been the site of a large trading post and Indian settlement, but no permanent European settlements were made until after the French and Indian War which ended with the Treaty of Paris in 1763.

The site of Fort Miro, named for the Spanish governor of Louisiana, Don Estevan Miro, is commemorated by a historic marker at 424 South Grand Street. A wooden stockade was built on the site by colonists in 1791. Their 1785 petition for the fort is on file at the Ouachita Parish Court House. In it the colonists voice their fears of "demons" and "savages." There is no record that the post was ever attacked or even threatened.

Probably no other person had as much influence on the early days of Fort Miro as Henry Bry. A native of Switzerland, Bry had been persuaded to emigrate to the United States by his cousin, Albert Galatin, who was Thomas Jefferson's Secretary of the Treasury. When the first steamboat, the *President Monroe*, chugged up the Ouachita in 1819, Bry suggested that the town's name be changed. As was true of most of his suggestions, this one was accepted immediately and Fort Miro became Monroe.

The railroad's arrival in Monroe in 1860 rivaled the earlier drama of the steamboat's coming. Several Civil War skirmishes were fought in the area. Two were fought in town, one on August 2 and the other on September 3, 1863. During the siege of Vicksburg, Federal gunboats came up the Ouachita and destroyed the courthouse and other public buildings.

One of the easiest ways for travelers to modern Monroe to explore the area's history is through visits to a series of buildings representing different eras, fashions and styles.

The site of old Fort Miro is on the banks of the river alongside the Isaiah Garrett Law Office Museum at 520 South Grand Street. The museum, circa 1840, is one of the oldest buildings in town. A delegate to the Secession Convention of 1860, Isaiah Garrett was one of seven Louisiana delegates who refused to sign the Ordinance of Secession, claiming that it violated the oath of allegiance he had taken as a cadet at West Point. However, two of his sons served in the Confederate Army, and local storytellers say Mr. Garrett's heart was with the South. The small building's interior is arranged pretty much as it would have been in Garrett's day. Displays of historic documents, photographs, clothing, furniture and miscellaneous memorabilia offer an intimate look at a portion of the city's past.

The Daughters of the American Revolution's Fort Miro Chapter House on the Courthouse Square, 300 block of St. John, shows up on maps as early as 1816 and its construction is of a style that can be dated prior to that time.

Layton Castle, in all its red brick splendor, didn't achieve its regal status until 1910-1912 when Eugenia Stubbs Layton returned from a prolonged stay in Europe. Her simple raised cottage home, circa 1814, had been expanded during the 1860s. With European inspiration as her guide, Eugenia used red bricks fired on the place to

DAR Fort Miro Chapter House.

cover the old walls and added a tower, an arcaded gallery, a turret and *porte cochère* with Romanesque columns. When Henry Bry built the place in 1814, he was a successful businessman and planter of cotton and sugarcane. He owned a commercial brick kiln and dabbled in horticulture. He imported many rare plants and even experimented with silkworm cultivation for awhile. In those days the place was known as Mulberry Grove, and a few descendants of the mulberry trees brought in for the worms can still be seen on the ground. A brick wine house with some of the original bottles Bry used is located next door to the castle. Bry was a delegate to the convention that drafted Louisiana's first state constitution in 1812. Layton Castle, which took its name from a later owner, is located at 1133 South Grand Street. An admission fee is charged but you must make an appointment for a tour.

In the same neighborhood, in the vicinity of the Lower Pargoud Plantation, is the Catalpa Tree Fence, an area also known as Lover's

Layton Castle.

Lane. At 1400 South Grand Street, the Masur Museum of Art houses a permanent collection of eclectic styles including pieces of sculpture, paintings, graphics and photographs. The museum also hosts changing exhibits and juried shows. Admission is free. The museum is closed on Mondays.

When the oak and catalpa canopied South Grand Street crosses US 80, it becomes Riverside Drive, but the quiet, neighborhood atmosphere of elegant old homes and ancient trees continues. At 2006 Riverside Drive the Emy-Lou Biedenharn Foundation opens the doors of its various attractions to visitors. Miss Emy-Lou, as she is remembered locally, was the daughter of the Biedenharn family of Vicksburg, Mississippi, who first bottled Coca-Cola. They moved to Monroe in 1913 and their home Elsong was built in 1914. It is now open for tours, as are its elaborate formal gardens. Miss Emy-Lou loved music and her operatic training prepared her for a successful singing career in Europe. Initially she set up the foundation to fund the Bible Research Center and Museum which is also located here. A large collection of rare Bibles and related artifacts will enthrall biblical scholars and laymen. There is a 16-volume ante-Nicene Christian Library, which contains writings from the first century A.D. to 325; comments on the scriptures written by the Venerable Bede, A.D. 673-735; Greek, Hebrew, Latin and Aramaic Bibles; an original Danish Martin Luther Bible (1550) and nine original Geneva Bibles from 1584 to 1615; originals of the *Biblia Sacra* (1523), the *Beza New Testament* (1596) and the *King James Holy Bible* (1617); and many other translations and versions from across the ages including modern times. Admission is free. The museum, gardens and house are closed on Mondays and national holidays.

The town proudly claims a number of gracious homes in styles ranging from the unpretentious Cox House, circa 1882, and the Greek Revival overseer's house, circa 1835, on the Lower Pargoud Plantation to numerous Queen Anne cottages and Colonial Revivals. Probably the most notable of the Colonial Revivals is the Governor Luther Hall home at 1515 Jackson Street. The Tudor Revival style (Masur Museum is an example), the California Bungalow and the Prairie style are also represented. The most notable of the latter is the Cooley House on South Grand. Built for a Ouachita steamboat captain, the house's layout is meant to resemble a steamboat. Few breezes escape the Cooley house in summer when all 100 of its windows can be opened.

If you're looking for a little bit of Monroe to take home with you, cross the river into West Monroe on DeSiard, and just beyond the cottonseed mill, on Trenton, you'll find a district of antique stores.

Boscobel Cottage.

Contact the visitors bureau for a directory/brochure of all area antique shops and their hours.

For a complete look at the history of the town, venture out into the countryside. About 14 miles south of Monroe on the Ouachita is Bosco, Louisiana, a quaint plantation community along US 165. Here Henry Bry, the same fellow who built what was to become Layton Castle, built Boscobel Cottage in 1820. Used as a residence by Bry until Boscobel the-big-house could be built, the cottage in time became the overseer's house. Owner Kay LaFrance says, ''Boscobel means beautiful woods.'' The cottage today sits in a grove of champion pecan trees and is surrounded by outbuildings including a *garçonnière*, a ''chapel'' which is used as an office and bed-and-breakfast lodge, and a shotgun house that is an inclement weather dining room for the tours and groups who come to lunch here. Usually the luncheons are under the pecan trees on the green expanses of lawn fronting the levee. To either side of the house are vistas of cotton fields.

The big house is no longer standing, but the details of the simple cottage offer clues of what its construction entailed. Framed with cypress and blue poplar, sassafras wood was used in the walls and ceiling of the drawing room and hall. Kay says in antebellum times it was believed the yellow sassafras wood repelled bedbugs and various other insects. The house reflected Federal-West Indies styles when it was built, and though Greek Revival touches were added later, the interior still has distinctly Federal touches. Tours of the house and luncheon are by appointment only. (Telephone 318-325-1550.) If you go, plan to slow down for a bit of storytelling. Kay LaFrance and her family are some of the best storytellers around.

Monroe is located on I-20 and US 80 at US 165. There are ample accommodations in town as well as restaurants and fast food establishments.

For more information contact: Monroe/West Monroe Convention and Visitors Bureau, 1333 State Farm Drive, Monroe, LA 71202. Telephone 318-387-5691.

4

I-20 Interludes

Interstate 20 shoots out across the flat fields of Louisiana from the Mississippi, running a course for the Texas border. Paralleled by US 80, the interstate makes quick work of the miles, while the older road winds along the railroad tracks which twist and turn like a prehistoric sculpture snaking across the earth.

Out on the interstate, hawks perch on utility wires, watching the road, waiting for breakfast to scurry across the open space. Eighteen-wheelers bear down on law-abiding drivers, pushing traffic over the speed limit. Cotton wagons with lint clinging to their sides cluster near gins, willows ring ponds, the smoky morning fog rises as the first light tinges clouds with pink.

The delta looks more immense, more all-encompassing from the interstate. Along US 80 there is an immediate relationship with the land, a closeness to the roadside towns that the interstate sacrifices for speed.

With the mournful lament of *"Jolie Blond"* on the radio you may not feel as far removed from the essence of Cajun Louisiana as you might have expected here in the northern part of the state.

About seven miles from the Mississippi border, Mound, a tiny plantation town, full of tenant houses and dominated by a general store, is one of the first interludes from the interstate. The town was named for the Indian mounds in the area. Most of them have disappeared now, but there is still one plainly visible mound near the general store. Topped with an abandoned farmhouse, it makes a poignant visual statement. Townspeople claim their community is the smallest incorporated town in America.

Moving closer to Monroe, you can detour to Rayville and the site of the first public library in the state.

About 30 miles west of Monroe, Ruston is home of Louisiana Tech University and the Old Dixie Theatre, famous for its Saturday night country music shows. The Lincoln Parish Museum, at 609 North Vienna, is also the local tourist information center. Admission is free. Hours are weekdays from 9 a.m. to 4:30 p.m.

Next stop down the interstate is Grambling, home to the famous

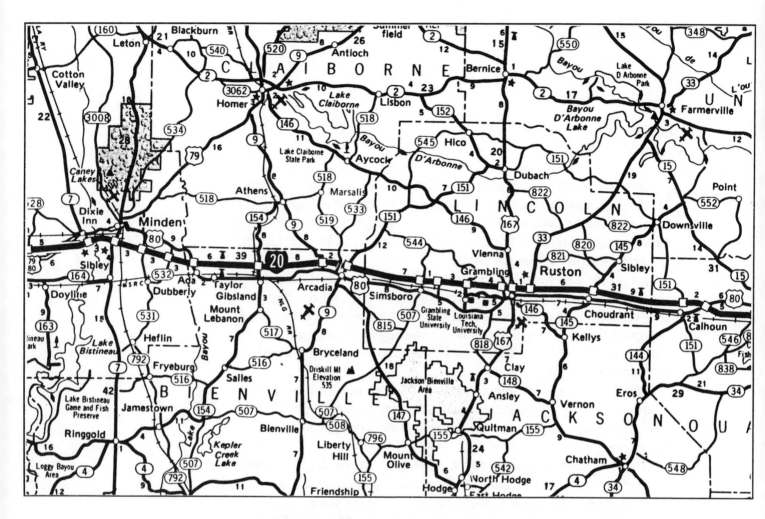

Grambling State University whose football teams and marching bands are legend.

Continuing westward, Mount Lebanon claims the distinction of being one of the few towns to issue its own postage stamps during the Civil War. On LA 154, the Mount Lebanon Baptist Church, circa 1837, is furnished with handmade pews equipped with dividers to separate men and women. The church holds special services including dinner on the grounds the first Sunday in May as part of the Mount Lebanon Homecoming and Tour of Homes. Also on LA 154 is the Stagecoach Trail Museum where the story of Mount Lebanon's days as a stagecoach stop is documented along with displays and exhibits of tools, farm equipment and other antiques. Open Friday—Sunday, 2 to 5 p.m.

The next interlude is at Minden, where travelers must dip deep into the woods to discover the Germantown Colony and Museum. Take

Webster Parish Road 114 northwest of Minden for seven miles. This road meanders through quiet, deserted pine forests before reaching the colony site where the Countess Von Leon, aided by a group of personal freedom devotees, pursued her dead husband's dream and established a commune in 1835.

Descendants of the colonists still live in the area though the commune was disbanded after only 37 years. The countess' cabin and the kitchen-dining hall remain on the site. Open Wednesday through Saturday from 9 a.m. until 5 p.m. and Sunday from 1 to 6 p.m. An admission fee is charged. Telephone 318-377-7564.

Interstate 20 runs east to west across the state from the Mississippi River at Vicksburg, through Shreveport, to the Texas border, a distance of about 195 miles.

For more information and a free map of the state with all the towns and cities along I-20 clearly marked, contact: The   Louisiana Office of Tourism, Box 94291, Baton Rouge, LA 70804-9291. Telephone 800-334-8626, or in Louisiana 504-342-8119.

5

Shreveport

The black towers of Shreveport's skyline could intimidate a history-loving traveler. Shining on the horizon, looming with technological splendor, they seem to promise a modern world devoid of the warmth and charm of the past. The highways and interstate ramps that loop and hurl fast-moving traffic into the heart of the city add to the illusion.

The skyline is misleading.

The traffic races in from the outlying areas to quiet, orderly streets patrolled by policemen on horseback.

Shreveport, on the Red River, has managed to merge high-tech business with a romantic past, dominated by cotton producers nestled on an overland route to the Texas frontier. The resulting lifestyle is dominated by an eclectic mixture of all the best from the past and present. The best nostalgic aspects of the good life, especially an unhurried lifestyle where the Deep South meets the frontier West, are guarded from the economic watchtowers/skyscrapers.

Before settlers of European heritage arrived, Caddo Indians lived in the area. A woodland people remembered locally for their conical earthen houses and sedentary ways, the Caddo became well known after the arrival of Europeans for their ability and expertise with horses. Twenty-five of their tribes belonged to a confederacy when La Salle met them in 1685. Caddoian culture had a clearly defined system of social castes and a religion that dominated daily life.

Caddoian artifacts are featured in displays in the Louisiana State Exhibit Museum in the Art and Historical Wing. Pottery, the implements of everyday life, jewelry, a 1000-year-old cypress canoe—capable of transporting 15 people—are tangible clues of a vanished lifestyle. Murals on the walls represent artists' interpretations of prehistoric Indian culture in the region as well as first encounters with European colonizers at Natchitoches. The museum, on Perishing Boulevard at the State Fairgrounds, is open Tuesday through Saturday, 9 a.m. to 4:30 p.m. Admission is free.

One of the first settlers of European ancestry in the area was Larkin Edwards, a Tennessean, who arrived about 1803. He built a

Louisiana Exhibit Museum.

home at the eastern end of present-day Olive Street. Edwards became an interpreter for the Caddo and as a reward for his service to
the tribe, they reserved a section of land for him when they signed a
treaty with the U.S. government in 1835 ceding their northwestern
Louisiana territory. Edwards later sold the land to the Shreve Town
Company, a group of eight men including William Bennet, James
Cane, Angus McNeil, Bushrod Jenkins, Thomas Sprague, Thomas
Williamson, James Pickett, and Captain Henry Miller Shreve, for
whom the town was named.

A hero of the War of 1812, Captain Shreve is remembered most
often as the man who cleared the Red River of the ''Great Raft''—a
gargantuan log jam that stretched for more than 160 miles (from near
Campti northward) and made the river unnavigable. Commissioned
by the U.S. government in 1832 to clear the raft because moving
military supplies northward was so difficult overland, Shreve, a
native of New Jersey and renowned as a steamboat builder, spent five

years clearing a path in the river from Campti to Fort Towson in Oklahoma. But about 40 years passed before the river was completely cleared of the log jam. Shreve became a founding father of the modern city. In 1836 Shreve Town was incorporated and then renamed Shreveport in 1837. All the while, Texas-bound emigrants were pouring through the new town.

You can walk in the footsteps of the city's founders and the pioneers on their way to Texas at Shreve Square. Tucked under and around the entrance to the Texas Street Bridge which crosses the Red River to Bossier City, the square is in the area of the earliest town site. The first stores, hotels and saloons were built here. A trading post is credited with being Shreveport's first business, while an establishment called the Catfish Hotel comes in a close second. The Old Texas Trail (originally a Caddo Indian trail along a ridge—also called the Texas Wagon Road) through northern Louisiana is easy to follow from the river crossing where the Texas Street Bridge was built, down Texas Street and Texas Avenue on to the Texas border. Commerce Street, which runs parallel to the river—one street up and on the east side of Shreve Square—still shelters some of the buildings known to the cotton factors who conducted their business along the street in the days when Texans hauled their cotton overland to the river. Merchants and livery stable owners who catered to the farmers and factors also had their businesses along the street.

One block south of Shreve Square, the Spring Street Museum is filled with memorabilia of the city's past. Originally built as a bank in 1866, the museum is one of the two oldest buildings still standing in Shreveport. The building housed Tally's Bank and later the original First National Bank of Shreveport. Admission is by donation.

Supposedly the first church services in Shreveport were conducted in 1839 by Episcopal Bishop Leonidas Polk. According to local stories the service was held in a general store/barroom. A cowbell called the faithful to worship. Holy Cross Church, on Texas Avenue at the corner of Cotton Street, contains the altar, pews, French glass windows, chancel rail and credence table from the first church occupied by this pioneer congregation on Fannin Street.

The Louisiana Hayride rang out from the Municipal Auditorium, on Milam, every Saturday night from 1948 to 1960 on radios across the country. Hank Williams, Sr., sang his way to legendary status here. Hank Williams, Jr., was born in the city while his dad was employed by the Hayride. And a little later, rock'n'roll king-to-be Elvis Presley came to town to sing on the Hayride.

The Caddo Parish Courthouse's Texas Street front is graced by the

Captain Shreve.

Confederate Monument, a spot said to be the place where the last Confederate flag was lowered in June 1865. The monument is dedicated to southern men who lost their lives during the Civil War and is topped with a young soldier, rifle in hand, with Clio, the Greek Muse of history, below. At each corner of the base is a bust of a Confederate hero—Robert E. Lee, Stonewall Jackson, P.G.T. Beauregard and Henry W. Allen, the last Confederate governor of Louisiana.

Although, according to local legends, scattered pockets of Confederate resistance remained in isolated areas, the lowering of the Confederate flag in Shreveport when Federal troops arrived June 6, 1865, to occupy the city marked the final surrender of the war.

The Confederate capital of Louisiana from January, 1863, to June, 1865, the city had been protected from Federal troops by major Confederate victories to the south at Pleasant Hill and Mansfield.

For a sample of life in frontier Shreveport, visitors will want to stop by the Pioneer Heritage Center on the LSU campus, 8515 Youree Drive, in the city. Here, volunteers explain how pioneers of primarily Scotch-Irish heritage settled the area, built log cabins or "dogtrots," and honed the skills that were necessary to survive on the frontier. There are demonstrations of some of the skills. Historic buildings that have been moved onto the site include a log dogtrot, a frame antebellum cottage, a detached kitchen, a 19th century physician's office, and a commissary. The center is open to the general public Sundays 1:30 to 4:30 p.m. but is closed major holidays and

Pioneer Heritage Center.

from mid-December through February. An admission fee is charged for adults; children are admitted free of charge.

The fact that this portion of Louisiana is so closely allied to Texas is celebrated at the R. W. Norton Art Gallery where two outstanding collections of paintings, watercolors, drawings and sculptures by Frederic Remington and Charles M. Russell, the most celebrated of American's ''western'' artists, are displayed.

The Norton Gallery also houses impressive collections of other American as well as European art, plus a reference and research library. The Norton Gallery is located in the 4700 block of Creswell Avenue. Telephone 318-865-4201. Admission is free. Open Tuesday through Saturday 1 p.m. to 5 p.m. Closed Mondays and national holidays.

Barksdale Air Base is home to the 8th Air Force Museum where uniforms, barracks, scenes from the World War II homefront, and a

8th Air Force Museum, Barksdale.

growing number of aircraft detail the history of the Strategic Air Command. Admission is free. Hours are 9 a.m. to 3 p.m. daily. Enter the base via North Gate Road.

A map for a driving tour of the Fairfield-Highland residential area is offered by the convention and tourist bureau. Originally called the Norris Ferry Road or the Norris Ridge Road, Fairfield Avenue and the surrounding area was the site of some of the city's first suburban homes.

Less than 20 miles northwest of town is Oil City, LA 1, where the Caddo-Pine Island Oil and Historical Society Museum is the prime attraction for history lovers. Exhibits depict life in a turn-of-the-

century Louisiana oil boom town. Also displayed are artifacts from
the Caddo Indian culture dating back into prehistory. A former
railroad depot of the Kansas City Southern Railroad houses the
museum. The grounds are used to display oil well paraphernalia.
The museum is located two blocks off LA 1 on Land Avenue. Admission is free. Hours are 9 a.m. to 5 p.m. Monday—Friday and 1
p.m. to 5 p.m. on Saturdays. Closed for lunch from 11 a.m. to 12
a.m. daily.

Shreveport is located on I-20 at the junction of US 71 and US 171,
about 310 miles northwest of New Orleans and about 190 miles east
of Dallas, Texas.

Accommodations, fast food establishments and restaurants are
plentiful.

For more information contact: The Shreveport-Bossier City Convention and Tourist Bureau, P. O. Box 1761, Shreveport, LA 71166.
Telephone 318-222-9391.

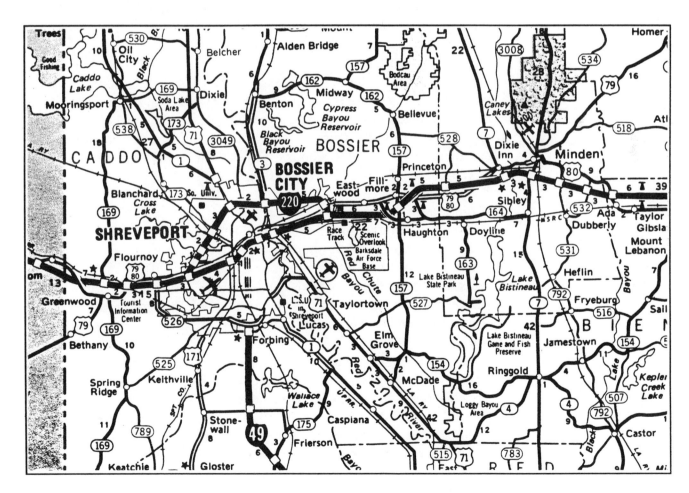

6

Mansfield

The scene is early morning over breakfast at the Dairy Queen in Many (man-ee). I am listening to the suggestions of local diners:

"Pleasant Hill? You really can't see anything there."

"Well, yes, there was a battle there, but you can't tell anything about it by just driving through."

"You need to come back, go there in April. That's when they have the re-enactment."

"Besides the best road to Mansfield is (US) 171 and it doesn't go through Pleasant Hill."

I eat my eggs and say I appreciate the advice.

I am not deterred.

I'm taking LA 175 through Pleasant Hill to Mansfield. I don't volunteer that I am briefly detouring east on LA 120 at Belmont to the Rebel State Commemorative Area, doubtlessly they would discourage me. In the guise of saving me time. "Nothing going on out there. Way out in the woods. Way out of the way."

They smile. I smile. We say, "Bye."

Such nice people.

But I know something they don't.

There are no direct routes to my destinations.

The country road of my choice is strewn with loose clumps of hay. Eventually I overtake a tractor pulling a hay wagon. The empty landscape stretches and expands the distances. The fields, pastures and deep woods are seldom relieved by a house. The pine woods grow deeper and denser as I reach the Rebel State Commemorative Area.

The commemorative area, or park, takes its name from an unknown Confederate soldier who was buried on the place. The story goes that the soldier became separated from his squad during a skirmish with Federal forces at Marthaville, known in those times as Crump's Corner. Supposedly, the young soldier became disoriented and wandered onto the farm of William Hodge Barnhill. He spoke with the Barnhill family, they gave him directions, and he continued his search for his squad. But while stopping for a drink at a spring on the farm, he was discovered by a patrol of Federal cavalrymen who shot and killed him on the spot.

The Barnhill family found the dead soldier and buried him. Near the park entrance is a marker which reads, "In memory of William Hodge Barnhill, his family and descendants. Here on his homeplace, April 3, 1864, he and his sons buried a Confederate soldier killed by Union forces." The Barnhills maintained the grave site for 98 years. The grave is located close to the center of the commemorative area, near the amphitheater.

The amphitheater hosts country and gospel music performances by nationally known, as well as local, entertainers throughout the year. The musical performances grew out of local memorial gatherings at the site of the unknown soldier's grave in the 1960s. Today a museum in the commemorative area features exhibits telling the story of the region's folk music, which has evolved from simple gospel to sophisticated "modern country" sounds. Also featured are exhibits honoring Louisiana natives who have made contributions to the field of popular country music.

Perhaps the nicest thing about the remote pastoral location of the park is that there are no neighbors to complain about the noise when there are performances.

Back on the road to Pleasant Hill, I look for the ghost armies sweeping across the fields. I imagine a thousand Confederate spying eyes watching the road. I see the fringes of woods across the rain-wet fields of winter rye. Range cattle graze in the gentle rain.

Pleasant Hill passes by my car windows, a peaceful village with open fields and vacant lots making elbow room between the houses. Perhaps a vacant lot between households makes for as good a neighbor as a stone wall.

North of Pleasant Hill the historic markers begin and continue all the way to Mansfield, strung out along the highway like Burma Shave signs for miles, occasionally appearing in clumps like surrealistic wildflowers in roadside bouquets.

The battle began at Mansfield, in the vicinity of the Mansfield State Commemorative Area, a park on LA 175, and spread southward over a period of several days in April, 1864.

Federal troops and a squadron of boats commanded by General N. P. Banks and Admiral D. D. Porter had advanced as far as Alexandria on the Red River and occupied that city on May 7, 1863, in the first Red River Campaign before orders were given to turn east and capture Port Hudson. Early in 1864 the second Red River Campaign began. The stated objectives were to secure cotton for the New

Mansfield Battlefield.

England textiles mills, to return Texas to the Union, to disrupt Confederate-Mexican trade, and to discourage French activities in Mexico where Napoleon III was conspiring with Mexican opponents of Benito Juarez to name the Austrian archduke Maximillian as emperor of a newly created Mexican empire.

General Banks and Admiral Porter steamed up the Red River from Alexandria to Natchitoches. Historians say they met little resistance along the way. Then at Natchitoches, Banks and his army (some local historians' estimates run from 27,000 to over 30,000 men, while others estimate the Federal forces were about half that size) swerved away from the river and headed toward Shreveport by way of Mansfield, which left them without the support of Porter's naval force. According to local history buffs, General Banks assumed the Confederate forces were massing in Shreveport and there would be no major action until his army reached that city. By splitting, Federal forces could make a two-prong assault on the Confederate stronghold.

Confederate General Richard Taylor, the son of U.S. President Zachary Taylor, commanded the Confederate forces in the area. The first engagement of the battle was between opposing cavalry units on April 7, at Wilson's Farm and lasted for about two hours. After which, General Taylor selected a site about four miles south of Mansfield to make a stand. Today the site is the Mansfield State Commemorative Area.

The story goes that in the early afternoon of April 8, with less than 6,000 men of his massive army with him (the rest were strung out along the road south of Mansfield), Banks faced nearly 9,000 Confederate troops in battle formation.

According to the official story offered by the museum in the commemorative area, ''The Union troops quickly formed a line of battle along a rail fence and a ridge known as Honeycutt Hill. On orders from Taylor, General Alfred Mouton's Division charged the rail fence. Mouton was killed leading the attack, but French born General J. C. Polignac continued the charge and overwhelmed the Union line.''

Though late-arriving Federal troops formed another line about a mile south of the first, they were quickly routed by the Confederates. The rebel forces took prisoners and, also seized guns, small arms and wagons abandoned by the fleeing Federal troops.

At Chapman's Bayou, two miles south of the second line, another group of Federal troops, locally estimated at about 6,000, formed yet another line and held it until dark. In the night they fell back to Pleasant Hill.

On April 9, the Battle of Pleasant Hill raged through the day and only after darkness fell did the fighting subside. Heavy losses were inflicted on both sides.

After the battle the Federal Army rejoined Admiral Porter's naval forces at Natchitoches. They then withdrew down the Red River destroying and burning much of what lay in their path. Confederate cavalrymen did their best to harass the retreating Yankees. They did manage to temporarily blockade the Red River with a sunken river-boat. The retreating Federal troops also encountered trouble with the river levels. The water was unusually low and special ''wing-dams'' had to be built to free the Union Navy from a series of rapids near Alexandria. Confederates continued to hamper the retreat with at-tacks at Mansura and Yellow Bayou. When the Federal forces crossed the Atchafalaya River, the Second Red River Campaign was considered at an end. The Confederates claimed a great victory, but Federal propagandists assured the world the battle was a draw.

The Mansfield State Commemorative Area nestles along LA 175 in a pine forest, appropriately surrounded by a split rail fence. The museum on the grounds contains mementoes of the battle as well as other artifacts from the area.

Confederate powder flasks, bayonets, flags and uniforms, a first sergeant's morning report, soldiers' Bibles, diaries, letters home, a surgeon's gruesome tools, a list of area homes and churches turned into hospitals after the battle, and maps tie the story of the battle together in frighteningly tangible terms. Models of ironclad ships and lists of the ships in the Red River Squadron offer a footnote.

A canvas likeness of CSA Major General Camille De Poligac, who was a French-born prince, watches over the entrance to the museum's main display hall. A uniform he wore at the British Court of St. James during Victoria's reign is displayed.

The most unusual piece in the museum has no connection with the battle but came as a gift from President Harry Truman. A massive mantel which had been installed in the East Room of the White House in 1902 and removed in 1955 when the presidential mansion was renovated rests just inside the main foyer. The local United Daughters of the Confederacy had written President Truman and requested a brick from the White House renovation to be used in the cornerstone of the museum. He sent the mantel instead. There is probably a moral in this story. But exactly what is it? Be careful what you request of a U.S. president?

The grounds of the commemorative area contain nature trails and picnic areas as well as the tombs of some of the men who died at the site, and memorials to such heroes as General Mouton.

Mansfield, located in De Soto Parish, is near several other spots of interest. A granite survey post, called the ''Dry Line Boundary,'' located 100 feet off FM 31, denotes the international boundary agreed on in 1841 between the United States and the Republic of Texas.

LA 509, northeast of town, leads to the village of Carmel, said to be the home of descendants of Jean Laffite's brother Pierre. Laffitte's Store, at the intersection with the Smithport Road, is the hub of community information. The clerk says there may be some Pierre Laffite descendants in the area. But, he explains, there are at least three different ''sets'' of Lafitte/Laffite/Laffitte families in the

Rock Chapel, Carmel.

area—each with their own preferred spelling of the family surname and not all claim Jean as a kinsman.

The drive to Carmel takes travelers to the site of a monastery, seminary and convent. These buildings are now gone and the forest has reclaimed the spaces they occupied. The Carmel Catholic church, The Church of the Immaculate Conception, near the site of the original buildings, sits in a field of wildflowers beside a lane off the main road. Far off the road, down the lane, back in the woods, along Bayou Lou, there is tangible reminder of the monks and their time in the forest.

The Rock Chapel, built by the monks as a place of quiet meditation and retreat in 1891, has been sheltered by time and nature in its remote setting. The path to the main door is lined with the graves of the holy men. As I open the door and step into the cool room, sun-blindness gradually gives way to a realm of frescoes, dim light, color and designs. Images and visual messages from the past cover the walls and ceilings. So far removed is the interior, whispering of ancient middle eastern worlds, from the wild forests of Louisiana that it is hard to reconcile their symbiotic existences—each re-enforcing the other's gift to silence, peace and meditation.

House on Old Wagon Road.

For exact directions to the Rock Chapel stop at Laffitte's Store. The clerk will lend you the key to the gate across the lane which leads to the chapel as well as the key to the chapel itself.

Northwest of Mansfield, Grand Cane lingers at the edge of yesterday, with its storefronts and village streets running to the edge of the fields and woods that seem to lead straight back into the past. There are sassafras orchards where leaves are gathered for the essential

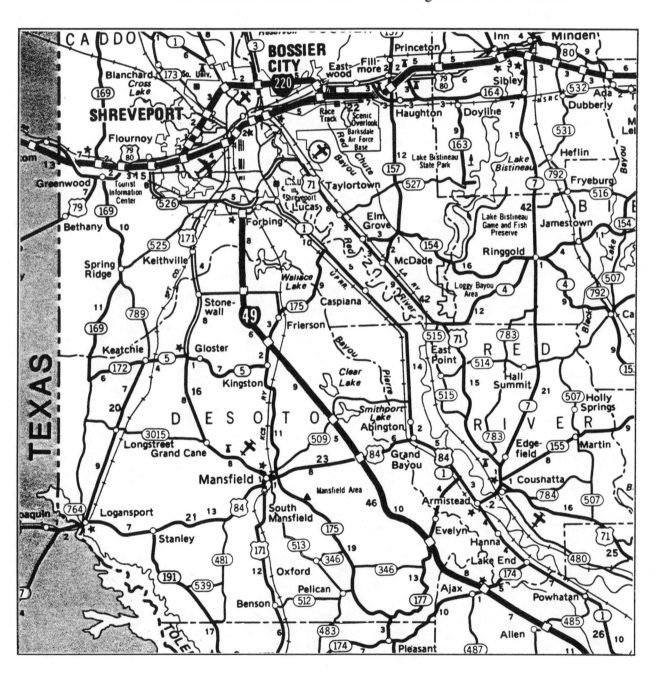

Louisiana herb filé, roots are dug for tea, and bark is stripped for flavoring. There are "old wagon roads" running like tunnels through underbrush and time to Keatchie, and stories about "old nesters from way, way back."

LA 175, once a stagecoach route to Shreveport, is my choice of roads out of town. Holly, Kingston and Frierson interrupt the fields, pastures and stretches of woods. The people I'm meeting in Shreveport are puzzled. Why did I take such an indirect route into town?

Mansfield is located on US 171 and US 84 about 30 miles south of Shreveport.

Overnight accommodations, fast food establishments and restaurants are available locally.

For more information contact: De Soto Parish Tourist Bureau, P. O. Box 1327, Mansfield, LA 71052. Telephone 318-872-1177.

Mansfield State Commemorative Area, Route 2, Box 252, Mansfield, LA 71052. Telephone 318-872-1474. The museum charges an admission fee.

Rebel State Commemorative Area, P.O. Box 127, Marthaville, LA 71450. Telephone 318-472-6255. The museum charges an admission fee.

7

Natchitoches

Conna Cloutier's early 19th century townhouse on Ducournau Square, Front Street, downtown Natchitoches, is crowded with history. Family portraits, swords, lace collars, furniture and other mementoes share space with Conna's dreams of Natchitoches as a choice destination for throngs of history-loving tourists.

Ducournau Square, Front Street.

Her bed and breakfast guests discover a town that ranks as one of Louisiana's best-kept secrets. Sitting on the front gallery, a second-floor balcony trimmed in lacy wrought iron New Orleans-style, guests have a panoramic view of Cane River, once the main channel of the Red River, now a placid lake stretching down the length of the parish, a thoroughfare into plantation country. From the center of town, red-brick Front Street, changing names to Jefferson and Washington at the south and north ends, follows the meandering river down a trail lined with antebellum and Victorian homes that wrap a visitor in the comforting ambience of nostalgia. Traffic lines up at the two downtown bridges to cross the river where on the opposite shore Williams Avenue with its comfortable and antique residences also follows the river.

On Conna's back gallery, the quiet Creole country town could be miles away. Visitors can feel they have truly escaped the stress of the modern world as they look out on the courtyard with its fountain and listen to the soothing sounds of cascading water in a green-filled world where ferns, geraniums and azaleas crowd together under a magnolia tree which rises up to shield the gallery with its glossy leaves all year long. The blossoms of late spring and early summer come as a bonus. On most any day the aroma of peppers and onions being sauteed at the restaurant downstairs wafts up to the back gallery teasing and enticing appetites.

Conna is building a museum in the carriage house at the back end of the courtyard. The museum will celebrate the history and the heritage of the area. In the meantime she keeps guests entertained with stories and memorabilia from the town's past. Ample reading material relating to the area is on every guest's night stand. Over the years local diarists and historians, plus an occasional novelist and playwright, have never lacked for exotic material and raw data to tantalize their imaginations.

Natchitoches, founded in 1714, is the oldest European town in the Louisiana Purchase. But its history can be traced back even further. It is located almost an equal distance to the east of the Sabine River as Nachidoches, Texas, is to the west. Legends claim the Sabine was the dividing line between the land of two Indian brothers. (According to the legends, Natchitoches means paw-paw eaters and Nachidoches means persimmon eaters.) The Natchitoches Indians, the southernmost members of the Caddo Confederacy, were well established in the area when the first Europeans arrived. There is some speculation, based on a mention of a village called ''Nacacahoz'' in *The Gentleman of Elvas* chronicle, that the De Soto expedition may have visited the area in 1542 . Some historical speculators also claim that La Salle visited the site in 1687. But the Italian-born, French soldier Henri di Tonti's arrival here in February 1690 is well documented and has earned him a historic marker on LA 1 in front of the U.S. Fish and Wildlife Service's National Fish Hatchery. He was looking for La Salle after the latter had failed to make a rendezvous at the mouth of the Mississippi River (unbeknowst to Tonti, La Salle had at first been lost, then murdered by his own crew). Tonti lingered with the Natchitoches long enough to negotiate a peace settlement between them and a warring neighbor tribe. His descriptions of the Indians and their village give anthropologists like Hiram "Pete" Gregory, here at Northwestern State University, valuable eyewitness accounts that can be put together with information from archaeological digs and findings to form a picture of the Native American town and lifestyle.

Dr. Gregory says the Indians made their rectangular homes of mud and moss. (They looked a lot like the *bousillage* houses the colonials built.) They made garments of bark cloth, had feathered cloaks and produced sophisticated pottery. Skulls were flattened, deliberately deformed during infancy, giving them what Europeans considered an awesome appearance.

Visitors in the Indian homes during those early contact days reported that the babies often cried during the night. Dr. Gregory says it may or may not have been because of the flattening process.

Tonti also reported that there was a temple here where toads and insects appeared to be enshrined. The Indian township is believed to have been washed into the river. The Fish Hatchery itself was the site of a number of burials that were examined by personnel from the Smithsonian Institution when the place was under construction. (The university has a collection of Native American artifacts, many from the immediate area, located in the Williamson Museum, Arts and Sciences Building. The museum is open free to the public during normal school hours.)

The next European visitors to leave a record of their visit to Natchitoches were D'Iberville's brother Bienville and Louis Juchereau de Saint Denis, who came up the Red River Valley in 1700.

The Frenchmen wanted to open up trade with the Caddos and other Indian tribes. The Caddos were just as anxious for commerce and a few years later found an excuse to move a large group of their people from Natchitoches to the shores of Lake Pontchartrain to facilitate the flow of goods. When St. Denis was ordered to establish a post at Natchitoches in 1714, the Indians moved back here with him.

St. Denis' mission was twofold: to build a trading center and to push French claims as hard up against the Spanish frontier as he dared. No sooner had St. Denis established the post than he set out to find the Spaniards. He marched all the way across Texas to the Spanish post of San Juan Bautista on the Rio Grande, with his valet, some Indian allies and a small group of Frenchmen one of whom, André Pénicaut, later wrote of the journey in a narrative which has been published under the title *Fleur de Lys and Calumet*, edited and translated by Richebourg Gaillard McWilliams.

The very elegant and well-groomed St. Denis, who did not neglect his appearance even on an arduous journey across the wilderness, finally arrived at a Spanish outpost where his intent to enter into trade put him at odds with the Spanish mercantile laws. His claim to have come at the request of a Spanish priest who wanted French help in re-establishing missions in east Texas was considered a very flimsy excuse for such a journey, especially since his party was loaded down with trade goods. Before he was shipped off to Mexico City and a confrontation with Spanish justice, the granddaughter of the local *comandante* fell in love with him. While he was away in jail, she tried to intervene for his release. When he was released, they were married and she eventually returned with him to Louisiana. But on the first trip back to Louisiana she waited at her grandfather's while St. Denis was accompanied by a number of her kinsmen,

Fort St. Jean Baptiste.

Commander's House, Fort St. Jean Baptiste.

Church, Fort St. Jean Baptiste.

countrymen and missionaries who established a Spanish fort at Los Adaes just a few miles west of the Natchitoches post. Though Spanish mercantilism outlawed trade with the French, the frontier outpost resorted to expediency more often than not. St. Denis' story is long and romantic, much like the history of Natchitoches itself.

A replica of Fort St. Jean Baptiste, the first fort built at Natchitoches in 1716, as well as the new buildings added within the palisade in 1732, is called the Fort St. Jean Baptiste Commemorative Area. It is said to be in the vicinity of the original fort. An admission fee is charged. A plan drawn by Francois Broutin, the engineer who made the additions in 1732, was used to build the replica. Eighteenth century methods were employed as much as possible in the reconstruction.

The wooden walls of the fort look more decorative than defensive, but in 1732 the fragile pine palisade of the original fort was all that stood between the French colonists and annihilation. A band of Natchez Indians laid siege to the fort. Their aim was to destroy the European colonists who had invaded their land. They nurtured a particular hatred for the French which they felt was well justified because of their nation's suffering under the oppression and brutality of the colonists at Natchez, Mississippi, where a French settlement had been established in 1716. As the Native Americans watched their culture degraded, their religion debased and the women of their nation forced into sexual servitude by the French, they grew more and more angry until they finally revolted in 1729 and massacred most of the French colonists at Natchez. Some French women, children and black slaves were taken captive. (A few of the French colonists' black slaves joined the Natchez in the uprising.)

In 1732 after several ruses to get inside Fort St. Jean Baptiste failed, the Natchez warriors raged outside the walls. St. Denis and his band watched as the Natchez burned alive a captive French woman in an attempt to lure the Frenchmen out of the fort to her rescue.

St. Denis' own brand of Indian policy had earned him the respect and admiration of the Natchitoches, and now in the fledgling colony's darkest hour they rallied to his side as did a token force of Spanish soldiers from nearby Los Adaes. When he did finally storm out of the fort, with his allies' aid, he did so with a vengeance, fighting ferociously, driving the Natchez into retreat. They fled down the river with St. Denis' forces in hot pursuit.

Between the edges of modern day Derry and Cloutierville, the Natchez made their last stand. The name of a hill, *Sang Pour Sang* (blood for blood), is their only monument. The lake at the base of the hill, now dry and called Dry Lake and/or Shallow Lake by locals, was said to have turned red with the carnage. The slain Natchez's bones are said to have bleached in the sun here, visible for generations.

To make the land safe for Frenchmen, surviving members of the Natchez's royal family were captured during the years of the uprising, taken to New Orleans, sold into slavery and shipped to the cane fields of Hispaniola. Other captured Natchez were sold into slavery also, some ending their days in the fields of Louisiana plantations.

St. Denis, his family and followers returned to their ongoing battle with the wilderness.

The fort continued as a defensive frontier outpost until after Louisiana was ceded to the Spanish in a secret treaty in 1762. (A year prior to the Treaty of Paris, 1763, which ended the French and Indian War and forced France to cede much of her American territory to Great Britain, France had ceded to Spain the Isle of Orleans and all French territory west of the Mississippi.) With the Spanish came mercantilism. The post became a center in the intracolonial trade network. No longer needed as a border defense, the fort fell into disrepair and was in ruins by the time of the Louisiana Purchase of 1803.

In a woodland setting, fringed by garden plots and animal compounds of the type the first colonists would have had, the modern pine palisade surrounds a collection of primitive buildings: dirt-floor barracks, warehouses, post commander's living quarters, a church and an outdoor oven. The loneliness of the frontier, the fear of the unknown wilderness, the desperate attempt of men to encircle all they had of what they considered the civilized world is memorialized in the fort. The earliest surviving original house in Natchitoches, the Wells House, circa 1776, at 607 Williams Avenue, poignantly reminds visitors that after 62 years the Europeans had still scarcely made a dent in the wilderness. Owner Carol Wells says the house was a trading post in the days of Spanish rule. In 1790 the man who lived in the house had a franchise from the Spanish government to trade horses and hides.

Cypress and *bousillage* (mud and spanish moss) were molded and shaped into the unpretentious home. Carol Wells offers candlelight tours of the house by appointment most evenings. (An admission fee is charged.) In the dim light, the Spartan rooms come alive with her stories of how things were in the days when the house was new. ''The people were ragged,'' she says. ''There was no cash crop. Tobacco was the medium of exchange. Looking off the porch, across the river was wilderness.''

Her tour lingers over period furniture, explanations of utensils lost to modern housekeepers, and the authentic touches such as a buffalo

Wells House, c. 1776.

robe blanket. The house was originally two rooms with galleries all around and one of the first in the region built off the ground. Deer hair was added to a type of homemade plaster to cover the earthen *bousillage* walls. Additional rooms were added over the years and galleries were enclosed, leaving the house with one long gallery across the front.

The essence of frontier Natchitoches lingers at the Wells House even in the yard. Planted in native wildflowers and plants the early colonists knew, the yard surrounding the house make it an island of the past.

Today, in Natchitoches, the Roque House, circa 1790, built by a former slave who earned his freedom late in life, rests beneath the bank of Front Street, along Cane River. The house is a prime example of the type of home early settlers constructed. The Roque House was moved to its present location from Isle Brevelle in the nearby countryside. The tall river bank is lined with wrought-iron benches emblazoned with *fleur-de-lis* emblems and the number 1714. There is no visible trace of the old steamboat landing which once conducted a viable trade with New Orleans and the world beyond, but a marker at the corner of Front and Lafayette streets tells the story of *El Camino Real* (the King's Highway) which ran from Natchez, Mississippi, through Natchitoches to San Antonio, Texas, and from there all the way to Mexico City.

Often colonial Natchitoches and the long shadow of St. Denis overshadow later times. St. Denis' home and *vacherie* (ranch) were located on land where Northwestern State University now stands. Historic markers on the campus are strategically located to remind visitors and students of St. Denis' sojourn.

The American Cemetery, at the corner of Demeziere and Second streets, was the site of one of town's earliest forts and contains graves of some of the first citizens, including St. Denis' wife, Emanuela. Architecturally interesting buildings, each with its own story, are the Immaculate Conception Catholic Church, corner of Church and Second streets; the rectory across the street (the building was a gift to the bishop of Natchitoches from a friend in New Orleans—it was dismantled and moved up the Red River to its present location); the Old Seminary-Bishop Martin Museum beside the rectory which is a despository for church records and artifacts dating from 1724; and Trinity Episcopal Church, circa 1857, nearby at the corner of Second and Trudeau streets. Townhouses, Greek Revival mansions and cottages, as well as local and Creole interpretations of popular architectural styles give the town a unique and pleasing demeanor.

Natchitoches' fame has been enhanced over the years by several films made in the area—*The Horse Soldiers* in the 1950s and *Steel Magnolias* in the 1980s. A local bank (corner of St. Denis and Second) has even begun a walk of fame to memorialize the visits of the actors, actresses, writers, directors and producers.

No visit to Natchitoches would be complete without sampling the local speciality ''the Natchitoches meat pie.'' Precooked ground pork, beef and spices are encased in a piece of pastry and deep fried. Order one to go and set out down the river to plantation country to get a more complete picture of the realm of Natchitoches.

LA 1, US 84, I-49, LA 6, all lead to Natchitoches located about 50 miles northwest of Alexandria and 70 miles south of Shreveport.

Accommodations are limited. Best bets are local bed and breakfast establishments. Lists of lodgings are available from the tourist commission. Restaurants and fast food establishments are plentiful.

Maps of the area, lists of attractions, and other information is available free of charge from the Natchitoches Parish Tourist Commission, P.O. Box 411, Natchitoches, LA 71457. Telephone 318-352-8072.

For information on organized package tours of the area contact: Unique Tours of Historic Natchitoches, 536 Elizabeth Street, Natchitoches, LA 71457. Telephone 318-352-5242 or 318-352-3797.

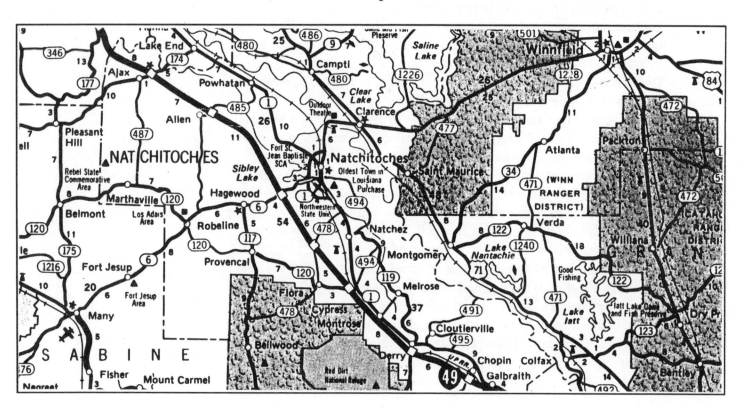

8

Cane River Country

The high red bluffs of Grand Encore, four miles above Natchitoches, mark the turn of the Red River away from its former main channel through the heart of the old Creole town.

The river changed courses in 1832 and the old main channel became the Cane River. After a modest start, the town of Grand Encore blossomed into a bustling center for the steamboat trade that had frequented Natchitoches. In 1863 Federal troops looted and burned the new town.

Civil War entrenchments can still be seen in the area, but the most dramatic monument is a grand amphitheatre, built in very recent times, especially for regular seasonal performances of a drama celebrating St. Denis' arrival and many adventures. Unfortunately, the performances have been discontinued.

The turning of the river left Natchitoches on a placid lake stretching through the town and beyond to the lush region that has become known as Plantation Country. Cane River, though a lake, still provided a thoroughfare for plantation goods to the main channel. Today in the winter months, sculling crews from as far away as Princeton University can be seen in training, racing their crafts downstream. The calm waters appeal to the trainers.

To reach the Planation Country, follow either LA 1 or LA 464 south of town. (Free maps are available from the Natchitoches Tourist Commission, 781 Front Street.) For an overall perspective of the area, take LA 119 (at Natchez, LA) south to Derry, then turn south to Cloutierville, which is about 15 miles south of town. For the history lover yearning for the places of yesterday, places where the past can be envisioned in its everyday dress, this is a path to fulfillment. Travelers may have the sensation of moving through the pages of an illustrated storybook of the past.

Perhaps time is kindest when it forgets a place, when nature forces a river to turn away, when combined nature and time push progress off in another direction. Along LA 1 the road hugs the river's edge, giant oaks swoop down to the water, pirogues are upturned on the bank.

Plantation houses, most often influenced by the West Indies styles, sit in their own dominions at the end of avenues of oaks. Commissaries, barns, gins, slave quarters, tenant houses, overseer cottages, *pigeonniers* and *garçonnières* cluster near the main houses. Each plantation has a long, convoluted and often romantic story. Travelers could spend days visiting and touring all the homes open to the public along Cane River.

Perhaps the most famous, exotic and poignant is Melrose on LA 119. This is the world of Clementine Hunter. Searching the countryside for her visions, the faces in her portraits, the bright splashes of the flowers encased in their dense thickets of green, reminds visitors that her visions were of an inner world where with paint she could bring a simplified order to the chaos of plantation life.

Clementine Hunter, whose primitive paintings have gained an international following, was a field hand on Melrose Plantation before she became a cook. Visitors to the plantation are shown a short movie which tells Clementine's story as well as that of three other women: her patroness Cammie Garrett Henry, Kate Chopin, the writer, who lived just down the river at Cloutierville, and Marie Therese Coincoin, the woman who established the plantation. But Clementine's story overshadows all the others. She had more to overcome. A child of poverty, her years were measured out in hard labor, then late in life she picked up some paints and brushes an artist visiting Melrose had discarded, and began her career.

Mrs. Henry, who was fond of collecting artists and writers and usually kept a retinue of creative souls as guests at her plantation, recognized Clementine's talent and uncluttered vision and encouraged her, as did the guests. Gradually her work was accepted as a significant contribution to folk art.

At first Clementine gave away her works. Later she sold them for very modest sums—so modest that nearly everybody who lived in the area when she began her painting career owns one. Gradually the prices rose. Today many of her works are still available through art dealers such as Robert Lucky, Jr., at the Carriage House Market, 720 Front Street, Natchitoches. Clementine Hunter's colors and forms dance across the walls of Lucky's store, an ode to the unaffected regions of the soul.

Clementine's friends at Melrose helped her manage her affairs and saw that she enjoyed some of the profits of her talent. She died, at 102 years of age, in 1987.

The small house she lived in while working as a cook at the plantation has been relocated to the grounds of the main house, where it fits in well with an eclectic group of other buildings. As well as creative

Melrose, c. 1833.

souls, Mrs. Henry also collected folk cabins and cottages and had them moved onto the main house grounds. But the one considered by many to be the most significant, The African House, circa 1800, was already on the grounds long before Mrs. Henry arrived on the scene. Some say it is the only structure of true African architecture on the North American continent dating to colonial times. The two-story building, with its overhanging eaves and thatched roof, contains murals of plantation life and religious visions by Clementine Hunter that many consider her very finest work.

The African House dates back to the days of Marie Therese Coin-coin, the lady who established Melrose plantation, only in her day it was called Yucca. Like Clementine Hunter, Marie Therese Coincoin was of African heritage. Both women twisted the tail of fate, but in very different ways.

Marie Therese Coincoin, born a slave, was the property of Louis Juchereau de St. Denis' daughter and the mother of at least two children, when according to the custom of the day she was leased to Thomas Pierre Metoyer. When a Catholic priest protested to St. Denis' daughter and threatened legal action over the unsanctioned

African House, c. 1800.

Yucca Cottage, c. 1796.

union, she in effect told him to mind his own business. Eventually Metoyer purchased Marie Therese, freed her, and later when he married a European woman, gave the black woman what was considered a generous settlement. He also agreed to free the ten children born to their illegal union. Marie Therese bought the freedom of the children she had before she was leased by Metoyer. With land grants, hard work and more sheer determination than anything else, Marie Therese Coincoin carved out a plantation for herself and her children and built a home. The *bouillage* cottage is called Yucca, circa 1796, and is just across the back yard of the antebellum plantation house called Melrose.

The community of Isle Brevelle, along the Cane River's La Côte Joyeuse, is still home to numerous descendants of Marie Therese Coincoin, as well as the descendants of other free people of color, who found it possible to carve out plantations, modest fortunes, and a respected society in antebellum Louisiana. The antebellum mansion that is the main house at Melrose today was built in 1833. Due to economic reverses, Marie Therese Coincoin's family lost the plantation in the 1840s.

A few families along the Cane River have managed to hold onto their plantations from colonial times to the present. One of the most notable of these is Oakland, circa 1821, which has been in the Prudhomme family for eight generations. The plantation itself is said to have been settled in 1718 by Emanuel Prudhomme. The details of the house and gardens give clues to evolving lifestyles. The flower

Oakland, c. 1821.

Plantation Commissary, Oakland.

beds in the front yard at Oakland are outlined with bottles—as they have been from the house's earliest days—most of the bottles are antiques, some contained ale imported from Dublin in the early 19th century, others are hand blown and have round bottoms.

The ground floor of the house contains a museum stuffed with family possessions from over eight generations. Antique cameras and photographic equipment including a machine used in the making of daguerreotype images, a 19th century surgeon's tools, toys and bathtubs, tools and clothing, baskets and cooking pots tell their own stories. The Smithsonian Institution has expressed great interest in acquiring some of the homemade well-drilling tools.

The Smithsonian has also expressed a great deal of interest in the antique cotton press at Magnolia Plantation in the Derry community on LA 119, where the original French land grant was made to Jean Baptiste LeComte II in 1753. His son Ambrose established the plantation in 1830 and built the "Big House," a complex of brick slave quarters, an overseer's house, *a pigeonnier*, a store, barns, blacksmith shop and the cotton press. Federal troops burned the "Big House" on their retreat from the Battle of Mansfield. But other buildings were spared and are still standing on the working plantation of 2,192 acres where cotton, cattle and soybeans are the chief products.

The "Big House" was rebuilt in 1896 using the original square brick foundation, the 18-inch brick walls, and the brick pillars, all of which had survived the fire. The brick pillars were shortened to act as supports for the front and rear galleries. The two-and-a-half story home has 27 rooms, including 14 fireplaces and a Catholic chapel where mass is still celebrated.

In its early years the plantation became famous for its racing stables. Ambrose LeComte's "Flying Dutchman" won the St. Charles Hotel Handicap at New Orleans in 1850. The horse lies buried between the oaks just outside the plantation house, not far from the dining room where his silver trophies are still displayed.

Other plantations in the area of the antebellum period are Starlight, Oaklawn, Cherokee, Beau Fort and Roubieu. The Bayou Folk Museum, Cloutierville, was once the home of Kate Chopin, author of early feminist novels as well as regionally oriented literature.

At Derry, Charlie Churchwell runs the Mercantile, is mayor and postmaster as well as part-owner and manager of the Bayou Camitte Plantation. The Mercantile, on LA 1, pleasantly old-fashioned and unpretentious, sports an updated snack bar. Visitors couldn't find a better spot to have a cup of coffee and conversation with the local residents.

Sang Pour Sang, the hill that marks the site of the terminal battle

of the Natchez Indians with the French, is located to the left of LA 1
south of Derry, directly behind Charlie Churchwell's hunting/fishing
camp. A historic marker on LA 1 at Emmanuel Road, Cloutierville,
points the way to the hill and tells the story. The base of the hill is
about two-and-one-half miles down Emmanuel Road, but the best
view is from LA 1 or from the junction of LA 119 and I-49 at Derry.

For free maps of the area, tour schedules and hours at the plantation homes (all charge admission fees) and other information, contact: The Natchitoches Parish Tourist Commission, P.O. Box 411,
Natchitoches, LA 71457. Telephone 318-352-8072.

Limited accommodations and a wide variety of eating establishments are located in Natchitoches.

Packaged tours of Cane River Plantation Country are offered by
Unique Tours of Historic Natchitoches, 536 Elizabeth Street, Natchitoches, LA 71457. Telephone 318-352-5242 or 318-352-3797.

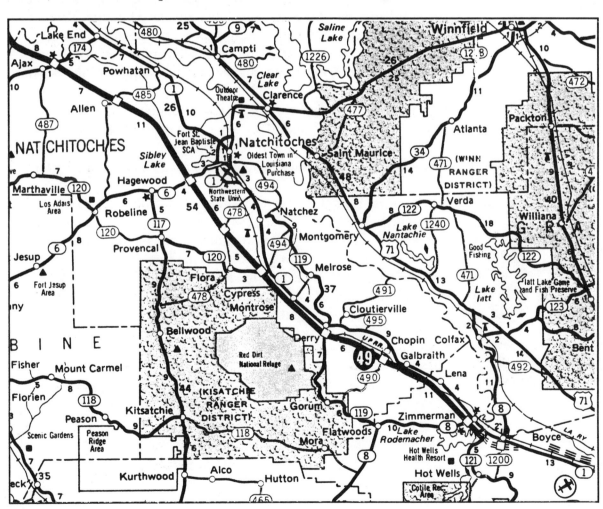

9

Los Adaes, Fort Jesup
and the Neutral Zone

The pine hills on the outskirts of Robeline shelter the quiet memory of Los Adaes, a Spanish town and fort established in 1717, which has long since dissolved back into the forest from which it was hewn. Today the site is still so isolated and lonely that it is not difficult to imagine the fears and the concerns of the first settlers huddled in the dense, dark forest.

The narrow paved road (LA 485) from LA 6 through the tall pines is worn down into the earth, a path pressed deep by time. Time heaped dirt, pine straw and falling logs over Los Adaes' remains until only the archaeologists could detect the placement of the mission, the presidio, the houses and attendant structures of the frontier Spanish outpost.

This quiet, green spot was once the far eastern outpost of Spain's Mexican empire. Its reason for being was twofold: to serve as a missionary outreach to the Adaes Indians and to guard against encroachments of the French who were located about 12 miles away from this site at Natchitoches.

Strangely enough it was the founder of Natchitoches, Louis Juchereau de Saint Denis, who led the Spanish expedition that established the outpost. Under the pretense of answering a letter to a Spanish priest who had written for French help in re-establishing Catholic missions in Texas, St. Denis, loaded with trade goods in violation of Spanish mercantile laws, foraged across the wilderness until he was detained at San Juan Bautista, the first Spanish post he came to on the Rio Grande. Between being detained, arrested and jailed in Mexico City for two years, St. Denis married the granddaughter of the *comandante* of San Juan Bautista, talked himself out of jail and into a position as the guide for a colonizing expedition to the Louisiana Border.

The route the expedition took across Texas, *El Camino Real*, had been hammered out of the wilderness in ancient times by buffalo herds. Later *El Camino Real* would become known as the San Antonio Trail and would be one of the favored routes of American settlers to Texas and beyond.

Cow's Skull.

56

Several of St. Denis' new in-laws accompanied the expedition, and one of them was in charge of the new fort. Without troubling themselves with the consequences of violating the mercantile law—they were so far from home, who would ever know anyway, and, besides, the supply lines to Mexico were so long and wrought with danger as to be untenable—the Spanish became a viable market for French goods. When Spain and France declared war on each other in 1719, M. Blondel, the post commander at Fort St. Jean Baptiste, Natchitoches, attacked Los Adaes. The story goes that most of the folks at Los Adaes were away doing missionary work among the Indians, and Blondel found only one lay brother and one soldier at the mission. Blondel is said to have captured the two Spaniards and some chickens, but was thrown from his horse and in the confusion the lay brother escaped, so the French commander returned to Natchitoches with one Spanish soldier and most of the mission's chickens. Shortly afterward the Spanish moved their operations west of the Sabine. But in 1721 they returned, rebuilt their mission and a new stone fort christened Neustra Senora del Pilar de los Adaes. The presidio boasted six cannons and 100 soldiers as befitted its position as the new capital of the Mexican province of Texas. To help provide a work force, Apache women and children from the west were brought in as slaves. (Their descendants can still be found in Louisiana.)

Though Spanish authorities no longer winked at violation of the mercantile laws, smuggling to and from nearby French territory kept the private and public storehouses full. In between smuggling, slave stealing and boundary feuds, many marriages took place between the opposing colonists and soldiers at the two forts, and the priests from one fort often performed ceremonies and masses at the other. But carving a living out of the pine woods proved nearly impossible for the Spanish colonists. The supply lines back to Mexico City were too long for the government to offer any real help, so slowly the colony dwindled until it was officially abandoned in 1773 and the capital moved to San Antonio. (In 1762 Natchitoches became part of the Spanish empire, but it was administered from Havana, Cuba.)

At a corner of the old site, an archaeology research lab is headquarters for an operation that seeks to extract the earth's and forest's surviving memories of the mission and presidio. Less than a half mile back down LA 485, at the junction with LA 6 (locally called The Spanish Trail), the police jury voting precinct house boasts a small museum and tourism information office. Artifacts from the site, especially French, Spanish and Native American pottery, are displayed. Other displays are mementoes from the life and times of the village of Robeline, which sprouted into a town with the coming of the railroad in 1881. But before then the area knew some rough times.

When the Louisiana Purchase made the area American territory in 1803, a dispute erupted with the Spaniards over the location of the western boundary. The Spaniards claimed the Arroyo Hondo (which is near the town of Hagewood on LA 6) as the boundary, the same boundary they had observed for years with the French, but the Americans insisted on the Sabine River. As a result, the area in between these streams was declared neutral until diplomats could work out a settlement. In the meantime the area became the home of outlaws and those who found it expedient to live beyond the bounds of any nation. Folks called the area Robber's Lane, the Free State of Sabine, and No-man's Land, as well as several other less flattering names.

The Florida Purchase Treaty of 1819 (also known as the Adams-Onis Treaty) fixed the United States' western boundary at the Sabine River, but due to a delay in the exchange of ratifications the U.S. was

Fort Jesup.

not able to take over the neutral zone until July, 1821. The American Fort Jesup, established in 1822 by Lt. Colonel Zachary Taylor, was built in an attempt to bring law and order to the former neutral zone. Historians say the troops at the fort had a variety of jobs over the years. They served as Indian agents, worked to prevent slave insurrections and kept the Sabine River clear of obstructions. But the fort's most important use may have been in 1845 when it served as a staging area for troops preparing to enter Texas at the beginning of the Mexican War. Abandoned in 1846 when Texas was annexed to the United States, Fort Jesup became a National Historic Landmark in 1961.

Located just off LA 6, about six miles northeast of Many, Fort Jesup was built along *El Camino Real*, the San Antonio Trail. Ruins of portions of the old fort and a reconstructed officers' quarters building are on a 22-acre park site called the Fort Jesup State Commemorative Area. (An admission fee is charged.) A museum and visitor's center is in the officers' quarters. Markers outline everything from the dragoon stables to soldiers' quarters to the storehouse and powder magazine. The fort was a complex of 82 structures. The native stone pillars of barracks, in various states of ruin, and a kitchen that served one of the numerous barracks are the only survivors of the original fort.

Fort Jesup Kitchen.

The kitchen, restored to its original appearance, tells the story of the frontier soldiers from a unique perspective. A large cooking fireplace dominates one end of the cabin, which is furnished as it would have been in the 1840s. Long wooden tables and benches are in the center of the room. Cooking and eating utensils round out the picture.

Records from the time tell us the soldiers had a very drab diet consisting mainly of stew, salt pork and beef. Men were issued extra shot and powder to hunt game for the kitchens in their spare time. Often soldiers were reported sick because of a diet that lacked green vegetables. The soldiers received a monthly ration of one pint of whiskey per man. The cooks were not always in the army. Sometimes even women were employed. One Marie Martone was a cook at Fort Jesup in 1842 when she was presented a tax bill for keeping a ''grog house.'' She protested, saying she kept a mess hall for officers within the fort.

Today, moss grows on the kitchen's shingle roof, ivy covers its shady sides. Across the well-manicured park, a rustic stone well nestles near the wooden picket fence surrounding the grounds. Oaks, pines and cedars, scattered around a pond, make rest stops for cawing crows on their way to nearby fields.

The parish road to the park passes an old-fashioned camp meeting ground with an open-sided tabernacle. Returning along the same route, visitors can continue at LA 6 on the old San Antonio Trail to Many.

Many, which locals remind visitors is pronounced man-ee, is just 20 miles from Texas. The community survived the rigors of life in the Neutral Zone to finally become an incorporated town in 1843. These days, Many is the center for a burgeoning tourist industry that capitalizes on the nearby Toledo Bend Lake with its resorts, natural beauty and outdoor recreation opportunities. Hodges Gardens, also near Many on US 171, attracts visitors who want to explore 4,700 acres of an experimental arboretum started by the pioneer conservationist A. J. Hodges in the early 1940s as part of a reforestation effort.

About five miles south of Many on US 171 is Fisher, a quiet turn-of-the-century sawmill town. The entire town, including the commissary, post office, depot, opera house, superintendent's home, workers' cottages and managers' slightly-grander-residences, is on the National Register of Historic Places. Trees, spacious commons and white picket fences make Fisher a place history-loving explorers may want to linger. The opera house is still in operation for special performances, and the whole town sparkles with exceptional vitality each year on the fourth weekend of May during the Fisher Sawmill Days.

General Merchandise, Fisher.

Fisher is still a sawmill town. Turn off US 171 at the Bosie-Cascade sign. The road makes a loop through the village and comes back to the highway.

Florien, a shotgun town lined straight down the highway, is just a few miles beyond Fisher on US 171. One of the best times to visit Florien, to get a flavor of the area and sample the history of the region is during the Florien Free State celebration the second weekend of November each year.

About ten miles northwest of Many, also on US 171, the town of Zwolle (zwa-ollie), named for a city in Holland, celebrates its Spanish heritage at the Tamale Fiesta the second weekend in October.

Many is located at the junction of LA 6 and US 171 about 20 miles southwest of Natchitoches. Both Los Adaes and Fort Jesup are just off LA 6. There are ample signs. Fisher and Florien are south of Many on US 171.

Opera House, Fisher.

Overnight accommodations, fast food establishments and restaurants are located in and around Many.

For additional information, contact: The Sabine Parish Tourist Commission, 920 Fisher Road, Many, LA 71449. Telephone 318-256-5880.

Fort Jesup State Commemorative Area, Route 2, Many, LA 71449. Telephone 318-256-5480.

Los Adaes Museum and Tourist Information Center, Robeline, LA 71469. Telephone 318-472-6843.

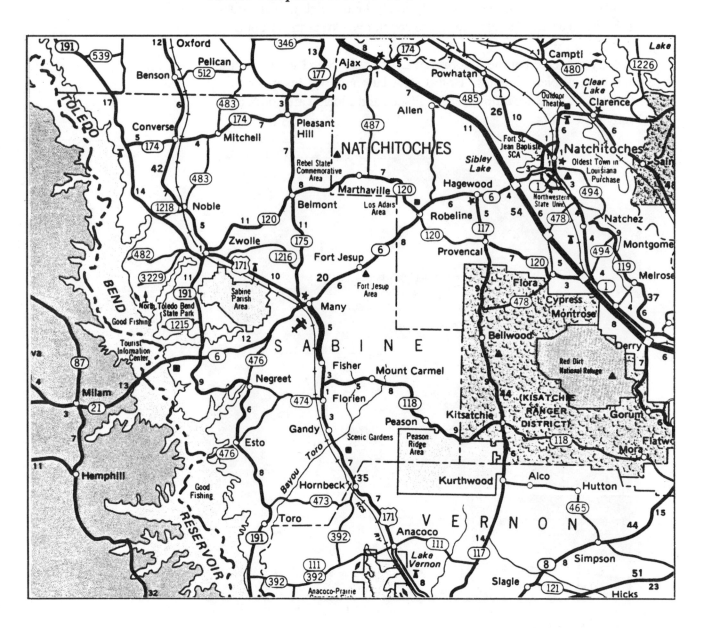

10

Alexandria—Pineville
and Cheneyville

You can slip across the border into Louisiana, nibble at the edges, gradually work your way deeper and deeper into the trails and paths of history, or you can strike for the heart.

Alexandria and Pineville claim to be located at the very heart of Louisiana. The twin cities on opposite banks of the Red River are at the crossroads of north and south Louisiana and along a route often favored by the great swarms of explorers, traders, and settlers from the east who swept out of Mississippi headed for Texas in the eighteenth and nineteenth centuries.

Here and now, those days seem as remote as a fairy tale. To the casual observer the twin cities appear firmly rooted in the ''new'' South, but looks can be deceiving. Much of the original towns were burned by Federal troops retreating down the Red River from the battles of Mansfield and Pleasant Hill in 1864. The citizens had to

Kent House, c. 1800.

begin again as far as industry and architecture went, but an earlier history survives in tradition and culture.

The first European settlement here, Les Rapides, came in 1723 when the French established a post at the rocky limestone shoals on the Red River. The shoals stretched over two miles and though they usually posed no problem during high water, low water often meant that boats had to be off-loaded and a portage made to a spot beyond the rocks.

One of the oldest houses in the town to survive the Yankee torch is Kent House, 3601 Bayou Rapides Road (LA 496) just off MacArthur Drive. When first built, Kent House, circa 1800, had two large rooms surrounded by a broad gallery, but the side galleries were soon enclosed, and in the 1840s pavilion rooms were added to either side of the front gallery. The house as it exists today is much as it was in the 1840s, though it has been moved about four blocks from its original location. The man who built the house, Pierre Baillio II, was the son of a French soldier stationed at Natchitoches. He received a land grant from the Spanish governor, Baron de Carondelet, in 1794, and built the house a few years later. In 1842 the property was purchased by Robert Hynson from Kent County, Maryland. He renamed the house for his old home county and established a successful cotton plantation.

Gardens and outbuildings including a kitchen, milk house, slave cabins, and carriage house offer a look at the everyday workings of an antebellum Alexandria household. An admission fee is charged. Open daily.

Another antebellum house, the Boyce Home, at 105 Main Street, Pineville, was the local headquarters for Confederate troops and a favorite target for Federal gunboats on the river. Local storytellers say courts martial were held in the house and those sentenced to die met their fate on the sandbars just above the present location of the bridge at the foot of Main Street.

The Louisiana Seminary of Learning opened at Pineville January 2, 1860. William Tecumseh Sherman was president. When he applied for the position he gave as references his good friends Colonel Braxton Bragg, Major P.G.T. Beauregard and Richard Taylor (son of Zachary)—all of whom shortly thereafter became Confederate generals. Sherman resigned his position with the school at the outbreak of the Civil War. The school buildings burned in 1869, at which time the school, a forerunner of Louisiana State University, moved to Baton Rouge. The old seminary site is located on US 165 North. A Veterans Administration Hospital is located on the old campus grounds.

Sherman is said to have retained a fondness for the school and manifested that fondness later by making a gift to the university of two cannons that had fired on Fort Sumter.

George Armstong Custer's troops certainly exhibited no fondness for their commanding officer when they mutinied in Alexandria shortly after the war. St. Francis Xavier Cathedral, erected in 1898 on the corner of Fourth and Beauregard streets in downtown Alexandria, is said to be on the very spot where the troops said they had had enough. Custer's headquarters in 1866 were in a home on the grounds of the Flint Thomas Plantation.

Near the cathedral, the tall, thick columns of Alexandria's Visual Arts Museum beckon like the portico of a Greek temple in the sunlight, promising souls a peaceful moment just beyond its doors. The building was a bank before becoming a museum. The bank, in turn, was built on the site of one of the town's first trading posts which had been erected in 1805 and destroyed by the Federal troops in the fire that wiped out the original downtown business district.

Folks who like to poke around the past's paper trail can visit the Alexandria Historical and Genealogical Library and Museum, located in the Carnegie Library, circa 1907, at the corner of Washington and Fifth Streets.

A historic marker at the O.K. Allen Bridge tells the story of Bailey's Dam built by Federal engineers during the Civil War to raise the water over the shoals so low water wouldn't interfere with the passage of boats.

The star of downtown Alexandria's historic architecture, the Hotel Bentley, commands a vantage point looking out over the Red River. The elegant Edwardian building, circa 1908, has been a landmark both physically and culturally in Alexandria for generations. During World War II the hotel dealt with overflowing crowds of soldiers and guests as five military training camps were established in the area. A spokesperson for the Bentley, says the hotel gave out blankets and pillows so the overflow crowds could bed down in the lobby or where ever they could find enough space. The roster of guests during those years tells a story of its own: Major General George Patton, Lt. Colonel Omar Bradley, Colonel Dwight Eisenhower, Lt. Henry Kissinger, General George C. Marshall and General Matthew Ridgeway.

A fountain and goldfish pond rest in the center of the Bentley's palatial lobby. Hotel employees say that in earlier years a traveling salesman from Florida dropped a baby alligator off as a gift at the hotel; it was placed in the fountain pool and was soon joined by other baby gators from various sources. The gators became the hotel mascots. Despite the potential for a unique attraction and the current owners' dedication to preservation and restoration, they have decided not to restore the gators to the pool.

Today the Bentley is a favored meeting spot for families and friends from the plantation country south of here when they come to town.

Cotton country laps up to the southern boundaries of Alexandria's suburbs. Twelve miles south of town on US 71 is LeCompte, named by Colonel Tom Wells of Wells Woods for his friend and fellow horse racing enthusiast Ambrose LeComte of Magnolia Plantation just south of Natchitoches. The story goes that when the railroad came through, the person marking the stations on the map misspelled LeComte, and it was just too much trouble to correct. Today one of the most famous establishments at LeCompte is Lea's, an unpretentious cafe, locally acclaimed for ham sandwiches and pies.

A few miles further south, Cheneyville, a plantation community, dominates the flat, fertile fields along Bayou Boeuf where generations of planters have made their fortunes. Established in 1811, the town was situated in an area already well populated by 1799. Anglo-Americans and some French protestant emigrants from South Carolina arrived in the early 1800s. The Anglo-American settlers were numerous enough for modern day historians to credit them with turning central Louisiana away from French-Spanish traditions to an "American" culture.

Modern landmarks are a cotton gin and grain elevator along US 71. Visitors to the town just a few generations ago always remarked on the number of dominoes players seen under the trees about the town. Though air conditioning has long since driven the majority of the players indoors, the game is still a local favorite. A championship tournament is a major feature of the Historic Cheneyville Tour, a pilgrimage-style festival, usually held the third Saturday of May each year.

Several different groups of Native Americans lived in the area as late as the time of the Louisiana Purchase. After the purchase, Indian traders Alexander Fulton and William Miller acquired 46,800 arpents of land in the area and hired Samuel Wells to survey it for one-ninth of the land in payment. Local historians say that after the survey the remaining Indians "were pushed further west" and the surveyed land offered for sale at $1.25 per acre. Jim Bowie bought a lot in town and stopped at Bennett's Store on Bayou Boeuf on August 5, 1817, where according to a local history brochure, he bought a bandanna handkerchief, a pocket comb, some buttons, thread, two-and-a-quarter yards of stocking net, cotton shirting and a quart of wine.

Hotel Bentley, Alexandria.

The unhurried country lifestyle still survives on the quiet streets running away from US 71. Across the bayou, Trinity Episcopal Church, circa 1853, recently restored, still boasts its original furnishings. Oak trees, lawns as wide as meadows, banana trees, and bright splashes of blooming flowers as well as unpretentious antebellum and Victorian cottages add to the ambience. Antique shoppers will want to linger in the many different shops in the area. Bob Cox's Antiques on US 71 is crowded with fixtures, furnishings and the stories Bob has collected with each piece. Daddy Sam's, Jackie's, Heritage House, Sadlers A-Z and Loyd's Hall are just a few of the shops where travelers can search for tangible bits and pieces of the past that can be had for a price.

Two of Cheneyville's antebellum plantation mansions are open for tours year round.

Walnut Grove, circa 1835, on Bayou Boeuf Road 1.7 miles out of town, has remained in the same family since it was built. Two antebellum slave cabins are located on the grounds. One, original to the site, houses an antiques and local crafts shop. The second cabin was moved here from another plantation. The grounds, shaded by ancient oaks and magnolias, are accented with azaleas, camellias and crepe myrtle that wrap the mansion in greenery and blossoms most of the year. Hours vary. An admission fee is charged. Inquire at Bob Cox's Antiques.

Loyd's Hall.

About five-and-a-half-miles north of town, US 167 turns south off US 71. One mile down US 167 a sign directs travelers onto a parish road which leads to Loyd's Hall Plantation. Still a working plantation, Loyd's Hall, circa 1810, was built by one of the Lloyds of the famous English insurance family, according to the present owner Anne Fitzgerald. This particular Lloyd, a black sheep of no small repute, spelled his name with one L at the insistence of his family.

Beulah Davis guides visitors through the home, along the way she demonstrates how to roll the lumps out of a Spanish moss mattress. Her ghost stories memorialize a suicide victim, a violin player who

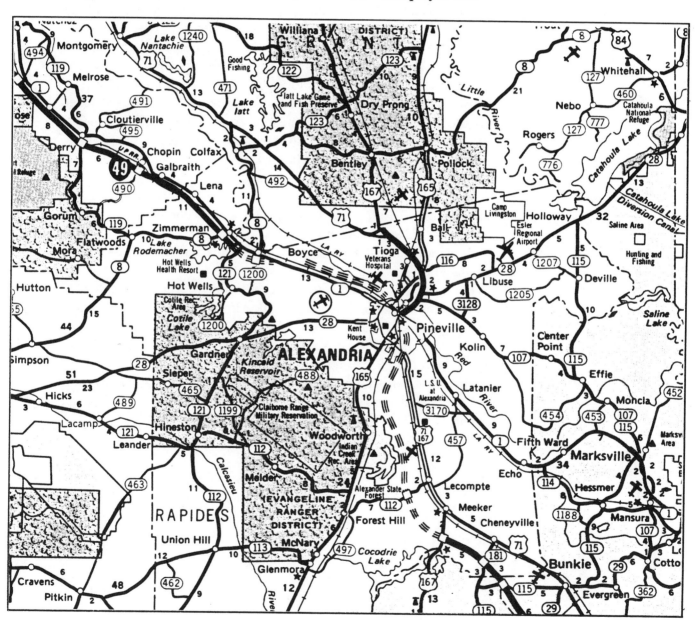

favors the second story balcony, and a Federal soldier who supposedly was in love with a daughter of the family. The soldier lingered behind after his unit moved out. Unflattered by his attention, a family member shot him and covered up the fact by burying him under the house. Beulah points out the blood stain still on the floor of the attic room assigned to the plantation's school teacher. Beulah says she has heard and seen too many mysterious happenings around the house to discount the ghost stories, but she is convinced that all the spirits are friendly.

The Yankees used the house as a headquarters for a while and left a couple of bullet holes in the first floor hallway as mementoes. Beulah also points out spots in the dining room door where Indian arrows are said to be embedded. Beulah says the house was under hostile attack by local Indians at least once during its life.

An antique and gift shop is located in a cabin behind the main house. Civic groups and clubs often enjoy lunch or dinner (by reservation) with their tour of the mansion. At evening meals a gospel trio entertains. Loyd's Hall also offers bed and breakfast accommodations. An admission fee is charged.

Alexandria and Pineville are located on the Red River at the junction of US 167, 165, 71, I-49, LA 1 and 28 about 188 miles northwest of New Orleans.

Accommodations, fast food establishments and restaurants are available in Alexandria.

For more information contact: The Rapides Parish Convention and Visitor's Bureau, P.O. Box 8110, Alexandria, LA 71306. Telephone 318-443-7049.

Hotel Bentley, 200 De Soto Street, Alexandria, LA 71301. Telephone 800-356-6835 (inside Louisiana 800-624-2778).

Historic Cheneyville, P.O. Box 176, Cheneyville, LA 71325.

Loyd's Hall, Route 1, Box 150, Cheneyville, LA 71325. Telephone 318-776-5641.

11

Marksville

Here on the high bluffs of Old River, an earthen wall has stood the test of time. For 2,000 years it has encircled a ceremonial center built by Native Americans. It varies in height from three to seven feet around the ancient site with the original breaks for gates still in place. Inside the wall, five mounds remain to tantalize our imaginations. The people who lived here were a southern branch of the Hopewellian culture once centered in Ohio and Illinois. According to anthropologists, they built this center behind these walls to perform their burial rituals.

The two flat-topped rectangular mounds within the walls were probably once the bases of temples, sanctuaries where ancient people prayed to their gods. We can imagine that the plaza, the wide flat field stretching across the prairie to the conical burial mounds, filled with people on holy days. Their songs and chants may have drowned out the bird songs.

We do know from evidence offered by anthropologists that the Indian religion centered on ancestor worship until about A.D. 700. Kin groups preserved family bones in special houses, eventually covering them with large conical earth mounds as final acts of veneration. After A.D. 700 a new concept, worship of the sun and other deities, became popular and large rectangular mounds were built as bases for wooden temples. The people believed spirits resided in all natural forces and in animals, and that these spirits controlled their actions. Shamans had power over these spirits.

This ancient place clings to silence even though hard pressed by encroaching residential districts. But archaeologists and anthropologists don't try to read silence. They read dirt, deciphering the mysterious streaks and lumps through layers of soil as if they were translating a book from a foreign language. Midden piles, the scientific name for ancient garbage dumps, are artifact files, tangible facts of ancient history safeguarded by neglect. Experts have read and studied this site so much they can guide visitors back across the barriers of time to the Marksville of A.D. 400 to 1000.

The journey is best begun in the white-painted brick museum in

Road Follows Curve of Ancient Wall, Marksville.

Flattop Mound and Plaza, Marksville.

the Marksville State Commemorative Area. The arched doors open into an alcove leading to an interior courtyard paved with red brick, planted with palms and centered with a well. A secret world, alien to the hardwoods encircling the ancient wall outside, unknown to the oaks and cedars rising from the mounds, waits inside. The museum walls are lined with cypress. The aroma of the wood subtly scents the air. The silent world of the ancients gains words here.

The scientists have left signs on the wall and displays in cases to guide us gently on our journey. The first sign reads, "Ideas are seldom created whole. They develop when man adapts and combines what he learns from other men or from observation. Archaeology is the study of prehistoric cultural ideas and how they developed in economy, social organization and art."

The signs go on to offer a short course in how prehistoric sites are located: by searching old maps, early explorers' reports and recent aerial photographs, as well as by interviewing farmers who know of surface features in a given area. Then archaeologists take to the field, collecting surface artifacts and making records on the spot.

According to the signs, "Man has lived in the Lower Mississippi

Museum, Marksville.

Valley for over 12,000 years. Long before De Soto's ragged army discovered the Mississippi River in 1541 and provided the first written records. Archaeological excavations have reconstructed this history in some detail to about 400 B.C. Before that it remains a fragmentary outline.''

The signs go on to tell us, some of the oldest pottery found in Louisiana was made about 2,000 years ago and was unearthed here at Marksville. Displays show samples of how the pottery was made and decorated, how it evolved and how it was used.

The people who lived here during the early years are described as being slender, with long heads. By A.D. 500 the population is described as being stocky, with round heads.

Their hunting, fishing, food preparation and agricultural endeavors are explored. The people's homes were circular thatched huts scattered in communities near their fields.

Ornaments found in burials and displayed here include shell and pearl necklaces, copper ear plugs and bracelets, feathers and bones, bits of cloth (they wove textiles at standing looms and made clothing from the resulting material).

Outside, wandering across the fields and through the woods along the paths of the park, communing with the same nature the ancient Americans knew, the lessons housed in the museum seem less matter-of-fact, more mystical.

Mound Number Four, the conical burial mound nearest the museum building, was excavated in 1927 and again in 1933. The official reports from that dig say some of the burials in the mound were made in a large square vault of earth which was covered by layers of cane and clay, and that this central chamber occupied the larger part of the mound.

Though the state owns the 39-acre park, due to a lack of operating funds it has been leased to the Tunica-Biloxi Tribe of Indians who live in the area. Their small reservation (134 acres) is part of an original Spanish land grant given to members of the tribe when they originally moved into the area during the late 1700s. Though they have no direct known relationship with the Marksville Indians and are originally from Mississippi, the tribe is spiritually in tune with the people and the place. The Tunica lived around Clarksdale, Mississippi, in a province called QuizQuiz, when De Soto and his cohorts came through the area in 1541. They had no known contact with Europeans again until the French arrived in the area over a century later. By then the diseases brought by the Europeans had ravaged not only the population but their cultural and social systems as well. The French found them living in small villages near the mouth of the

Conical Mound, Marksville.

Yazoo and reported that they were a good natured and pleasant people. They became fast friends of the French and it is speculated that because of that friendship they were driven from their homes around the Yazoo by the Chickasaw at the suggestion of the English. They moved south of the Natchez Indians' stronghold in southwestern Mississippi, to the Fort Adams/Tunica Hills area to escape the Chickasaw. Later they moved to the Pointe Coupee area before moving into their present location.

They aided the French in wiping out the surviving bands of Natchez Indians after the Natchez uprising in 1729, and made themselves valuable trading partners by offering a supply of salt, horses and other commodities. Anthropologist believe the Tunica became very successful and wealthy in their dealings with the French because of the vast amounts of European goods found buried with their dead. One Frenchman reported of the Tunica, "He has learned of us to hoard up money."

The Tunica Treasure, an archaeological cache of ancient ornaments and artifacts found at Angola, has been returned to the tribe and will be on display at the Tunica-Biloxi reservation as soon as a suitable museum can be built for it. (The Tunica and Biloxi merged in historic times through intermarriage and common cultural practices.)

The traditional Corn Festival, also called the Fete du Blé, an ancient religious celebration, has been adapted into a modern festival and is held at the reservation each year around the first of July. Rose White, a daughter of the tribe's last hereditary chief (the tribe is now governed by a council headed by a chairman), recalls that the festival was celebrated "late into the 1940s" and then discontinued for a number of years. One of the ancient religious aspects of the festival that has been revived is, as Rose puts it, "Sharing the feast with ones who have gone. We put fresh corn in little packs and put one on each grave. The first year we did it after not having done it in so long, we just felt so good."

Native American ballgames, dancing and performances, plus corn eating and corn cooking contests are just some of the activities that highlight the festival each year. There is a Catholic Mass which incorporates the modern religion of the people with their ancient celebration.

Native arts and crafts are for sale at the commemorative area's museum as well as at the festival. Rose White can usually be found near the center of tribal activities and is a great storyteller and resource person for those with more questions about the Tunica-Biloxi.

Also in the modern town of Marksville is the Hypolite-Bordelon

Hypolite-Bordelon Home, c. 1820.

Home, circa 1820, which is both a museum and the town's tourism information office. This Creole home is considered typical of early Avoyelles Parish, and the Bordelon family, who built the house, was one of the parish's pioneer families.

The house's charm is enhanced with an herb garden plot in back, along with a chicken coop, outhouse, sugar pot, and martin boxes on tall poles. The house itself is of *bousillage* construction and rests on cypress blocks. The roof is wood shingled and the windows are covered with shutters. The front is whitewashed but the sides and back proudly sport a grey patina only age brings. The house is shaded by live oaks and encircled by an unpainted cypress fence. Rose trellises offer the promise of blossoms in season. Up on the front porch benches await weary visitors who might want to linger within the boundaries of the old homestead and watch the world go by. Admission is free, but hours are limited. Closed on weekends. Located on LA 1 in town.

On the courthouse square a plaque commemorates Fort De Russy, a Civil War out post, four miles away.

Marksville is located on LA 1 about 30 miles southeast of Alexandria.

Fast food establishments and some restaurants are located in town. Best bets for overnight accommodations are in Alexandria.

For more information contact: Marksville State Commemorative Area, 700 Martin Luther King Dr., Marksville, LA 71351. Tele-

phone 318-253-9546. Located east of LA 1 and LA 452 at the end of
Allen Street. The route is well marked through town.   Hours vary.
An admission fee is charged.

   Tunica-Biloxi Tribe, Hwy. 1 South, Marksville, LA 71351. Telephone 318-253-9767. Admission fees are charged to the Corn
Festival and will also be charged to the Tunica Treasure Museum.

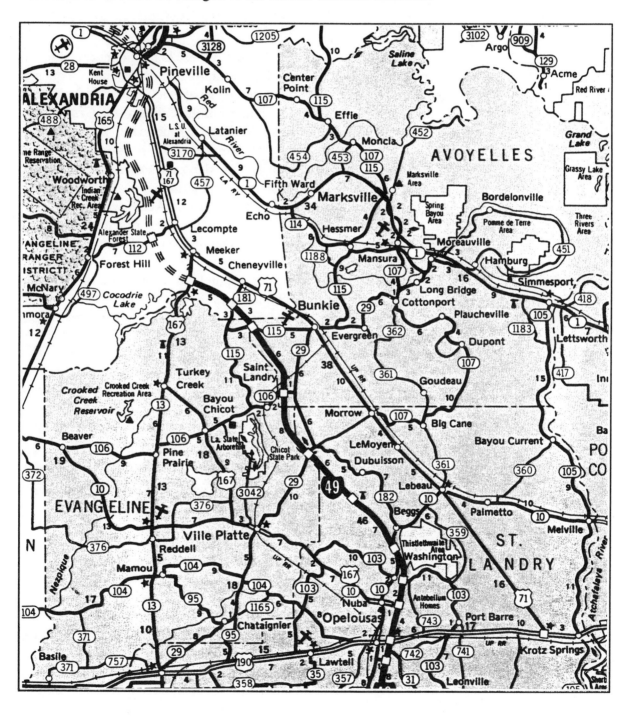

12

Eunice, Ville Platte
and the Cajun Prairie

Where does Cajun country begin? Where is the boundary, the line, the invisible wall that marks the beginning and end? That's a question that's about as easy to answer as, what is a Cajun? Technically, we all know. Cajuns are descendants of the exiles of the *Grand Derangement* when the British mercilessly rounded up and expelled the French inhabitants of Acadia (Nova Scotia). A goodly number of those refugees made their way to Louisiana and carved out an existence for themselves in the swamps, along the bayous and up in the prairie country of St. Landry, Evangeline and Acadia parishes. But in modern times Cajun has also become the name of a culture, of a lifestyle that embraces a myriad of people from different ethnic and national backgrounds.

If there is a boundary between Cajun land and the rest of the world you might find its northern boundaries here on the Louisiana prairie—in the grocery stores, at the cafes, on the radio programs and on portable signs that boldly announce fresh cracklins' and hot *boudin*.

A few scattered signs gradually proliferate. You might see the first ones as far north and east as Bunkie in Avoyelles Parish. From Bunkie, a railroad town looking like a western movie set along its main street, you can head south into a profoundly different cultural zone. The tourist information center, US 71, located in the Epps House, circa 1853, makes the point that visitors are nearing the outer edges of plantation country. Head south on LA 29. Bunkie's southern outskirts are blessed with ancient oaks. At Eola a faded red school house sits in a plowed field of red dirt. Soon the rust red soil will give way to the black dirt of the coastal plain.

LA 29 runs to Ville Platte where a portion of the old Spanish Trail, a road with many arms and branches, came through from New Iberia headed to Natchitoches and then westward. Ville Platte boasts a contingent of folks with British and French, but not Acadian, ancestors who become very excited about the casual and indiscriminate use of the word Cajun. The town's first mayor, Marcellin Garand, served as an officer in Napoleon's army.

The importance of cotton to the local economy is celebrated at the Louisiana Cotton Festival here each year during the second week of October. This festival may be the best time for visitors to explore the cultural heritage of the town. In fact, throughout this section of the state festivals and special celebrations are probably the very best time and way to explore area history. Parades, *fais do dos*, a harvest Mass, and the *Tournoi de la Ville Platte* make the Cotton Festival unique. The *Tournoi*, which has been held locally for almost a hundred years, is said to be derived from the "ancient sport of French kings." During the *Tournoi* mounted horsemen race over a circular course spearing rings to gain points.

Ville Platte, the flat town, basks in the elegance of white board fences along its roadways enclosing fields where horses romp.

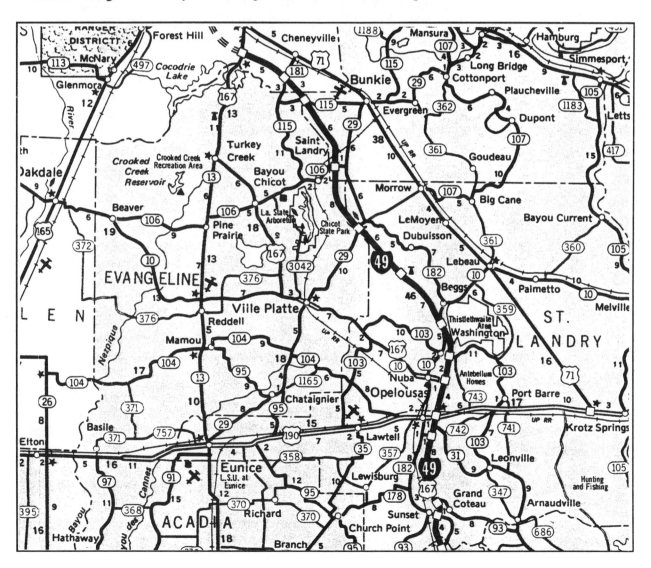

Horses are so dear, even Mardi Gras comes on horseback. The *Courir du Mardi Gras* is celebrated on Mardi Gras Day each year in Louisiana country style with costumed riders roaming the country-side soliciting contributions to a community-size gumbo. The contributions are made after the riders entertain with songs and dances at local farmhouses.

This old custom is the backbone of Mardi Gras from Mamou to Church Point and any number of places in between. At Mamou the *Courir du Mardi Gras* is an occasion when costumed male riders jealously guard their frolicking ride from female interlopers. The alcoholic spirits do flow at these country carnivals.

Eunice's *Courir du Mardi Gras* is just one of the activities of its Fat Tuesday celebrations. Tourists will find a special welcome at the day-long activities, many family oriented, that include several parades and a Young People's Cajun and Zydeco (an African-American interpretation of Cajun) Music Talent Contest. As a matter of fact, the Cajun and Zydeco music are as plentiful as the costumes, crawfish and *boudin*.

At the junction of LA 29, US 190 and LA 13, Eunice has declared itself "the capital of the Cajun Prairie." Jean Lafitte National Historical Park, Acadian Culture Center, corner of South Third and Park Avenue, is setting up shop in an old farm implement store and will feature exhibits and videos, as well as crafts and music workshops.

The Eunice Museum, located in the old depot next door to the chamber of commerce, 220 South First Street, is very near the site where on September 12, 1894, C. C. Duson proclaimed that the town would be established and named for his wife Eunice and then proceeded to sell lots. The museum contains much memorabilia on the customs of Cajun Mardi Gras, pioneer farming, homemade crafts and toys, as well as information on the local railroad's and newspaper's histories.

In keeping with the Louisiana tradition of celebrating good food, Eunice plays host to The World Championship Crawfish Etoufee Cookoff the last Sunday in March, at the Northwest Community Center. Amateurs and professionals vie for awards to the accompaniment of Cajun and Zydeco music.

Eunice even celebrates Saturday night, every Saturday night. "Let the *Bons Temps Rouler*," a weekly Cajun music radio show, is broadcast from the Liberty Center for the Performing Arts, a 1924 movie house at the corner of South Second Street and Park Avenue. Sponsored by the city of Eunice and the Jean Lafitte National Historical Park, the two hour show from 6 to 8 p.m. features Cajun and Zydeo music in Grand Ole Opry and Louisiana Hayride style. Cajun humorists spell the musicians and time is also reserved for local cooks to share their favorite recipes. Admission is by donation, children under 12 are admitted free.

If you wear your dancing shoes and want to participate in Cajun entertainment history-in-the-making, there is a wide selection of Cajun dance halls, with live bands, along US 190.

Eunice is located at the junction of US 190 and LA 29 and LA 13 about 18 miles west of Opelousas. Ville Platte is located at the junction of LA 29 and US 167 about 18 miles northeast of Eunice.

Some overnight accommodations are available at Eunice. Fast food establishments and restaurants are plentiful throughout the Cajun Prairie Country.

For more information contact: Eunice Chamber of Commerce, 200 South First Street, Eunice, LA 70535. Telephone 318-457-2565.

Evangeline Economic and Planning District, P.O. Box 90070, Lafayette, LA 70509.

Louisiana Office of Tourism, Box 94291, Baton Rouge, LA 70804-9291. Telephone 800-334-8626 or in Louisiana 504-342-8119.

13

Opelousas, Washington and Grand Coteau

Towns fall in love. Opelousas did. Jim Bowie swept her off her feet. Mesmerized her. She's still carrying the torch after all these years. Every chance she gets, she names something in his honor. Why she loved him and still loves him so, like all romances, is a mystery. Maybe it was chemistry.

Jim Bowie's brother John wrote a brief essay for *DeBow's Review* in 1852 about his famous sibling. He described him as "a stout, rather raw-boned man, of six feet height, weighed 180 pounds, and about as well made as any man I ever saw." John went on to say his brother's hair was "not quite red," that his deep set grey eyes were "penetrating in their glance," his complexion fair, his cheekbones high, "...altogether ... a manly, fine-looking person."

John doesn't disclaim his brother's wild nature or love of excitement, which he thinks developed during the years Jim lived on nearby Bayou Boeuf, where some of his favorite activities were catching bears, roping alligators and breaking wild horses. John assures us that his brother was possessed of a good temper "unless aroused by some insult, when the displays of his anger were terrible, and frequently terminated in some tragical scene."

Jim Bowie was born in Cumberland County, Tennessee, and as soon as he was old enough raised hell on the Mississippi from Natchez to New Orleans with a dueling knife of his own special design. He became a slave trader who in his early thirties moved on to Texas where a few years later (1836) he died at the Alamo. But none of these facts have disqualified him as Opelousas' favorite son. His family moved to Louisiana in 1802, when he was about seven years old. His brother says Jim spent his formative years in Catahoula Parish. The family came to Opelousas after the War of 1812. Their massive plantation operations included more than 20,000 acres, beginning just south of South City Park on the west side of LA 182. Their old home place stood on the east side of LA 182, on South Union Street, and is now the site of the Jim Bowie Branch of the First National Bank. Even though Jim moved on to Texas in 1827, the town clings so tightly to his memory that in the hearts and minds of many townspeople he will always be here.

But Opelousas, the European outpost established in 1720 by the French for its advantageous location more than 70 feet above sea level, has a far more ancient past. The Opelousas Indians, for whom the town was named, had a village here when the French arrived. One of the more dramatic legends still lingering from pre-European times tells the tale of how a group of Attakapas, allegedly cannibals, lived here until the Opelousas united with several groups of other Indians, including Choctaw and Alibamons, to rid the area of the Attakapas. The Opelousas may have been kinsmen of the Attakapas. There is considerable debate over the meaning of "Opelousas." The most commonly accepted meaning is "black leg." However, there are those who adamantly claim "Opelousas" means salt water. The Opelousas were joined first by the French, then by the Spanish, and eventually by the Acadian exiles and the Americans at their village site. One of the more glamourous settlers, Louis Garrigues, was a general in Napoleon's army.

A letter written from Opelousas in 1806 by a newly arrived Methodist minister relates that the local people were very dissatisfied with the American government and that "three-fourths" of the people hoped the Spanish would regain the territory. He wrote that "three-fourths" of the people were French and that the country was "three-fourths" prairie. He also said, "The people are rich in cattle. They have from one to three thousand head of cattle to a farmer..." He went on to note that it would be possible to carry off all their possessions from their homes "on your back." He concluded that, much to his dismay, locals spent the Sabbath in frolicking and gambling.

After the fall of Baton Rouge in 1863, Opelousas served as the Confederate capital of Louisiana for one session of the legislature before the capital was moved to Shreveport. The Governor's Mansion, circa 1850, at Grolee and Liberty streets, is an architectural reminder of those days. The Greek Revival mansion was home to Louisiana's Confederate Lt. Gov. Homere Mouton. Thomas Moore, the Confederate governor, resided with the Moutons while Opelousas was the capital.

One of the oldest surviving houses in the area is the Michel Prudhomme Home, circa 1810, 1152 Prudhomme Circle, built by a native of Strasbourg, France, who arrived at the Poste De Opelousas sometime before 1774. During the Civil War, Union soldiers were quartered in the house, which is credited with saving it from the Federal torches.

Another of the antebellum homes in town, Estorage, circa 1827, blends Creole and Greek Revival architecture. St. Landry Catholic

Jim Bowie House, Opelousas.

Church, Main and Church streets, circa 1908, houses records dating from the mid-1700s.

In keeping with the legends close to the town's heart, the Jim Bowie Museum, US 190 East, shares a park-like setting with the St. Landry Parish Tourism Information Center. The center is housed in a small Cajun-style cabin, where visitors can find information on all area attractions and view artifacts from the town's Indian past as well as from its days as a European outpost on the frontier.

The Jim Bowie House, an antique Louisiana frontier home, once the property of a free woman of color remembered as ''Venus,'' can be viewed from the outside. (The house was never Jim Bowie's home.) Many mementoes of the Bowie family are on display in the tourist information center. Pavilions, an old train engine, picnic tables, shade-offering pecan trees, and rest rooms make the site a pleasant stopping place.

Maps and other information available at the center can guide you into the surrounding countryside. Just west of I-49, LA 182 leads south to Sunset. A true relic of the past, regular public cock fights are said to be a popular local entertainment during the summer months in an arena off LA 182. The tourist information center personnel can mark the exact spot on a map for you.

Also at Sunset, is Chretien Point Plantation, circa 1831, said to have been the first plantation in the area to switch from the cultivation of cotton to rice after the Civil War. Stories claim the stairway at the house inspired Tara's in the movie *Gone with the Wind*. The house is an eclectic mixture of Creole, Greek Revival and Georgian architectural influences and is open to the public daily. An admission fee is charged.

St. Landry Parish still practices Creole frontier customs. Everyone knows the *fais do dos* (dance parties) and the *boucherie* (butchering time get-together), but other less well known customs such as the *coup de main* are still practiced. The *coup de main* is the Creole version of a barn raising or cabin raising as practiced on the American frontier, but it extends to almost any project, even planting a garden. In fact as you drive about the parish you may see a *coup de main* in action. A brochure published for the 1984 World's Fair claimed that French was still spoken in the area to the extent that local dogs usually understood only French commands.

Traveling back to Opelousas, take US 190 east to Port Barre. Located on bayous Courtableau and Teche (tesh), Port Barre served as a crossroads for the area. French traders, seeking business with the Opelousas Indians, were the town's first settlers in about 1740. During the American Revolution the trading post here was the staging area for the Opelousas militia and their Indian allies as they prepared to cross the Atchafalaya swamp to Baton Rouge, where under the command of the Spanish governor, Bernardo de Galvez, the American allies fought and defeated the British. There is a park here to mark the "birthplace" of the Teche.

From Port Barre, travel north on LA 103. The road twists and turns like a bayou itself as it meanders around fields and farms to the town of Washington.

Discovering Washington may be worth a trip to St. Landry Parish—all by itself. Wrapped in the mysteries of the past, the old steamboat town lies waiting in the shade of its ancient oaks, hoping company will call. LA 103 curves into town around the base of an ancient Indian mound with a white Greek Revival farmhouse atop, then runs past Steamboat House to LA 10, Main Street. Steamboat House in a Dutch Colonial style, exotic in this part of the world, is a landmark travelers can't miss.

This country town, population 1,434, with white clapboard houses and an old-fashioned Main Street, is heady with the perfume of garden flowers on a lazy summer day. The Washington Museum and Tourist Information Center, at the corner of Main (LA 10) and DeJean (LA 103), offers visitors insight into the town's beginnings with displays of area artifacts and a video. (The museum itself is situated on the site of Plonsky's Opera House and is actually made from the old Opera house's bricks.) The River Opelousas/Bayou Courtableau gave the town life. According to the story told at the museum, the town is situated on land originally granted to Jacques Courtableau. The river underwent a name change to Bayou Courtableau, and the gentleman deeded the site to a "guardian of the church" and the church started selling arpent-sized lots in 1822. At first the settlement was called Church's Landing, but when it was incorporated in 1835 it became Washington. Bayou Courtableau was navigable to New Orleans on the Mississippi via Grand Lake and Bayou Plaquemine and also through the Old River. The town, about six miles north of Opelousas via LA 10, was head of navigation on Bayou Courtableau and the starting point of the southwest Wells Fargo stage line. Many of the steamboats listed Washington as their homeport and their captains and crew built homes in the town.

Warehouses lined the banks of the bayou. One still survives as the Steamboat Warehouse Restaurant, Main Street, and displays antiques and relics of the steamboat era as well as serving local renditions of Louisiana cuisine.

The last steamboats made their journeys up the muddy red bayou around the turn of the century. After that, the produce and products of the area left via rail, usually from Opelousas to the south. Then the miracle happened. Without the steady input from the outside world, Washington evolved at its own pace, taking what it needed or wanted from modern technology, rejecting whatever seemed unnecessary. All visitors are the beneficiaries of this turn of fate.

Comfort spreads out under the oaks surrounding the Hinckley House, circa late 18th century, which became the residence of a steamboat captain. From the gravel street to the low meadow across the road, to the deep, cooling shade, there's no doubt this house is a home. This home is open to tourists for an admission fee and contains family heirlooms, antiques and steamboat memorabilia.

Other homes at Washington open to tourists for a fee are: Nicholson House of History, built by the first mayor of Washington and used as a hospital and Confederate headquarters during the Civil War; Arlington, circa 1829, one of the largest antebellum homes in the area; Paradis, circa 1852, West DeJean Street; Camellia Cove, circa 1825, 205 West Hill Street; and Etienne de la Morandiere, circa 1830, a two-story French planters'-style home with two galleries across the front, built of native cypress.

The museum offers free maps of the town plus listings of more than 50 in-town attractions, most of which are architecturally signifi-

Hickley House, Washington.

cant. Three miles from Washington on LA 746 at the confluence of bayous Boeuf and Cocodrie is Starvation Point, built in the late 1700s as a trading post and overnight stop for travelers.

One of the most delightful stops any visitor to Washington can make is Magnolia Ridge Antebellum Home and Gardens, circa 1830, on Highway 103, at the western edge of town. The most amazing feature of the establishment is that it is free—and privately funded. Visitors can park at the gatehouse and follow walking paths through four miles of plantation grounds. The paths loop back and forth around houses, wildflowers, identified trees, the main house, the sundial garden, a 400-year-old oak, a lily garden, the stables, an Indian mound, a cotton patch, a cypress swamp, site of a Civil War skirmish, a cemetery, across a coulee (a small stream), around a big bass pond and numerous other attractions.

If you need to stretch your legs, breathe some fresh air, and get in touch with nature this is the perfect place. You might also marvel at the generosity of the owners, who open their world of white board fences, red roses and green grass meadows to strangers—just for the joy of sharing.

Magnolia Ridge, c. 1830.

The museum/tourist information center provides maps of the town and information about any of the homes you might wish to visit. There are horse-drawn carriage rides available for tours of the town on the weekends. Check at the museum for details.

But there are even more treasures and hidden delights in St. Landry Parish. From Washington, head south on US 167 or I-49 to Grand Coteau, take the LA 93 exit, and drive into the village of oak alleys and serenity.

Most everything here is old, and settled, most everything is peaceful and calm. The Academy of the Sacred Heart, circa 1821, is one of the oldest schools in Louisiana. The school sits in formal gardens patterned after French gardens. The main building, circa 1830, has three stories, with dormer rooms under the pitched roof. Galleries across the front of the three floors are supported by iron posts and decorated with wrought-iron railings. The Jesuits built a college for their order here in 1840, and the first rector of the school is credited

Academy of the Sacred Heart, c. 1821, in Early Morning Fog.

with planting the avenue of oaks fronting the academy grounds to give shade to the priests who walked from the college (novitiate) to the academy to say mass for the nuns and students. Other avenues were also planted. Today the alleys beckon to visitors as avenues of meditation.

The academy was able to stay open during the Civil War due to the intervention of Union General Nathaniel Banks' wife. Their daughter attended a Sacred Heart school in New York. The superior of the convent there asked Mrs. Banks to have her husband "look after" the nuns at Grand Coteau. He did, going so far as to supply them with provisions from the Union commissary. A year after the war ended, what is considered a miracle in the Catholic church occurred at Grand Coteau. According to the story a young woman was dying, and the nuns prayed for intercession through John Berchmans, a Jesuit novice who had died sometime earlier. The girl was healed and in time John Berchmans became a saint.

In the early morning fog, under the protecting canopy of the oaks, you can feel you are wandering near a universal sense of peace no matter what your religion. In April the damp air smells of roses and wild Carolina jasmine. The nearby fields are freshly furrowed, the kudzu is beginning its annual outreach. Morning joggers and walkers

Avenue of Oaks, in the Morning Fog, Grand Coteau.

meander along their exercise routes. Quaint Cajun houses, Creole
cottages and turn-of-the-century storefronts line the streets. St. Charles Church sits at the edge of a pine grove, at the end of an oak alley.
Down another alley, in an oak grove, Our Lady of the Oaks Retreat
House awaits guests. The fog becomes as heavy as rain. Down from
Edwin Smith Square and the community bulletin board, village
streets need to be explored. Fields of wildflowers, orchards of
pecans, people who smile and say hello tantalize the imagination. If
you linger for lunch at the Kitchen Shop Tearoom, you might find
even more excuses to stay, to extend your visit, to draw closer to the
peace.

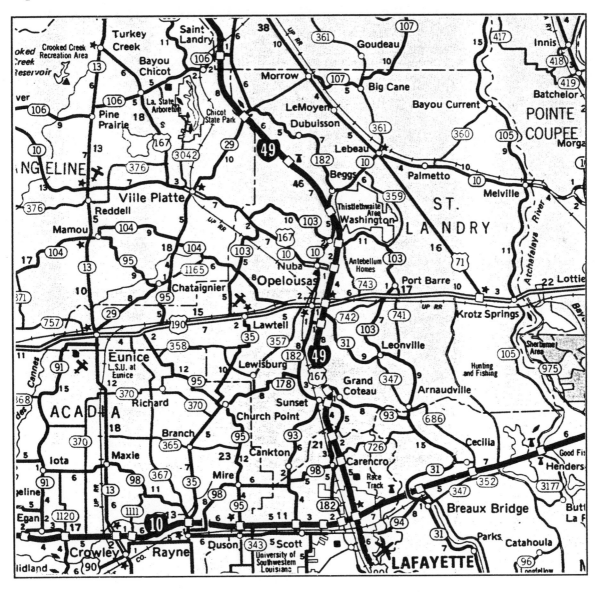

Opelousas is located at the junction of US 190 and I-49 about 136 miles northwest of New Orleans. Washington is located about six miles north of Opelousas on LA 10. Grand Coteau is located just off US 167/I-49 on LA 93 about ten miles south of Opelousas and ten miles north of I-10 at Lafayette.

Accommodations are available at Opelousas. There are some bed and breakfast establishments in the parish. Fast food establishments and restaurants are plentiful.

For more information contact: St. Landry Parish Tourist Commission, P.O. Box 1415, Opelousas, LA 70571-1415. Telephone 318-948-6263.

Washington Museum and Visitor Information Center, Washington, LA 70589. Telephone 318-826-3626.

Academy of the Sacred Heart, P.O. Box 310, Grand Coteau, LA 70541. Telephone 318-662-5275. (Fees are charged for tours of the academy.)

14

Lafayette

You can get to the crux of the matter in Lafayette. You can lift the mossy veil and look unabashedly into the Cajun soul.

But you will need a guide to take you across the swamps of creeping shopping malls, one who knows the bayous of the soul, the coulees of the heart. Just such a guide lives here. His name is George Rodrigue. An artist, a captor of Cajun essence, a distiller of Cajun soul, a translator of Cajun thought, he guides with his paintbrush. Actually, you don't even have to leave home to travel into his Cajun world. For your first journey his book, *The Cajuns of George Rodrigue*, is all you need.

History is essence and soul, mirrored through culture, cherished in attitudes and details of ongoing daily life. George Rodrigue's history of the Cajuns is pure essence and soul, poignantly accurate, reaching beyond the specific, touching the universal.

We are all attracted to the legend of survival, of being thrown into an impossible alien environment and adapting, making do and finding a unique joy in being alive that nothing can destroy. That may be one reason why so many people want to come here, to bask in the Cajun world. Another reason may be that once people have seen the paintings of George Rodrigue they want to search out the real-life dimensions of his world of stark contrast, haunting shapes and poignant stares.

So we come, looking for a memory of quiet bayous and soft-spoken country French. We find a modern city deep into technology and commerce. Lafayette in the morning is thick with traffic, a treadmill of fast-paced cars streaming past acres and acres of motels along the bayou, swiftly flowing past the meadows of shopping malls, running up past the university and the great throngs of students working up their courage to dash across the paths of speeding cars. Don't give up. The memory is here.

The tourist information center, situated in an island dividing north and south traffic on US 90 at 16th, offers help. The white frame building, a version of an Acadian-style cottage with its silvery tin

Acadian Village.

roof gleaming in the sun, is the site of a historic marker commemorating the generosity of General Franklin Gardner, a native of New York City who married into Lafayette's Mouton family, and when the Civil War broke out "offered his sword to the South." Inside the cottage the Lafayette Convention and Visitors Commission offers free maps, brochures and real people who'll look up phone numbers and even draw you a map if necessary. They tell me how to get to George Rodrigue's studio and gallery on Jefferson.

Alice answers the bell and opens the door. Posters and prints line the walls, along with recent paintings. Alice says she's the artist-historian's girl Friday. She can answer any question. She says the artist lives downstairs in the three story turn-of-the-century Victorian house, has offices and gallery space on the second floor and a studio on the third floor. He's away in New York today, but the paintings, the transport to the Cajun world are here.

The paintings in the book, *The Cajuns of George Rodrigue*, especially record what the artist believes the culture was like when it was pure, before it bumped up hard against the outside world around the time of World War I. The images of special occasions, Sundays on the bayous, the meeting of a gourmet club, and just plain folks in their environment tell the story of a people, their unique land and the interwoven ties between the two.

A number of books containing the artists' works are on sale at the gallery, as well as posters, prints and notecards that are moderately priced. Rodrigue's work is available at a number of other galleries in Lafayette, New Orleans and southern Louisiana.

The gallery/studio/home, 1206 Jefferson, is very near the heart of downtown Lafayette where history lovers will want to search out other memories.

A town called Petit Manchac was here in the mid-1700s where the old Spanish Trail waded across Vermilion Bayou. The Acadians, descendants of the French who settled Nova Scotia in 1605, began to arrive in the area as early as 1765, with the largest groups arriving in 1785. One of these refugees in particular shaped the future of Lafayette. In 1821 Jean Mouton donated five acres of land in the area to the Catholic church and a chapel was built. A community called Vermilionville began to sprout up around it. In 1836 Vermilionville was incorporated, in 1884 the name became LaFayette, later it would be written Lafayette. The tourist information center has a brochure outlining a walking tour of the heart of the early city, Lafayette Centre.

The first stop on the tour is The Lafayette Museum, 1122 Lafayette Street. This was the home of Alexandre Mouton and Alfred

Mouton, a Confederate general and hero who died at the Battle of Mansfield. The museum is a house that grew. First it was a "maison Dimanche"—a Sunday house—for Jean Mouton's family. They lived out on a plantation in the Carencro area and came to town on Sunday for church. Since they needed a place to freshen up and rest after their trip, they built a "Sunday house" (circa 1800) consisting of one room with a kitchen separated by a dogtrot. After expanding the house to some degree, the Mouton family sold it in 1836 and the succeeding owners added their own touches, including a cupola, until it evolved into the structure that has become the museum. Inside, visitors will find memorabilia from early Lafayette.

The walking tour takes visitors past several different styles and samples of local architecture from the 19th century, including commercial establishments and private homes. The cathedral of St. John the Evangelist, circa 1913, is located at 914 St. John Street on land donated to the community by Jean Mouton. To the right of the cathedral is St. John's Oak, a 400-year-old tree and a charter member of the Live Oak Society. The Live Oak Society was founded by Dr. Edwin L. Stephens, first president of the University of Southwestern Louisiana, here. Members of the society are live oaks in Louisiana and nearby states believed to be at least a century old. Where documentation is unavailable on a tree's age measurements of 17 feet in girth four feet from the roots is generally accepted as being 100 years old. Each member has an "attorney" (a human being) who promises to secure the history of the individual tree, work for preservation and not permit the tree to be whitewashed. Annual dues are 25 acorns from each tree, which are planted in a nursery to provide future supplies of oak seedlings.

CODOFIL, Council for the Development of French in Louisiana, makes its home at 217 West Main, in a building called "the First City Hall." CODOFIL is a cultural organization which works to preserve Louisiana's French heritage through the French language.

A statue of the Confederate General Alfred Mouton stands at the corner of Jefferson and Lee streets. Outdoor murals on buildings spice up Lafayette Centre's visual impact.

Lafayette has long been home to a number of oil-related businesses and fortunes. Before the Civil War, cattle were one of the main industries in the area. Raising cattle and rustling cattle seem to have been equally popular. For awhile, rustling was so popular honest folks didn't stand a chance. Then, according to local legends, an army of vigilantes managed to gain possession of a cannon, and with that decisive weapon the tide was turned against the outlaws. Yellow fever and the Civil War took their toll on the community's popula-

Acadian Village.

tion, but through it all the underpinnings of the Cajun culture stayed intact.

Houses, buildings, furniture, fixtures, and tools of that culture can be explored at the Acadian Village, 200 Greenleaf Drive, off Ridge Road. This village, with its haunting charm, is unique in many ways. It is a project of the Lafayette Association for Retarded Citizens and serves as a training area for the handicapped, and it is also a museum dedicated to the preservation of Acadian culture. Music, language, crafts and architecture of the Cajun are honored here. The six houses along a tiny bayou are said to reflect Acadian architectural styles, and have been moved here from their original sites where they were homes to a diverse group of people. The general store, the white-steepled chapel and the blacksmith shop at the village are replicas. The buildings are constructed of cypress and/or *bousillage entre poteaux* (mud and Spanish moss mixture between posts). The general store (a gift shop) also utilizes pine and bricks.

The oldest house in the village, the Aurelie Bernard House, was built around 1800 at St. Martinville. Paintings in the house depict the expulsion of the Acadians from Nova Scotia as well as their arrival and settling in Louisiana. There are also Cajun music exhibits in the house.

The LeBlanc House was the birthplace of the remarkable Dudley J. LeBlanc. Mr. LeBlanc was a politician, an author and most importantly of all the inventor of "Hadacol," an elixir with about 12 per cent alcohol that was guaranteed to cure most anything. A major sponsor of radio programs, LeBlanc was well known throughout the South, as was Hadacol. Pictures in the house celebrate LeBlanc's fame; one of the more interesting is a black and white photograph of Hank Williams, Sr. and his Drifting Cowboys Band.

The Billeaud House, built before the Civil War, came to the village from the Billeaud Sugar Plantation at Broussard. Displayed inside are looms and homespun clothing and linens. Weaving is considered by many to be the premier Cajun craft. The St. John House, circa 1840, which was originally located in downtown Lafayette, is outfitted as an early school house.

The peaceful, romantic village, with a flock of cackling guinea hens running about the yards, ducks on the ponds and Cajun music playing in the general store—on an average day—surges into celebrations at special festivals throughout the year. The celebrations are especially wonderful occasions for children to visit the village.

The *Courir du Mardi Gras* is celebrated at the village every year on the Saturday before Mardi Gras Day. The *Bal de Maison* (house dance), a gathering of friends and neighbors at a home for a party

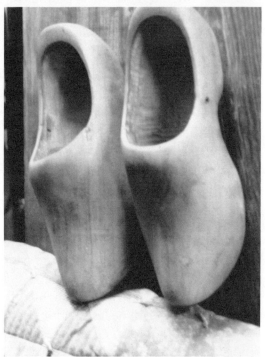

Details from a Cajun Home, Back Door Entrance, Cistern and Wooden Shoes Worn by Early Settlers.

Along the Bayou.

featuring music and dancing, is re-created the last weekend in August. *Jambalaya de Musique*, a celebration of music created by Cajuns, African-Americans and other cultures of south Louisiana, is usually held the third weekend in September in conjunction with Lafayette's *Festival Acadiens*. The Lafayette Association for Retarded Citizens celebrates its Cajun Festival, with everything the name implies, from food to music plus a flea market, on the third weekend of October. Christmas transforms the village into a fantasy land where homes and the church, the Chapel of New Hope, are decorated for an Acadian Christmas, and special celebrations are the order of the day. The event, dubbed *Noel Arrive!*, is sponsored by the Junior League of Lafayette.

The willows by the bayou, the clumps of irises at the water's edge, the outbuildings, the cane and red roses, the wild jasmine spilling over picket fences, slop jars under the beds, cowhide seats in straight chairs, and storytellers who emphasize the moral—all contribute to an informative and carefree visit both adults and children can enjoy at this recreated Cajun village.

Vermilionville, "A Cajun-Creole Attraction," will open at Beaver Park during the summer of 1990 and offer travelers to Lafayette even more opportunities to explore living history at a Creole plantation and in a Cajun village setting. Live music performances will be ongoing. And food will not be neglected: a restaurant, food court, and cooking school are guaranteed to give the new Vermilionville a very special appeal.

Lafayette is located at the junction of I-10, I-49 and US 90 about 130 miles west of New Orleans.

Accommodations, fast food establishments and restaurants are plentiful in the area.

For more information contact: The Lafayette Convention and Visitors Commission, P.O. Box 52066, Lafayette, LA 70505. Telephone 318-232-3737; outside LA 800-346-1958; Canada 800-543-5340.

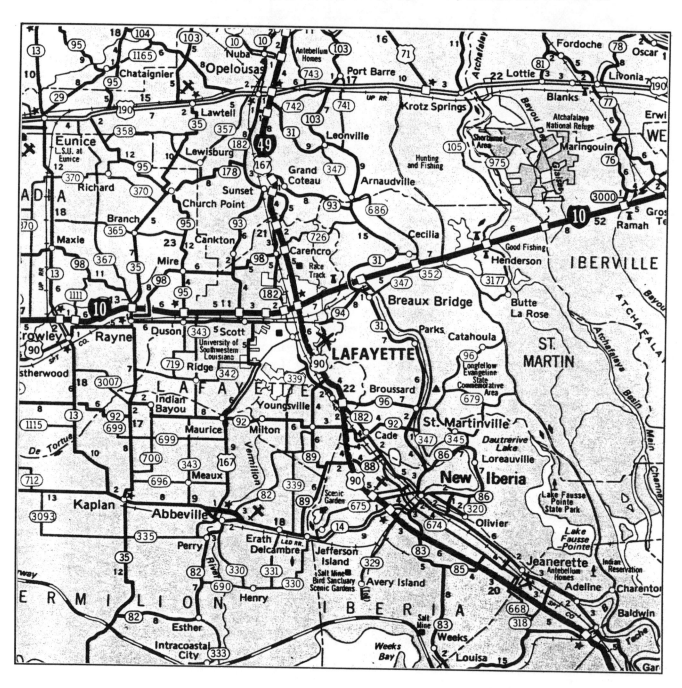

15

St. Martinville

"This is the forest primeval," whispers Henry Wadsworth Longfellow, as he guides us through the epic tale of *Le Grand Derangement*. He takes us to Nova Scotia, Acadia, to the village of Grand
Pré, to the church where the villagers are locked in by the British.
The Acadians, more than a hundred years from their French mother-
land, will not swear allegiance to the British crown that now controls
their American home.

Longfellow paints the word pictures. The torches fire the village,
the flames consume the town. There is mass confusion. Chaos.
People in turmoil. Upheaval. There are ships in the harbor. The
people are ordered to board. No concessions are granted, not even to
families. Mothers and children are separated, sons and daughters,
wives and husbands, lovers and their beloved are pried apart by the
British, driven apart by the wind, kept apart by the sea.

Eventually, after years of unceasing wandering some of the people
of Grand Pré find their way to south Louisiana. And the one person
Longfellow chose to symbolize a world ripped apart, Evangeline,
found her way to this small town of St. Martinville on the banks of
Bayou Teche.

Some historians say Longfellow's poem, first published in 1847,
overstates the cruelties involved in the British expulsion of the Acadians, that he chose the more emotional Acadian accounts of the
historic events on which to base his story. Few people living in this
small town would think the cruelties are overstated. However,
Longfellow is not free from criticism here; after all, he wrote his
story without ever having visited Louisiana or traveling the winding
trail he pushed his heroine down as she came south on the river.

Here, at St. Martinville, local people say there was a real
Evangeline—her name was Emmeline LeBiche and her lover, Gabriel, was Louis Arceneaux. The legend goes further, has many ins
and outs. But there is a house here which was allegedly the plantation home of Louis Arceneaux, and there is the Evangeline Oak at
the landing on Bayou Teche.

The oak is the magnet that draws thousands of travelers here each year. At the foot of Port Street, the oak sits in a patch of grass, roped off, encircled by concrete sidewalks (which go by the more romantic name *banquette* here). The bayou is just a few feet away. The police station is a next door neighbor on one side, La Place d'Evangeline Restaurant on the other. At the far edge of the shade, a couple of local musicians sit in straight-back chairs and make ''chank-a-chank'' tunes with their accordion and fiddle. Tourists sit on a park bench making conversation between sets, satiating their hunger for Cajun French words. Up in the oak's limbs (more of a Druid presence than Longfellow's pines and hemlocks of Nova Scotia) around the fuzzy edges of the resurrection fern, is blue sky. It is the same blue sky Evangeline saw when she lifted her eyes heavenward after falling asleep under the tree and missing a chance meeting with Gabriel who was passing on the bayou. We can move this close to the edge of heartbreak.

A statue of Evangeline, as portrayed in an early movie by Delores del Rio, sits in a tiny remnant of a graveyard behind St. Martin of Tours Church, less than two blocks away from the Evangeline Oak.

Evangeline's Statue. Posed for by Dolores del Rio. St. Martin of Tours Church.

Evangeline Oak.

Evangeline's memorial, enshrined in bronze, surrounded by red geraniums, shares the cemetery with a memorial to the officers of the Attakapas Militia who served under Spanish governor Galvez at the capture of Baton Rouge (New Richmond) and the Battle of Manchac in 1779 during the American Revolution. (Spanish Louisiana was loosely allied with the Americans against the British.) Chameleons dart back and forth across the monument, changing colors as rapidly and as often as the citizens of this district were called on to change nationalities over the years.

In front of the presbytère, the priest's home, circa 1856, on the square shared by the church and Le Petit Paris Museum, five flags and plaques tell the story of the nationality changes. One of the more confusing changes came in 1800, when Spain returned the Louisiana territory to France secretly (Spain had gained control of Louisiana in another secret treaty in 1762), with France only publicly acknowledging the transfer shortly before the land was sold to the Americans in 1803.

A statue of an Attakapas chieftain stands under the oaks of the church square. Strings of oak pollen cling to his face. An old-fashioned shopping district surrounds the square's green lawn and pink-beige church. Storefronts with porches and overhangs to offer shade, tout their goods with discreet signs. Herbert's Quality Jewelry, Thibodeaux's Café, F. C. Foti Grocery (''Live chickens and fresh shrimp''), Tancé Meat Market.

Le Petit Paris Museum with Statue of Attakapas Chief in Front.

Street Scene, St. Martinville.

Inside the Petit Paris Museum mementoes from the town's earliest days tell the story of how St. Martinville became known as a "little" Paris. (Many Parisians moved here to escape the French Revolution, bringing their culture and lifestyles with them.) Mardi Gras costumes are featured exhibits. The gift shop sells local crafts and a wide variety of books on topics related to the area, including an extensive, scholarly Cajun/English dictionary.

There is parking for tourists at the foot of Port Street. The La Place d'Evangeline is not only a restaurant, but also a bed and breakfast with a gift shop, as is the cottage across the street. La Place, originally the Castillo Hotel, probably built in the late 1700s, has enjoyed a wide variety of occupants. For a while it was a Catholic girls boarding school.

A short distance away, at 1200 North Main (LA 31), is the Longfellow-Evangeline State Commemorative Area, a 157-acre park on Bayou Teche. Here is the raised Creole cottage, circa 1836, that has on occasion been named the plantation home of Louis Arceneaux.

Here the story of the Acadians' arrival in the area is told. Though *Le Grand Derangement* is dated 1755, it was not until about 1765 that the Acadians began to make their way into this area, where they joined an established French Creole community. Coming into the park, which was once a *vacherie* (a Louisiana version of a cattle ranch), travelers first stop at the visitors center, where a museum exhibits area crafts and work methods as well as the resulting artifacts. One exhibit explains different house styles in the region. Spinning wheels, looms and weaving demonstrations highlight what many consider the top Cajun craft. Furniture, dishes, pipes, more Mardi Gras costumes, fans, walking canes, weapons, old clocks, saws, St. Martinville's first fire engine (1850), a Spanish moss gin and countless other pieces round out the display of area artifacts.

A brick-paved patio at the museum, fronts on the dark waters of the bayou, where antique cypress pirogues brave the elements within an outdoor cafe atmosphere. A gift shop in the museum/visitors center offers a unique selection of local handmade crafts ranging from baskets to voodoo dolls.

The raised Creole cottage-style plantation house is considered to be the centerpiece of the park. The plantation became prosperous under the ownership of Charles du Clozel, a Creole planter who purchased the place in the mid-1800s. Now, crows cry a morning wake-up call. The grassy meadow is speckled with white clover and dew. There is the smell of early southern morning—damp oaks and wet magnolia leaves. Soft, crumbling, antique bricks pave the walkway to the rustic cottage. Grinding stones, hand-pumps, herb

Creole Cottage, Frontside and Rear Views,
Longfellow—Evangeline State Commemorative Area.

gardens, and outbuildings round out the story of daily antebellum life. This is a house without pretensions. The resurrection fern clings with its brown tendrils to the oak branches, waiting for the rain. The rain is coming. The dark clouds are rolling in from the west. Clumps of wild yellow irises and crawdad chimneys share space in the low damp spaces in the house's front meadow. Gnarled cedars stand sentinel. The open windows let out the musty odors of age. Rustic pioneer furniture, pie safes, wash stands, lumpy beds and worn quilts stand inspection for the curious.

Just a few miles away, two miles from town on LA 96, another lifestyle of French-colonial Louisiana is remembered. But here, down the oak and pine alley, visitors need a generous dose of imagination. There are several versions of this tale. One is that a M. Charles Durand, wishing to give his daughter a grand wedding, imported spiders from China so the oak alley could be festooned with certain types of elegant spider webs. When the spiders had done their work, the webs were sprinkled with gold dust, and the alley was used for the grandest wedding procession ever seen before or since in the region. In another version of the story, the wedding was M. Durand's, not his daughter's.

Durand plantation house is gone now, but the oak/pine alley remains. The tiny remnants of the wedding story contrast sharply with the austere lifestyle attributed to Evangeline, but it is Evangeline, with her bronzed wooden shoes planted firmly on her pedestal behind St. Martin's, who rules local folklore.

St. Martinville is located on LA 96 off of US 90 about 15 miles southeast of Lafayette and about 14 miles north of New Iberia.

Some bed and breakfast accommodations are available at St. Martinville. Ample accommodations are available both at Lafayette and New Iberia. Restaurants and fast food establishments are located in the town.

For more information contact: Petit Paris Museum, 103 south Main Street, St. Martinville, LA 70582. Telephone 318-394-7334. An admission fee is charged to a portion of the museum.

Longfellow-Evangeline State Commemorative Area, 1200 N. Main Street, St. Martinville, LA 70582. Telephone 318-394-3754. An admission fee is charged.

Lafayette Convention and Visitors Commission, P.O. Box 52066, Lafayette, LA 70505. Telephone 318-232-3737; outside LA 800-346-1958; Canada 800-543-5340.

Iberia Parish Tourist Commission, P.O. Box 9196, New Iberia, LA 70562. Telephone 318-365-1540.

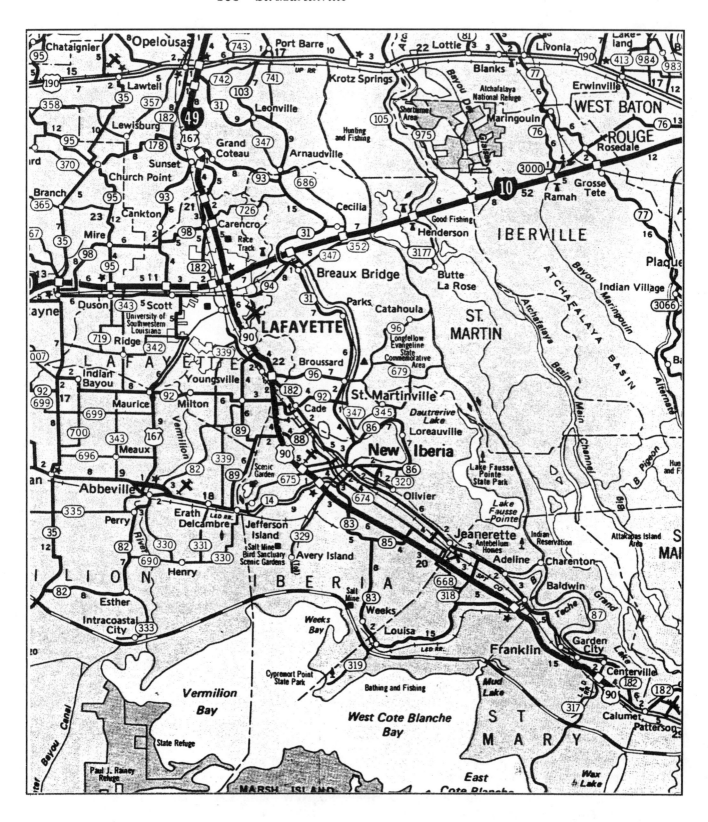

16
New Iberia

Sooner or later we have to talk about food. Sooner or later the tantalizing aromas and sample tastes will overwhelm even the most restrained appetite. Overindulgence is seldom far behind. Dieting and sin seem synonymous here, rather than the vice versa situation that exists in most of the world beyond the bayous.

Modern Louisiana cuisine, sometimes Cajun, sometimes Creole, often blurs the definite borders between the two main cooking styles. The end results speak to the palate in such seductive terms that most people don't care. Jambalaya, filé gumbo, crawfish etoufee, mounds and pounds of fried shrimp, oysters on the half-shell, stuffed crabs, broiled flounder, baked redfish, bread pudding in rum sauce, red beans and rice, pralines—what more could you want? A little hot sauce?

You've come to the right place. This is the home of Tabasco.

Hot sauce, usually Tabasco, sits on Louisiana tables with salt and pepper, an essential condiment. In the best Louisiana dishes, when it is added by the cook it is done so with restraint to enhance flavor rather than overwhelm the taste buds. Most often it is associated with Cajun-style dishes. To get an idea of how highly the sauce is esteemed, visitors should include a stop at the Tabasco factory on Avery Island a few miles outside New Iberia.

Avery Island, in reality a land-locked salt dome, rises above the horizon south of New Iberia on LA 329, just seven miles southwest of town. The highway runs like a levee above the flat, wet fields to the dome. The toll booth entrance to the compound sits across a bayou. Fisherman cluster on the public side. Beyond the toll booth gate lies a well-groomed compound of workers' houses, the pepper sauce factory, exotic gardens, native plants and a bird sanctuary. The salt dome does qualify as an island of tranquility.

Excavations around the salt works have unearthed the remains of long-extinct species such as prehistoric horses, mastodons and giant sloths. Some of the more intriguing finds have been man-made artifacts—bits of baskets and woven matting—several layers of earth beneath mastodon bones. Though prehistoric Americans were obviously well acquainted with the salt works, John Hays, who settled here in 1791, said the Indians of his day could not be persuaded to go near the place because of their legends that some horrendous event had occurred here in the prehistoric past.

John Hays "re-discovered" the salt springs. In the late 18th century, John Marsh acquired the dome as a land grant from the Spanish. Marsh, a sugar planter, supplied salt from the springs to American troops in the War of 1812. When rock salt was discovered in 1862, Confederate troops were stationed in the area to stand guard while salt was quarried for the South. Later, in 1863, the salt works were destroyed by General Nathaniel Banks' troops during the Federal invasion of the area.

The island is still owned by descendants of John Marsh, the most famous being members of the McIlhenny family. Their name appears on the Tabasco sauce label.

Edmund McIlhenny, a banker from New Orleans, married the heir to the island, Mary Eliza Avery, and moved here after his retirement. He "invented" the pepper sauce, put the finished product in cologne bottles and sent it off into the world. In 1868 the business sprang to life with the sale of 350 bottles. Today the sales are around 60 million bottles a year.

A family legend claims that the seeds for the original peppers were brought from Mexico by a soldier returning from the Mexican War in 1849. Large plots on the island are still planted in peppers, and the McIlhenny family still uses the original recipe for the sauce. The seeds used for each new crop are said to be direct descendants of the first seeds brought from Mexico. To make the sauce, the peppers are mashed with a small amount of salt and then aged in oak barrels. After three years, if the mash passes a sight and aroma inspection, it is poured into mixing bins along with white vinegar, where it is whipped into sauce. Vinegar, salt and peppers are the only ingredients. The modern bottles are still very similar to the first cologne bottles, down to the eight-sided screw-on top.

After a tour of the pungent pepper sauce factory, visitors may tour the gift shop store, both are open free to the public. For a fee you may tour other parts of the compound which contain the Jungle Garden and the bird sanctuary started by Edward Avery McIlhenny, son of Edmund. An author and adventurer, Edward is credited with saving the snowy egret population in this area with his advanced conservation methods.

Back in town, just off LA 182 South, the Konriko Rice Mill offers tours of its premises for a fee. Admission to the Konriko Country Store and gift shop, next door to the mill, is free. Just a few blocks

Avery Island, Home of Tabasco Sauce, and Sanctuary for Snowy Egrets.

away, on LA 182 North, is the Trappey Factory and Cajun Store where further dimensions of the cuisine can be explored. (Trappey processes and cans a wide variety of vegetables, among other items.) There is an admission fee to the factory but the store is free. Food is a major tourist attraction here. Both factory stores offer unique souvenirs and interesting perspectives.

Down LA 14, ten miles away, is Delcambre. Area markets and restaurants purchase their seafood at the shrimp boat landing here, while Delcambre, unpretentious, unaffected, waits out the seasons as it always has, content to be a fishing village.

South of New Iberia about eight miles on LA 182, at Jeanerette, the Le Jeune Bakery makes real French bread the old-fashioned way, in brick ovens.

All the ingredients are here. The Iberia Tourist Commission suggests that travelers who want to sample the culture of Acadicana make their headquarters in New Iberia, where there are ample accom-

Town Hall, New Iberia.

modations at more moderate prices than those available in larger
cities, as well as plenty of restaurants. Many attractions are just a
short distance away. Headquartering here for a day or two may not
be a bad idea.

New Iberia, a bustling small city, is said to have originally been
settled by Canary Islanders who raised hemp and flax before switch-
ing to cattle ranching. Their efforts are remembered with a historic
marker on LA 182 just north of town. Henri Frederic Duprier, a
sugar plantation owner, is credited with founding the town in 1839.
A generous sprinkling of antebellum homes have survived along
Bayou Teche. Those open to the public vary from time to time. But
Shadows-on-the-Teche, the most famous, located right downtown, is
open year-round. Surrounded by a high wall that makes viewing
from the street difficult, the Shadows gained fame as one of the
South's first private restorations in the 1920s. The house, circa 1834,
is said to have been built as the showplace of planter David Weeks'
plantation system. The architectural style of the house is described as
''a local interpretation of the Classical Revival style with Tuscan
columns and French and English influences.'' Cross ventilation was
one of the most important local considerations, due to the semitropi-
cal climate. The builders achieved it with many opposing doors and
windows. During the Civil War, Federal troops occupied the house.
After the war, it fell into disrepair until its restoration began in 1922.

The Shadows, at 317 East Main (LA 182 North), shares a street
with many gracious old homes in a massive oak grove along the

Shadows-on-the-Teche, c. 1834.

bayou. The imposing city hall, built in a modern interpretation of Louisiana planter architectural style, is just a few blocks away. Across the bayou City Park's green expanses make an enticing view.

Another short jaunt out of town, down LA 14 about six miles, then follow the signs, is Jefferson Island and Live Oak Gardens. Joseph Jefferson, a well-known actor during the Civil War period, purchased the salt dome that was to become known as Jefferson Island in 1865, and had a house built for a winter retreat in an eclectic style that combined Georgian, Moorish and Steamboat Gothic styles. The intricately landscaped gardens now cover 20 acres adjacent to Lake Peigneur.

One of the more intriguing exhibits at Live Oaks is a video shown at the reception center that documents how in very recent times a large portion of the gardens disappeared, vacuumed off the face of the earth. In 1980 an oil rig out in Lake Peigneur accidentally punctured the salt dome. The 1,300-acre lake, giant oaks, lakeside homes and some 64 acres of the gardens were sucked into the earth—gone—disappeared like science fiction—in just a few hours. Television news crews did capture part of the action on video. Repairs have since been made to the salt dome and the gardens.

Legends claim that Jefferson Island was once a hideout for Jean Laffite. Supposedly a cache of gold and silver coins found here in 1923 near the Lafitte Oaks lend credence to the stories.

Going south out of New Iberia on LA 182, take LA 86, and follow the signs to Loreauville. The flat countryside, with its occasional stand of trees, has a special morning appeal as the sun begins driving away the fog with shafts of light thrust through the mist. The Heritage Village Museum, across the street from the school at Loureauville, displays artifacts from prehistoric times to the turn of the century. There is an admission fee.

LA 86 loops back to New Iberia, or you can take a back road, LA 345, to St. Martinville. Along either way are flooded rice fields, crawfish ponds, sugar cane fields, and egrets having their breakfast.

Southeast of New Iberia, LA 182 runs quietly through the fuzzy fields of April on its way to Jeanerette. About eight miles away, Jeanerette offers travelers a look at an uncommercialized Cajun lifestyle in a small town setting. The clean streets, turn-of-the-century architecture, and good food make for real, not manufactured, memories. The Bicentennial Museum on Main Street (LA 182) shares stories and artifacts from the town's past with visitors.

Between towns and communities along the highway are oak groves and grazing sheep, Victorian and antebellum homes, historic markers of people come and gone. The highway follows the bayou for most of its journey south. Across the black earth fields waiting for their seeds, blindingly white churches rise, sometimes all alone, sometimes surrounded by a cluster of gravestones, sometimes down unpaved lanes, all of them just waiting, all of them a nearly irresistible lure.

At Charenton, just off LA 182 about five miles south of Jeanerette, follow the signs to the Chitimacha Indian Reservation. The reservation is a unit of the Jean Lafitte National Historical Park. According to the park service, Chitimacha comes from words which mean ''men altogether red.''

The Chitimacha have been located along the Atchafalaya and Lake Chitimacha (Grand Lake) since prehistoric times. The arrival of the Acadians in the area altered the Chitimacha lifestyle, and, they believe, eventually eroded their culture. The Cajuns intermarried with the Chitimacha and brought their language and their religion to the marriages. Many of the Native American traditions soon disappeared.

The reservation contains about 280 acres of traditional Chitimacha homeland. The tribal membership roles list 525 people. Around 190 of these live on the reservation. To be a member of the tribe a person must prove one-sixteenth Chitimacha blood. The tribe maintains a school, a trading post, a tribal center, a museum and a roadside park

Church Near Indian Village, Charenton.

on the reservation. A five-person council with a tribal chairman governs the tribe. A modern, massive bingo hall is also on reservation lands but is managed by a British firm.

The museum, in the tribal center, displays artifacts and relics of the Chitimacha past as well as modern samples of Chitimacha basketry. Baskets are the chief craft of the tribe. Double-weave designs are used for the Chitimacha's most distinctive pieces. Native canes and natural dyes are used by the basketmakers. The ranger at the museum can refer visitors wanting to make purchases to individual basketmakers. Each year, usually over the Fourth of July, the tribe celebrates the rites of the ancient green corn festival. This is a time of much celebration, and the public is invited to the festivities, which include Indian ballgames, Native American cooking and special foods, and a wide variety of Indian-style dancing. Native American craftsmen from all across the country set up booths and offer their goods for sale.

On down the road less than three miles away, Franklin, a town founded in 1808, still has signs posted on lamp posts warning horsemen "Do not hitch." An economy built on sugar cane fortunes in antebellum days has left a legacy of mansions and plantation homes in the area. Some are open to the public by appointment, for a fee. For a perspective on the area's architectural styles drive through the town's historic district. A map available from the Lower Bayou Teche Tourist Commission outlines a short tour over several blocks running parallel to Main Street (LA 182). Along with the antebellum styles are Victorian, Queen Anne, Eastlake, as well as shotgun houses, raised cottages and bungalows. The commercial district is equally interesting architecturally. Several of the buildings have been unchanged since the last century. The historic district contains 420 "notable structures" and is comprised of the original mid-19th century town and the "railroad town" which developed in the late 19th and early 20th centuries.

On down the highway, LA 182 runs into US 90 at several intervals. LA 182 roughly parallels US 90 for much of the way from Lafayette to the approaches of Morgan City. From New Iberia to Berwick LA 182 follows the Bayou Teche. Teche is supposedly from a Native American word meaning "snake." According to legends, in prehistoric times a fantastically huge snake lived in the area, and when he died his death throes carved out the bayou. There is no doubt that the bayou snakes its way to the Atchafalaya.

At Patterson, on LA 182, the State Aviation Museum preserves and documents artifacts and planes connected to Louisiana's aviation history. Charter boats and tours of the Atchafalaya Delta depart from Berwick.

And then across the bridge, Morgan City sits in a nest of bayous, lakes, swamps and marshes all interconnected to the Atchafalaya, which is considered one of America's greatest natural treasures. There is some debate over whether the area is a wilderness, or, due to the intrusions of modern man, a semi-wilderness. From either point of view you can get mighty close to nature here.

Morgan City claims a lot of firsts, including the first offshore oil well in the South, circa 1947. The first Tarzan movie, starring Elmo Lincoln, was filmed here at Belle Isle and Wax Bayou in 1917. The Turn-Of-The-Century House, also called the Morgan City Museum, at 715 Second Street, has regular showings of the silent film and videos of the local Mardi Gras. Much of the museum is given over to displays of Mardi Gras paraphernalia. The museum, which was originally a home, is furnished in late Victorian and Edwardian styles. An admission fee is charged.

Morgan City's history stretches back to the mid-to-late 1800s.

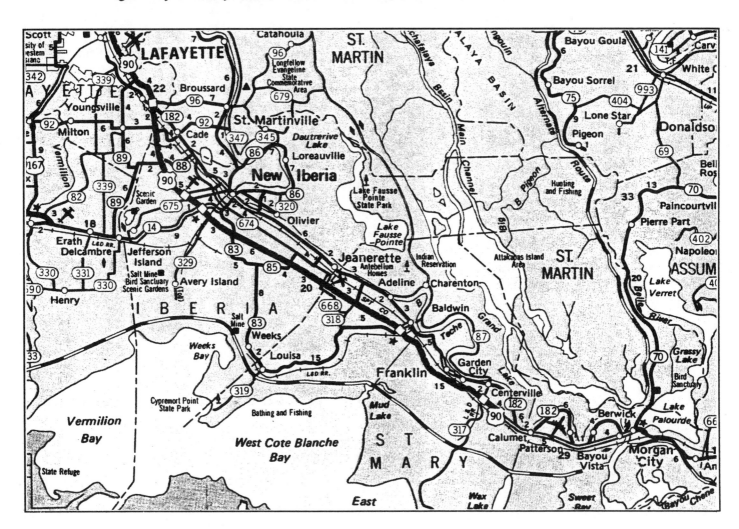

First known as Brashear City, it was a terminus of the New Orleans, Opelousas and Great Western Railroad. The city, originally laid out on the Brashear family plantation, was renamed for the president of the railroad, Charles Morgan. People and goods from New Orleans, bound for Texas, often transferred from the train to steamboats here in those early days.

The Swamp Gardens, located at Morgan City, shelter a living natural history museum in a preserved area of swamp. Life as the Acadian exiles first knew it here, as well as that of historic Indian tribes, is depicted. A zoo includes alligators, pelicans, deer, bears and raccoons. A guide leads tours through the three-and-one-half acre park. An admission fee is charged. Closed every Monday and legal holidays. Opens 10:30 a.m.

New Iberia is located on US 90 and LA 182 about 20 miles south of Lafayette. Morgan City is about 50 miles southeast of New Iberia.

Ample accommodations are available at New Iberia, Morgan City and Lafayette. Restaurants and fast food establishments are plentiful throughout the area.

For more information contact: Iberia Parish Tourism Commission, P.O. Box 9196, New Iberia, LA 70562-9196. Telephone 318-365-1540 or 318-365-6931.

Lower Bayou Teche Tourist Commission, P.O. Box 706, Franklin, LA 70538. Telephone 318-828-1395.

Atchafalaya Delta Tourist Commission, Dept. B, P.O. Box 2332, Morgan City, LA, 70381. Telephone 504-385-5787 or 504-385-5785.

17

Meandering in the Southwest
Abbeville, Lake Charles,
Jennings and Crowley

History's trail through southwest Louisiana slides over the prairies, down the bayous, hugging the coastline, seeking refuge in forgotten corners. This is a lowland sanctuary, a place where seldom-charted streams and landlocked islands offer solace and respite. Pirates, buccaneers, freebooters and privateers were among the first Europeans to slip out of the main shipping lanes into the back waters. Then there were the Acadians, exiles, people stripped from their homes and property, who needed a place to begin again. And in at least one instance, there was a Catholic priest who got tired of bickering with his congregation, packed up his sacraments and headed downstream to the flatland refuge.

South from Lafayette, on US 167, Abbeville is a town founded in the mid-1800s by a Catholic priest who became disillusioned with the folks at Vermilionville (Lafayette), moved down the Vermilion River seeking more receptive audiences, built a new church and eventually a new town. In 1843 Father Antoine Desirè Megret bought a strip of land four arpents wide and 40 arpents deep along the Vermilion River. (An arpent is equal to about one acre.) Father Megret designed the town around two public squares in a style similar to those of Provence in his native France. The town had Vermilion Parish's first newspaper in 1852. *The Independent* was published by Megret's assistant, Valcort Veazey, who, after Megret's death in a yellow fever epidemic, decided not to become a priest but to marry a wealthy widow instead.

Megret held outdoor mass under the oaks in the area around 337 North State Street until his church was built. Legends claim these oaks also shaded a popular dueling ground. St. Marie Madeleine's Church, Port Street, across from Madeleine Square, sits on the site of Megret's first church, which was destroyed by fire in 1854. The present building, circa 1910, is "modified French Gothic" in style.

The Vermilion Parish Courthouse, located on the second town square, is a modern building in a Greek Revival style. Murals on the main floor celebrate south Louisiana.

The Riviana Rice Mills complex, on Washington Street, is said to

119

be one of the largest rice milling operations in the United States.

C.S. Steen Syrup Mill, 121 North Main, on the Vermilion River, makes syrup from sugar cane from about mid-October to Christmas. The aroma of cane cooking hangs so heavy in the air you'll fear that every breath is calorie laden during the season. Tours of the mill are available.

Along the back roads that slip out of Abbeville, the rice fields and cane fields stretch into a distant line of trees. The land, flat and low, seems to be sinking even lower. The highway is bordered by utility poles and emptiness. An occasional house has isolated itself on the flat open fields and built a barrier of open space around its walls. Ahead the road runs straight, disappearing into a shimmer.

Kaplan, LA 14, is a rice town. Rice mills lined up along the railroad send their products out to the world. Farmers park their pickups along the main street, while they take a break and do a bit of lounging in cafes and hangouts behind the mills. Most of the year Kaplan is a quiet farming town, but on Bastille Day you'd never believe it. For many years Kaplan claimed to be the only city in Louisiana, or in

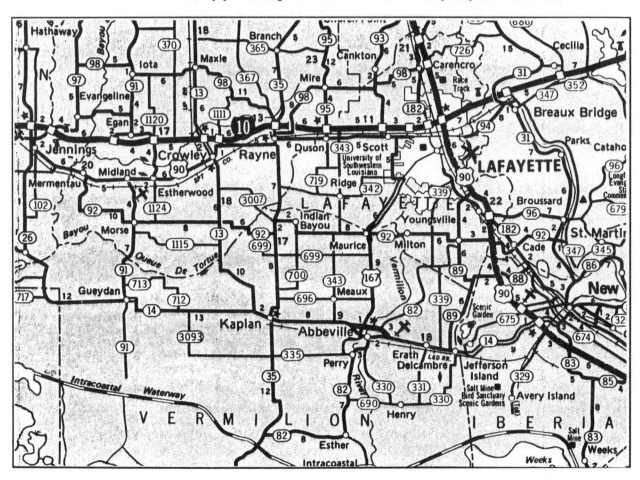

the entire United States for that matter, that had an annual Bastille Day celebration. Now there are others, but Kaplan's fervor and tradition keep the town's Bastille Day very special. On the weekend closest to July 14, the celebration includes a Friday night *fais do do* in the streets, fireworks, various contests of strength and endurance, bicycle races and a two-day softball tournament.

Mardi Gras Day at Kaplan brings the *Chic-A-La-Pie*, a parade by a women's krewe with a Cajun country motif. This is unusual, because in many of the region's Cajun Mardi Gras traditions and practices, women are excluded.

Go south on LA 35 from Kaplan to LA 82, and then cross the Intracoastal Waterway, down the "Hug-the-Coast Highway" where natural history exhibits one of its more intriguing sides. Birdwatchers can rack up a high count of varieties along the road. Patient wildlife photographers can capture fleeting images of birds and mammals. Nature lovers can soak up the glory of the wildflowers, especially in the springtime when the wild irises and water hyacinths splash the flat, wet, green world with color.

At Pecan Island, a chenier, defined as a sand and shell ridge rising out of the marsh, is another style of inland "Louisiana island." Pecan Island is about 18 miles long and ranges from a quarter of a mile to about two miles in width. One of the first visitors to document his sojourn on the island reported that the place was covered with bleached human bones.

All sorts of stories sprang up, almost instantaneously, to explain the mysterious bones. One of the more interesting explanations is that the Attakapa Indians, who were reputedly cannibals, stewed up some of their favorite dishes here. Perhaps this legend gained credibility because in pioneer days twenty-two large Indian mounds were easily discernible on the chenier. The Smithsonian Institution sent a survey team to explore the area and do some excavation work in 1928. From material found they decided that very advanced and sophisticated cultures predating the Attakapa had dwelled on the chenier in prehistoric times.

Jean Laffite wrote in his autobiography that he had buried treasure on Pecan Island, but that he couldn't remember just where. Several legends tie the mystery of the bones to Laffite and his band of enterprising privateers. One version claims that the privateers were actually pirates who frequently used the chenier as a dumping ground for murdered prisoners; another claims that Laffite's men dumped the bodies of smallpox victims here. The piles of bones have long since disappeared, but they may be memorialized for some time to come in the ongoing legends.

Just west of Pecan Island along LA 82 is the Rockefeller Wildlife Refuge and Game Preserve, a 84,000-acre area that is a seasonal home to ducks, geese, and numerous wading birds. Nutria, raccoons, muskrats, otters and alligators are at home in the refuge throughout the year. Waterfowl, deer and alligator display pens are located at the refuge headquarters, on LA 82 at Grand Chenier. Visitors can obtain entrance permits to the area here also. Sightseeing is permitted within the refuge and preserve during daylight hours. Contact the Rockefeller Wildlife Refuge, Grand Chenier, LA 70643 (telephone 318-538-2276) for more information.

At Oak Grove, travelers can follow the Creole Nature Trail north on LA 27 to west LA 384, then north again on LA 385 toward Lake Charles, or continue westward to Cameron on LA 27 and LA 82. There is a free 50-car ferry, usually operated 24 hours a day, that crosses the Calcasieu Ship Channel at Cameron. The Creole Nature Trail continues west for about nine miles, then turns north. Stay with LA 27 through Hackberry until you reach Sulphur where the trail ends (or begins).

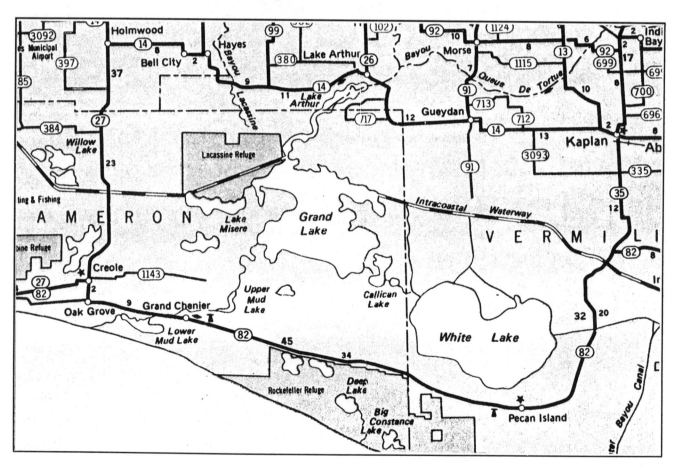

Sulphur, circa 1913, named for a nearby sulphur dome, came into being as a result of successful mining operations in the area. An old railroad station in town houses the Brimstone Museum, which boasts a unique collection of exhibits on the sulphur industry. Sulphur has one of the best-named Catholic churches around—Our Lady of Immediate Succor.

US 90 runs roughly parallel with I-10 from the Texas border to Lake Charles. US 90 in many spots follows one of the original paths of the Old Spanish Trail, a route favored by cattlemen driving their herds to shipping/marketing centers. West of Vinton on LA 109 North, Niblett's Bluff Park overlooks the Sabine River. A busy river port and crossing site prior to the Civil War, Niblett's Bluff was fortified by the Confederates, becoming a supply route to north central Louisiana when the Mississippi and Red rivers were blockaded by Federal troops. Camping hook-ups, picnic spots, a boat launch and restrooms are offered in the park. Fees are charged.

LA 109 runs into LA 12 at Starks; follow it northwest to De-Quincy. The DeQuincy Railroad Museum, 218 East Fourth, displays train souvenirs ranging from uniforms to silverware. Usually open on weekdays 9 to 5. Admission is free.

Beauregard Parish Jail, DeRidder.

From DeQuincy, LA 27 runs north/northeast to DeRidder. A free museum shares quarters with the DeRidder Tourist Center. Some say the Gothic-style Beauregard Parish Jail, circa 1914, on the Court-house Square, is the most elaborate prison in the state. One of the best times to visit DeRidder is during the Beauregard Parish Fair, usually held in late September. An annual fiddlers contest at the fair spotlights Louisiana, folk and country music.

Fort Polk, just off US 171, near Leesville, opens its Military Mu-seum to the public free of charge, usually seven days a week. Of special interest are the flags and uniforms dating from the American Revolution. Named for the "fighting bishop of the Confederacy," Episcopal priest Leonidas Polk, over the years the fort has numbered Dwight Eisenhower, Omar Bradley, Mark Clark, and George Patton among the officers serving here.

Travel back down US 171 to Lake Charles, where the Imperial Calcasieu Museum celebrates the history of the area with artifacts and relics as well as original Audubon prints. The Sallier Oak, on the grounds, is said to be more than 300 years old and was named for Charles Sallier (Carlos Salia), one of the area's first European set-tlers. The town, incorporated in 1867, was named for Sallier, who came to the area around 1782 from New Orleans.

Jean Laffite and his band of egalitarian privateers favored the area, and their legacy is celebrated in the ten-day-long festival called Con-traband Days, usually held at the end of April or first of May each year. For folks seeking high-spirited fun, this is one of the best times to visit. The weather is nearly perfect for the invasion of the rowdy

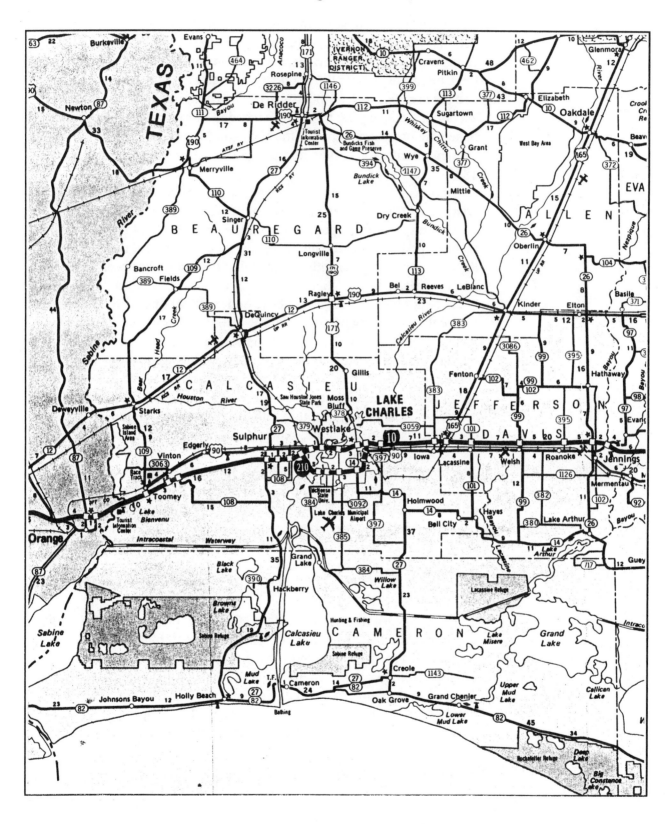

privateers, led by an actor playing Jean Laffite himself. The Contraband Days also feed on the legends springing from the time after the Louisiana Purchase, when there was some debate between Spain and the United States over the boundary between the U.S. and Mexico and the area fell into a "neutral zone." Though the Adams-Onis Treaty of February 22, 1819, which ceded Florida to the U.S., established the boundary between the U.S. and Mexico, a delay in exchanging ratifications held up the treaty's enforcement until July 1821.

All during the year visitors can enjoy the downtown Charpentier District, a 20-block area of homes built around the turn of the century. Built by area carpenters who mixed and matched various architectural styles and patterns to suit their clients and themselves, the houses are so pleasantly unusual that their style has been designated "Lake Charles."

Eastward meanderers can choose either US 90 or I-10 to Jennings, where the discovery of oil in 1901 is celebrated at the Louisiana Oil and Gas Park, LA 26 at I-10. Admission to the park, usually open daily, is free. A replica of the original wooden oil derrick is the centerpiece of the park. The derrick is complete with antique drilling equipment similar to that used on Jennings' first well. A visitors center, an Acadian-style house with displays related to the history of the oil industry, picnic area, and half-mile jogging trail are some of the park's attractions.

Jennings' Zigler Museum, 411 Clara Street, features works by Audubon, as well as a collection of waterfowl carvings and dioramas of Louisiana wildlife. The west wing of the colonial-style building houses a fine art collection of works by European and American artists. The Louisiana Gallery features works by artists from the state. Admission is free. Hours are 10 a.m. to 12 noon and 2 p.m. to 4:30 p.m. Tuesday through Friday; 2 p.m. to 4:30 p.m. weekends; closed Mondays.

Continue eastward along US 90 to Crowley, the town of rice mills, rice fields, the LSU Rice Experiment Station, the International Rice Festival and the Rice Museum. Named in honor of Pat Crowley, a section foreman on the Southern Pacific Railroad, the unpretentious town marks a boundary in southwestern Louisiana where cowboy hats become more numerous than ball caps. LA 13 loops around the gray-block parish courthouse then wanders through the business district, past the shopping malls and fast food outlets, before setting its path across the rice fields again.

The Rice Museum, US 90 West, displays exhibits on the area's predominantly Acadian culture, as well as the history of the town and the rice industry. Open by appointment only. An admission is charged. The Rice Experiment Station, US 90 East, offers free drive-through tours. The International Rice Festival, usually in October each year, features rice eating contests, stock shows, parades, a ball, and a street fair, among other activities.

From Crowley, take I-10 east. Louisiana is one of the few places where the ubiquitous interstates actually follow scenic routes. East of Lafayette and Breaux Bridge, I-10 travels across the wilderness of the Atchafalaya Basin, offering a unique opportunity for modern travelers to get a sense of the vast, wild swampland.

Lake Charles is located at the junction of I-10 and US 171 about 200 miles west of New Orleans. DeRidder is located at the junction of LA 27 and US 190/171 about 50 miles north of Lake Charles. Leesville, on US 171, is about 20 miles further north.

Abbeville is located about 27 miles southeast of Crowley at the junction of US 167 and LA 14. Kaplan is about nine miles west of Abbeville at the junction of LA 14 and LA 35.

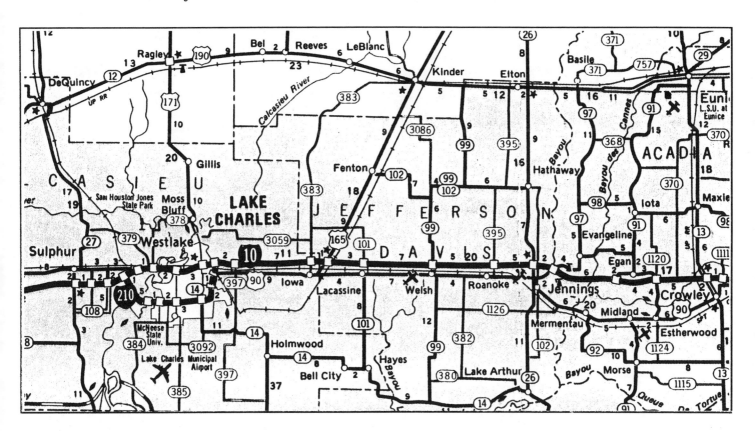

Accommodations are available in all larger cities. Fast food establishments and restaurants are available in towns and cities. But travelers along the Hug-the-Coast Highway and Creole Nature Trail might want to bring picnic lunches and make sure their gas tanks are full before venturing into the empty spaces.

For more information contact: Southwest Louisiana Convention and Visitors Bureau, P. O. Box 1912, Lake Charles, LA 70601. Telephone 318-436-9588.

Vernon Parish Tourism and Recreational Commission, P.O. Box 1228, Leesville, LA 71446. Telephone 318-238-0783.

Beauregard Tourist Commission, P.O. Box 1174, DeRidder, LA 70634. Telephone 318-463-5534.

Jennings Tourist Commission, 100 Rue Acadian, Jennings, LA 70546. Telephone 318-824-9533.

Evangeline Economic and Planning District, P.O. Box 90070, Lafayette, LA 70509.

Louisiana Office of Tourism, Box 94291, Baton Rouge, LA 70804-9291. Telephone 800-334-8626 or in Louisiana 504-342-8119.

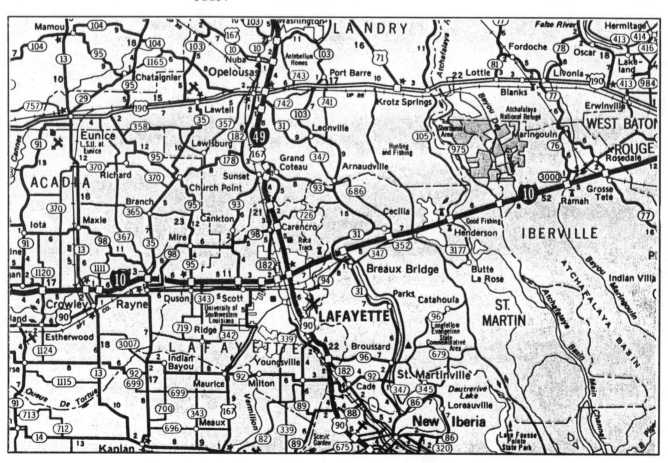

18

Bayou Lafourche

Nature made a road. European settlers named it Bayou Lafourche. This way through the wilderness became a vital path of commerce for early European settlers, pirates and smugglers, just as it had been for the Native Americans. Often labeled "the longest street in the world," the bayou stretches from Donaldsonville and the Mississippi to the Gulf of Mexico.

Paincourtville, Napoleonville, Thibodaux, Raceland, Galliano, Golden Meadow and Leeville residents have used the bayou as a main thoroughfare for generations. Now, LA 1 runs down the high ground on the west side of the stream all the way to Leeville, where the bayou swerves southwest through the marshes and the highway continues south and then east/northeast to Grand Isle. The distance from Donaldsonville to Grand Isle is almost 120 miles. On the east side of the bayou, LA 308 runs from Donaldsonville to Golden Meadow.

Bayou Lafourche linked the Mississippi directly with the Gulf of Mexico until a levee built at Donaldsonville severed the streams. Cut off from its life source, the bayou became a long sliver of lake until 1954, when a pumping operation was installed at Donaldsonville to keep the bayou supplied with fresh water.

The Sunshine Bridge at Donaldsonville, LA 70, is the only bridge across the Mississippi River between Baton Rouge and New Orleans. Built by Louisiana's singing governor, Jimmie Davis, whose popular song "You Are My Sunshine" became the trademark of his administration, the bridge appears to be a giant's tinker toy dropped on the empty, flat landscape. Vertigo sufferers will not find crossing the steep steel incline a pleasant undertaking. But other travelers will be able to enjoy a highly elevated view of the Mississippi and the surrounding countryside.

Just across the bridge, off River Road, is Lafitte's Landing, a popular restaurant in a raised Creole cottage, circa 1797. Jean Laffite is said to have frequented the house. He often moved ill-gotten gains up the bayou to Donaldsonville and the river. His own motherless, teenaged daughter lived with the Martin family (who acted as guardi-

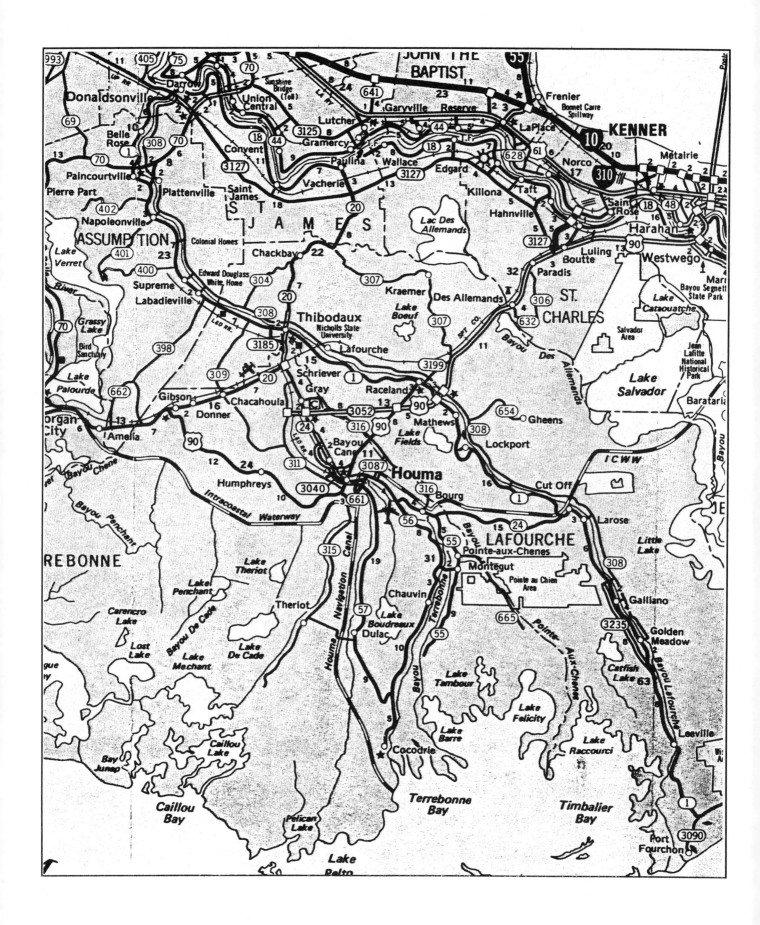

ans) at Donaldsonville. Evidence suggests Mr. Martin was at one time Laffite's agent on the Mississippi above New Orleans.

Donaldsonville came into being because the location was perfect for a trading post. When the first European traders settled in the area around 1750, an Indian village was nearby at a spot where there was a fork in the bayou. The village was known to the French as La Fourche des Chitimachas. According to legend, the bayou was named La Fourche (the fork) for its location. Ten to twenty years later, Acadian exiles were given land grants in the area by the Spanish government. The town took its name from William Donaldson, who bought a tract of land from some of the Acadians for a town site and then offered it to the state for a capital. Incorporated in 1822, Donaldsonville was the site of two meetings of the state legislature in 1830 and 1831. Federal gunboats shelled the town during the Civil War.

Ascension Museum, Chitimachas at Nicholls, a parish jail built in the late 1860s, contains building tools, architectural memorabilia and artifacts from the area. The museum is usually open Thursday through Sunday from 1 p.m. to 5 p.m. Admission is by donation. The Ascension Catholic Church, circa 1896, is on the site of the trading post community's first church, which was built in 1781.

Following the bayou on LA 1, travelers will follow the trail of sugar cane plantations, some with their antebellum mansions or more modest planters' homes still vibrant and occupied, others with their mansions and outbuildings abandoned and in disrepair. Each vision, each view writes its own story, whispers of its own mysteries.

Down the opposite side of the bayou (bridges cross back and forth fairly frequently) are a large number of antebellum plantation homes. Belle Alliance Plantation, circa 1846, just below Donaldsonville, a massive house with fancy lace-like wrought iron framing its galleries, is one of the more famous Greek Revival mansions in the area.

Just outside Paincourtville on LA 1 is the Dugas & LeBlanc Sugar Factory. Tours available by appointment. Telephone 504-369-6450.

Paincourtville, which translates from the French as ''short-of-bread-town,'' supposedly got its name because a traveler couldn't find a loaf of bread for his supper in the entire settlement. Spanish immigrants were among the first settlers here. One block off LA 1, on LA 43, is St. Elizabeth Church, circa 1890, where murals painted in fresco by an exiled Mexican priest symbolize the church's battles with heresies.

Plattenville, LA 308, boasts of being the site of the first church ever built on Bayou Lafourche. The Church of the Assumption, circa 1856, built in the Gothic Revival style, is said to be on the site of the original church.

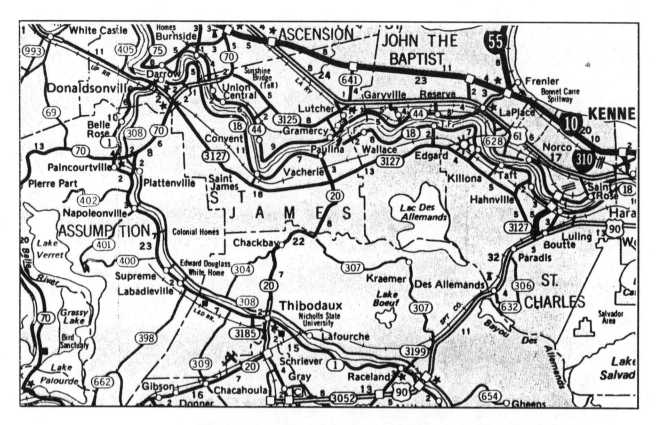

On the other side of the bayou, at Napoleonville, Christ Episcopal Church, circa 1853, was consecrated by the fabled fighting bishop of the Confederacy, Leonidas Polk. Federal troops stabled their horses in the sanctuary during the Civil War and allegedly used the stained glass windows for target practice. The glass was repaired after the war. The cemetery behind the church is noted for its neoclassical-style tombs and memorials.

Napoleonville, the seat of Assumption Parish, founded by a veteran of Napoleon's army, is just a short distance above Madewood Plantation on Bayou Lafourche. Madewood, circa 1840, is considered a "traditional" Louisiana plantation mansion. The house's name is said to be derived from the fact that the cypress timbers were hewn or "made" by hand, a process that took several years. The walls vary in thickness from 18 to 24 inches. The beams are said to be 14 inches square. Six Ionic columns grace the front. The original kitchen and carriage house, as well as the family cemetery are on the site. The house is open daily, 10 a.m. to 5 p.m.; closed holidays. An admission fee is charged. Telephone 504-369-7151.

On down LA 1, just above Labadieville, the Supreme Sugar Factory may also be toured by appointment. Telephone 504-369-6796.

According to legends, Labadieville was the site of a village of Washi Indians, one of the tribes who smoked the calumet with D'Iberville in 1699. Early French and Spanish settlers in the area were soon joined by Acadians and Germans. After the Louisiana Purchase, large numbers of Anglo-Americans came into the area. The town saw action, briefly, during the Civil War when, according to local historians, 500 Confederates tried to stop an advance of 4,000 Federal troops.

Among the early "American" settlers was the White family. Edward Douglass White (1845--1921), chief justice of the United States Supreme Court from 1910 to 1921, was born here. The Edward Douglass White State Commemorative Area, LA 1, south of Labadieville, is the site of the raised cottage, circa 1790, where White was born. The house contains a museum of mementoes and souvenirs from Chief Justice White's life and career. White served in the Confederate army, practiced law, was a state senator, associate justice of the Louisiana Supreme Court, and a U.S. senator, before President Grover Cleveland appointed him to the U.S. Supreme Court in 1894. President William Howard Taft appointed him chief justice in 1910. White's tenure as a Louisiana politician was marked by his opposition to the Louisiana State Lottery. As a supreme court justice he was known for his conservative views. The park-like commemorative area offers well-shaded picnic areas for travelers who might want to bring their lunch and linger awhile. Telephone 504-447-3473.

Thibodaux sits on the bayou surrounded by flat, wet farmland and sprawling modern suburbs itching to stretch across the planters' fields, aching for one more shopping mall with an assortment of new fast food outlets. Truck farmers seem to be holding their own, at least temporarily. The Cajun accent is still thick, the everyday manners charming. Kindness is still a virtue. People smile and say hello.

Thibodaux, named for the gentleman who donated land for the courthouse, jail, and town market in 1820, was, according to local legends, the first European trading post between New Orleans and the Bayou Teche region. The town is the home of Nicholls State University and another of the Louisiana churches consecrated by Leonidas Polk. St. John's Episcopal Church, 718 Jackson at West Seventh, circa 1844, is one of the oldest Episcopal churches west of the Mississippi. The Lafourche Parish Courthouse, circa 1856, corner of Third at Green, nestles under copper domes, bolstered by Doric columns.

The Leighton Sugar Factory, LA 1, two miles north of Thibodaux, offers tours by appointment between October and December. Telephone 504-447-3210.

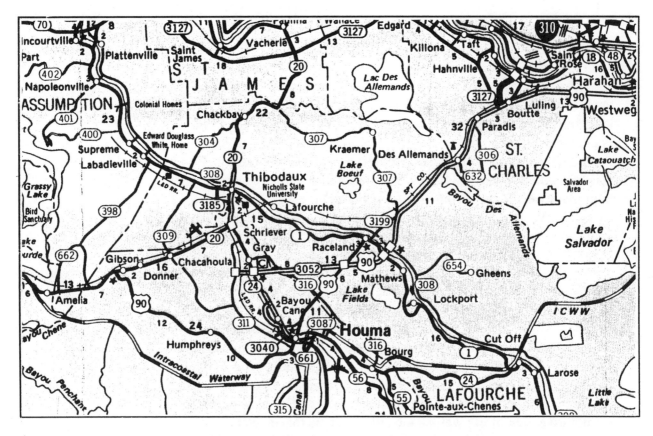

Leonidas Polk also has ties to the Leighton Plantation. He purchased it in 1841, a few years after being named Episcopal missionary bishop to the Southwest. In 1842 he became Episcopal bishop of Louisiana. After a series of natural disasters and bouts with cholera and yellow fever, he sold the plantation and moved to New Orleans in 1854. He had originally been educated at West Point and after conferring with Jefferson Davis at the outbreak of the Civil War accepted a commission as a major general in the Confederate army.

Rienzi, circa 1796, one of the most elegant and romantic plantation mansions along Bayou Lafourche, is about two miles from Thibodaux on LA 308. The gleaming white mansion, with its gracefully curved front stairs leading to the main entrance, according to legend, was built at the order of Queen Maria Louisa, consort of Charles IV, king of Spain. One version of the legend claims she had it built for one of her ladies-in-waiting and named for her friend, the Duc de Rienzi. Another claims she had it built for herself as a possible home in exile. She might very well have been considering seeking refuge in America during the early years of the Napoleonic Wars when Louisiana was Spanish. Spain was defeated by France in those wars but before that happened, in a secret treaty in 1800, Spain returned Louisiana to France. So even though the queen's worse fears were realized, and she needed a safe haven in 1811, Louisiana had probably long since lost its appeal as a sanctuary. A representative of Maria Louisa, Juan Ygnacio de Egana, was the first occupant of the house. After Louisiana became U.S. territory in 1803 he purchased the house and his family lived there for the next 50 years. You can view the house from the road, but it is a private home and not open to the public.

Just off LA 308, on Parish Road 33, is Laurel Valley Plantation, said to be the largest surviving 19th century sugar plantation complex in the South. Seventy-six original outbuildings wearing the patina of age form the core of a living-history rural life museum. Travelers wanting to cross the time barrier and move back to an earlier era for a while will find an open gate to the past here. An admission fee is charged. Telephone 504-446-8111.

More plantations line the banks of the bayou. Wild, thick, tall, green growth laps at the edges of road and the water every chance it gets. At Raceland, St. Mary's Catholic Church, LA 1, circa 1850, guards its antique cemetery of above- ground tombs. Here, the shrimp boats on the bayou begin to be more plentiful. The pirogues, casually pulled up on the grassy bank between uses, are the favorite and often most convenient means of transportation for neighbors wanting to visit back and forth across the bayou. Lush vegetable gardens grow in spare patches of ground along the waterfront. Docks cluster at the water's edge. Houses, usually modest cottages, line the highway which is the no-man's land between the bayou and the front lawns. Raceland, too, has a sugar factory, the Georgia Sugar Refinery, LA 308. Tours are by appointment. Telephone 504-532-2527.

For a special view of life on the bayou, *La Vie Lafourchaise Festival*, each October at Raceland is highly recommended. The festival re-creates life on the bayou in the 1850s. Priests arrive by pirogues. They perform an open air mass. Just about everyone wears period costumes. Antebellum music sets the mood. Operators of an antique syrup mill squeeze cane and cook juice. There's soap making. A blacksmith works at his forge. Then, everything is topped off with a *boucherie* (hog butchering).

LA 1 follows the bayou southward through Larose, Lockport, Galliano and Golden Meadow. Keep an eye out for speed limit signs. Sometimes they are hidden or obscured, but none-the-less the posted speed limit is enforced. At Golden Meadow, an old shrimp boat, said to have been built around 1854, is on permanent display beside LA 1.

The road cuts across the bayou at Leeville, to continue across vast expanses of marshland dotted with pools of open water and slivers of floating islands. Bird watchers may name this paradise. Those who've never indulged in the sport will probably take it up before the journey is over out of simple awe at the number and variety of birds in the area. This lonely, houseless, townless, stretch of marsh occasionally pushes some rusting hulk of man's intrusion toward the roadbed, but mainly it ignores man's passing and makes no allowances for the few people who want to linger. This land belongs to mother nature. She has begrudgingly permitted the highway to be built, but she may send a hurricane to reclaim it at any moment.

Grand Isle is an outpost, the far edge of man's claim to the marshland and the barrier islands that stand between solid ground and the Gulf of Mexico. There are sandy beaches here, summer homes, year-round island residents, heliports servicing the offshore oil rigs, and an isolation that speaks to the quiet corners of the mind. Surfing, fishing, crabbing and boating are activities recommended to visitors. There are boat launches and camping hook-ups. Charters are available. The seafood restaurants (take your pick) pluck their offerings straight from the Gulf. Grand Isle East State Park, LA 1, at the east end of the island, has a sand beach, swimming, primitive camping, restrooms, showers and a 400-foot-long fishing pier. An admission fee is charged.

The most historic figure associated with Grand Isle is Jean Laffite. His commune headquarters was just across the way at Grand Terre. (Grand Terre can be reached only by private boat.) Commune members and lookouts also lived here on Grand Isle, where, with the forces on Grand Terre, they guarded the entrance to Barataria Bay. In those days, the network of bayous along the coast and bay seemed to be allied with Laffite and his cohorts much to the dismay of U.S. Customs collectors. Descendants of the buccaneers and privateers still call the island home.

The greatest appeal of the wet, sultry, windy stretch of sand with its handful of dwarfed oaks and oleander bushes is that here for a brief spell we can pretend we are as free and untethered as Laffite himself.

The distance from Donaldsonville to Grand Isle along LA 1 is about 120 miles. Thibodaux is about 60 miles west of New Orleans. Grand Isle is about 110 miles southwest of New Orleans.

Accommodations are available at Thibodaux and Grand Isle. Fast food establishments and restaurants are found in towns along the bayou.

For more information contact: Lafourche Parish Tourist Commission, P.O. Box 1334, Thibodaux, LA 70302. Telephone 504-447-6776.

Grand Isle State Park, P.O. Box 741, Grand Isle, LA 70358. Telephone 504-787-2559.

Grand Isle Tourist Commission, P.O. Box 776, Grand Isle, LA 70358. Telephone 504-787-2559.

Louisiana Tourism Office, P.O. Box 94291, Baton Rouge, LA 70804-9291. Telephone 800-334-8626 or in Louisiana 504-342-8119.

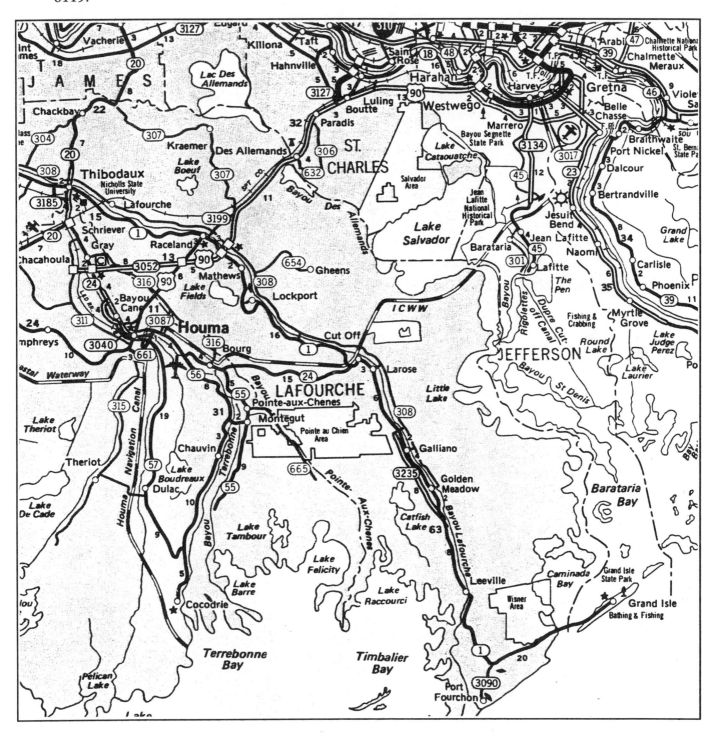

19

Houma and Terrebonne Parish

South Louisiana's deep bayou country sheds her green camouflage in winter, exposing the gray, bare bones of her swamps, marshes and woods.

"But winter is not our best side," folks in Houma say.

Unless tourists are coming for the bright splash of Mardi Gras on local streets, homefolks say, "Wait till the spring."

Spring has its moments. The swamps burst forth with a thousand shades of green, the wild irises bloom, the alligators come out of hiberation and the mosquitoes swarm. All the seasonal wonders of nature have their appeal; that's why I like the deep-south Louisiana winter. There's an unexpected magic, a natural high, waiting for the visitor to this stripped-down, exotic winter world.

The sullen, gray skies of January and February are reflected in the bayous and on the marshes, making a silver landscape, a monotone world. With a good guide by your side, you can see one of the great wonders of the untamed world, a bald eagle. Terrebone Parish bird watchers have counted at least nine nesting pairs of bald eagles in the area in recent years. This time of year a knowledgeable local guide can take you across a maze of swamps, floating marshes and back bayous to within eyeshot of at least one of the nesting pairs.

From a boat on a narrow bayou passage, binoculars in hand, you can visually tour treetop aeries. The giant nests are so deep the great birds can disappear entirely from view inside their homes as they hatch their eggs or feed their young. A patient wait may be rewarded by the witnessing of a changing of the guard as one member of the pair swoops in from a fishing trip and perches near the nest for a treetop meeting with his mate before he takes up the watch and she goes off fishing and hunting.

One of the best guides in this part of the world is Annie Miller. As she nears her 80th birthday her reputation has grown to legendary proportions. She is the reigning queen of the swamps and is most commonly called "Alligator Annie." During her long life Annie has been a deputy sheriff, licensed commercial pilot, trapper, wife and mother, as well as a tour guide, amateur naturalist and animal trainer.

She never lacks for stories as she glides her flat-bottomed tour boat over the watery byways of Terrebone Parish. When Annie's husband Edd was disabled some years ago in an accident flying supplies to an off-shore oil rig, Annie found the simplest and easiet way for her to earn a living for the family was to take to the swamps and marshes she had learned as a child and become a trapper. Though there was relatively easy money to be made from the fur pelts, she found killing the animals distasteful, so when she learned of markets for live animals she phased herself out of the fur trapping business and became, primarily, a snake catcher "for zoos and private collectors." In the meantime, a couple of otters she had trained and lived with as house pets became stars in a Disney movie.

When the oil bust hit Terrebone Parish, tucked away in its maze of bayous, tourism seemed the most viable alternative to the local business community. Someone suggested to Annie that with her knowledge of the swamps, she'd make a perfect guide. She was 70ish then and Edd was recovering; it was a business they could run together from their home, so they got started.

Now, she's here with me in a flat-bottomed boat on a January day telling me about the eagles. I think they are her personal friends.

Alligators Hibernate in Winter, Then Make Up For Lost Time in Summer.

She knows where their other nest was, before a tornado ripped it from its tree.

"They lost their baby that year," she says. She stares into the distance. "They still go back there, and just sit in the trees. They seem so sad."

Bald eagles mate for life and usually lay their eggs and hatch their fledglings in the same nest each year. We watch one of the great birds swoop into the water, fishing. Annie says it is the mama. We are content to sit for an hour watching the eagles play out a slice-of-life drama.

Then Annie starts up the outboard motor and we are off, racing across the bayou towards the floating marsh, cutting across the Intracoastal Canal in front of barge traffic. Flocks of egrets and ibises drift up and down like thick clouds of tossed confetti. "There are hardly any birds here this time of year. You should be here in the spring when the rookeries over on the floating marshes are full," she says.

The temperature is in the 50s (Fahrenheit), but racing against the wind is a chilly business, so we've come well-bundled. Within the watery wilderness we pass a trapper, a black ski-mask hides his face. There is the noise of the motors and the wind, so we exchange waves, silent greetings as he glides to the hummocks where we have seen his handiwork, his traps and snares in the dry patches. The swamp is teeming with nutria. That is his main quarry, according to Annie.

She would know. She takes the boat up a canopied arm of a bayou, to show me where the irises bloom in the spring. An egret stands on one leg against a backdrop of palmettos and cypress knees. We move across open water to the rookeries, see roseate spoonbills, and then go on to the spot where she feeds the alligators. They are sleeping now. Once in awhile on a warm winter day they'll come out, lazily perusing the rookeries, but Annie doesn't count on seeing them until spring. Then she entertains her customers by calling the alligators by name, and when they respond by coming up to the boat, she feeds them chicken.

Back at her house she shows me photographs of the gators, Mike, Pete, Sam and Dee, snapping their chicken snack off the stick from which she serves it. There's a picture of her holding a snake. I cringe. "They are God's creatures, too," she says. "If you'd just hold one in your hands once, feel its heartbeat, you'd change your mind."

I smile politely. There's no need to disillusion Annie by telling her that one of the reasons I like south Louisiana so much in the wintertime is because the snakes are scarce.

Annie doesn't run regular tours of the swamps in the winter; most folks want the high drama of the gators snapping at the boats, Annie snatching a snake (non-poisonous) out of the water, and the rookeries teeming with new life. But whenever you are coming down, give her a call (504-879-3934) and see if one of her two/two-and-a-half hour trips is possible.

Many other area guides also offer visitors intriguing journeys through the Terrebone swamps and bayous. They are all characters. Jimmy Sothern sometimes acts as a guide. A college professor before he retreated to his "camp" on the bayou, where you can now find him most of the year performing Cajun music, playing a mean game of *bouree* (a card game), hosting a *fais do do* (a Cajun dance party that translates "make sleep" in French baby talk—Jimmy says the name came from the Cajun custom of bringing children to grown-up parties and telling them to go to sleep while the adults partied), restoring an antique pirogue or working on a novel. He knows the bayous and area history equally well.

Nutria.

If you want a pure, unadulterated Cajun guide, ask for Shaffer Domanque. He knows, believes and shares the Cajun version of everything from creation to oil exploration. He doesn't see swarms of nutrias in the swamps, he sees nutria-rats. He knows the plants, the birds, the alligators and the wilderness from a very pragmatic perspective.

The people at the Houma-Terrebone Tourism Commission can put you in touch with any of the tour guides currently operating in the area and tell you what their fees are. They can also tell you about all the other area attractions, among which restaurants rank high. Redfish courtboullion, frog legs, jambalaya, crawfish bisque or etoufee—ohh my—fried speckled trout and alligator tails.

Fried alligator tail cutlets are on the menu at Gino's. They are tasty, with a delicate flavor reminiscent of frog legs. Gino's is a Cajun pizza parlor where the most formal dress is tee shirt, blue jeans, cowboy boots and ball cap. On Saturday nights there is dancing to the wail of Cajun fiddles inside the metal building with its concrete floor. The speciality of the house is a shrimp and crab pizza.

The Sportsman Paradise, down the bayou at Cocodrie, turns speckled trout into a gourmet delicacy. The chef claims that a coating of finely ground cornmeal (not available commercially), fresh vats of oil for every batch of fish, and carefully monitored cooking thermometers do the trick.

If you want your Cajun dishes spiced with folklore and a nostalgic atmosphere, The Cajun Cabin, also called *La Trouvaille*, out the road to Chauvin (LA 56) serves a fixed menu luncheon daily. On Sundays the food is dished up with a song. Wylma Dussenberg and her family (nine daughters and three sons, plus in-laws) operate the place and sing. The cabin was originally a modest Cajun home; now all the small rooms are dining rooms, or you can eat in the kitchen. Decorations are Cajun crafts and arts. After lunch, if it's not during the shrimping season, Wylma's son, Louis, offers tours of local bayous on his shrimp boat for a fee.

The tourism commission offers a free map of a 75-mile automobile tour visitors can take up and down the area's main bayous that will lead past shrimp-canning factories, netmakers' workshops, sugar and rice plantations and a modern-day Indian village.

The town, Houma, takes its name from the local tribe, the Houmas, a Choctaw people, who came to this area in the 1700s after some disturbances with the Tunica. They had originally lived along the Mississippi River. Houma means red in Choctaw. A crawfish has been the tribe's totem (symbol) since they were first encountered by Europeans. Henri di Tonti, an early explorer of Louisiana, said the Houma were ''the bravest savages on the (Mississippi) river.'' Today most of the Houma live in and around the village of Dulac. Several stores in the area sell palmetto hats, reed and palmetto baskets, wood carvings and other handmade crafts of the Houma. Sometimes crafts are also available at the Dulac Community Center.

The first settlers of European ancestry to make their homes in the area probably arrived in the 1760s. According to local records, a group of 250 Acadian exiles under the leadership of a Captain Dautrive arrived by way of Santo Domingo on February 4, 1765. Terrebonne Parish was created in 1822 and Houma became the parish seat in 1834. Seven bayous (the town has 52 bridges) converge at Houma, and for many years they were the thoroughfares to and from the town. According to local historians, tow paths developed along the bayous so that when there wasn't enough wind to move the sail-driven vessels upstream they could be towed. The paths evolved into roads, and today modern highways run up and down the bayous along these same trails.

Hurricanes have devastated the parish a number of times since records have been kept. In a locally published booklet that commemorates the 150th anniversary of the parish's founding, a headline reads, ''Hurricanes Gave Us Hell!'' Now, two of the gravest dangers threatening the area are shoreline erosion and salt water intrusion into the marshes. Acres and acres of ghost swamps where dead trees raise their barren limbs against the sky offer testimony to what the sea will do to the land it penetrates. The erosion and intrusion are said to be primarily the by-products of modern civilization. Conservationists are working overtime to come up with solutions.

History can scarcely be separated from natural history in Terrebonne Parish. The area is a living and dying natural history museum. Men have taken fortunes in timber and oil out of the swamps and marshes. On the drier patches, in the black, wet muck planters made their fortunes with sugar cane. The U.S. Sugar Cane Experimental Station is here, as are several antebellum and Victorian mansions built with sugar cane fortunes.

Southdown Plantation has figured prominently in the sugar cane industry over the years. Southdown Plantation House, LA 311 at St. Charles Street., is the Terrebonne Museum. William Minor of Natchez, Mississippi, built a one-story Greek Revival home here in 1859. His son added a second floor in 1893 and altered the architecture to reflect the Queen Anne style which was popular at the time. Much memorabilia from the area is on display here. The museum is open daily from 10 a.m. to 4 p.m. Closed major holidays. An admission fee is charged.

Blessing of Shrimp Fleet, Chauvin.

All those recommendations for springtime in Terrebonne Parish haunted me, until I came back one April for the Blessing of the Fleet at Chauvin. Picnickers lined the banks of the bayou. The delicacy of the day was crawfish boiled with new potatoes. Boats, decked out like Mardi Gras floats, paraded up and down the bayou. Fiddles, squeeze boxes and triangles made their magic. Willows and cypress were draped in green, and there was so much noise the gators kept their distance and there was not a snake in sight. But I might well argue that the spring was not better than the winter, just different.

Located on US 90, Houma is a little less than 60 miles southwest of New Orleans.

Accommodations are plentiful. Restaurants and fast food establishments abound.

For more information contact: Houma-Terrebone Tourist Commission, 1701 St. Charles St., P.O. Box 2792, Houma, LA 70361. Telephone 504-868-2732.

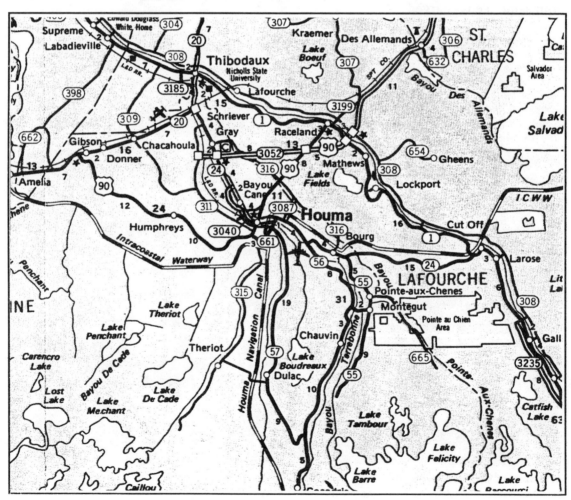

20

River Roads
Along the Mississippi,
Above New Orleans

This is where you wrap yourself in the dream, the place you slip into the fantasy, the place you shake the bonds of reality and indulge in the romance and mystery that the antebellum south evokes.

Great mansions, architectural jewels, symbols of staggering wealth once lined the Mississippi's banks from Baton Rouge to New Orleans. There are tangible memories of those houses, survivors made of cypress and stone. The Great River Road, US 61 south from Baton Rouge, and the River Road, LA 1 south from Port Allen to Donaldsonville then LA 18 south, follow the river to New Orleans. With just a few detours off these main routes travelers can fill their visual banks with enough images of a lost world to excite their imaginations for a long time to come.

The only bridge across the Mississippi between Baton Rouge and New Orleans is at Donaldsonville, but there are free ferries at several points. Ferry schedules vary widely, due to weather and other circumstances. If you will be inconvenienced by having to adjust to the ferries' schedules, take the bridge routes. Start at New Orleans, follow the river to Baton Rouge, cross there, then come back down the west bank of the river to New Orleans and cross back into town on the Huey P. Long Bridge. The great houses, restored, abandoned, or fiercely private are awe-inspiring just seen from the road. Some are open to the public and welcome visitors for a fee.

Destrehan Plantation, 9999 River Road (LA 48), just off Airline Highway (US 61) via Ormond Boulevard, on the outskirts of New Orleans, is said to be the oldest plantation home still intact in the lower Mississippi Valley. Circa 1787, the house incorporates cypress and *bousillage-entre-poteau* construction. Deep, recessed galleries and massive columns comfort and cool the memories and spirits lingering about the elegant, understated house. Old records show a D'estrehan came to Louisiana with Bienville, so the family name was well established by the time the planter's mansion, in the West Indies style, was built.

The three sons of Philippe Egalité, Duc d'Orleans, were enter-

Destrehan, c. 1787.

tained here in 1798 during the time when the future of the surviving French nobility was uncertain. (Philippe went to the guillotine in 1793.) Later, when the monarchy was restored, one of the sons, Louis Philippe became king, reigning from 1830-48. Thank-you gifts sent by Philippe's sons for the hospitality and temporary refuge they enjoyed at the plantation are on display in the house.

Another guest at the house a few years later was Jean Laffite. Supposedly, he buried gold on the place and his ghost has been seen wandering the grounds.

The house is open for tours daily from 10 a.m. to 4 p.m. except major holidays. An admission fee is charged. There is a gift shop on the premises. Telephone 504-764-9315.

Follow LA 48 back to US 61, take US 61 to Laplace then take LA 44 back to the river. Interspersed with industrial developments, factories and refineries are cane fields and plantations. Hard by the road, on a curve, near Reserve, San Francisco Plantation's mansion shatters the stereotypical image of elegant Greek Revival or pragmatic West Indian-style Louisiana mansions. Circa 1856, this house has a unique style that defies tags and labels. Some folks say the house was built and decorated in a style inspired by the more ostentatious riverboats of the era, and it has been dubbed a representation of Steamboat Gothic. The pinkish building probably has more outside ornamentation than any antebellum building surviving in the area.

The house was originally called "Sans Frusquin" ("one's all") by the family of the builder, Edmond Bozonier Marmillion, because of the vast fortune spent on the construction and then the maintenance of the place. The house is noted for its five frescoed ceilings and its authentic period furniture. It is open daily for tours from 10 a.m. to 4 p.m. except major holidays. An admission fee is charged. Telephone 504-535-2341.

Perique tobacco is grown in patches between the cane fields and the sugar refineries at Lutcher. This is the only area in the world where this particular type of tobacco is grown commercially. A strong, dark variety, perique is sold primarily to foreign markets. Supposedly, perique can be grown anywhere, but it is only here in this rich, wet, black earth that it develops the flavor desired by connoisseurs.

The levees running in both directions from Gramercy are stacked

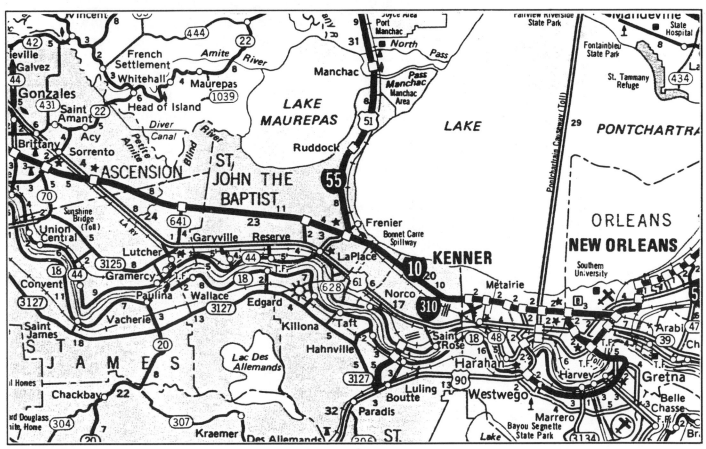

with logs for bonfires during the Christmas season, and on Christmas Eve the wood is torched to light the way for *Peré Noel* as he makes his rounds up and down the river.

Lighting the way for *Peré Noel*, sometimes called *Papa Noel*, is a pretty big job in Louisiana. The kind-hearted old fellow who brings gifts to children down here doesn't have a bird's-eye view or a flying reindeer to aid in navigation. Instead he travels the dark waters in a pirogue which he paddles himself. Not only does he travel the river, he's got a maze of bayous to negotiate as he makes his appointed rounds. The nights are mighty dark, but by following the bonfires on the levee and bayou shores *Peré Noel* can find his way to even the most remote trapper's camp if a deserving child is there.

No one seems to remember a time when there weren't bonfires on the levee at Christmas. Their beginnings have been lost in time. One young man putting the finishing touches on a 20-foot pile of stacked willow logs stuffed with bamboo said, "I read in the paper that it (the custom) came from France way back in the 1700s."

The Gramercy firemen who issue permits for the blazes in their town say they aren't sure what the history is. "It's just something we've always done," they say.

Local historians suggest that the present customs were a marriage of European traditions and New World slave celebrations. "Gifts, new clothing, a major Christmas party, highlighted with a bonfire, were considered necessary rewards for the slaves along the river each year," they say.

The traditional bonfires are teepee shaped, made of stacked willow logs and stuffed with bamboo. (When the bamboo burns it crackles like fire crackers.) These teepee shaped/abstract Christmas trees can be seen up and down the river, as well as on the banks of nearby bayous. But at Gramercy, where the firemen oversee the event, the bonfires have taken on new dimensions. Log cabins and lofty galleons replete with sails and banners share space with the more traditional teepees. Intense competition between clubs and civic groups results in fanciful structures, in the grand style of Mardi Gras floats, lining the levee on Christmas Eve. But no matter how spectacular, everything is built to burn. While the buses of tourists and caravans of motorists up from New Orleans to see the sight wait for dark and the cry, "Torch the bonfire!" the firemen and their wives serve up gumbo and jambalaya at the firehall for a modest fee.

If you arrive early on Christmas Eve, take the St. James ferry across to Vacherie so you can see how the bonfires on the other side of the levee are shaping up. Down on the river, from the ferry's deck you can get a close-up view of the working river, a sense of where you are, as you cross the paths of mammoth freighters and tankers plying a course for the refineries and factories facing the waterfront.

Hunting is a traditional Christmas Eve activity here and chances are you'll share your ferry trip with hunters laden with kills of rabbits and squirrels, heading home with their hounds. The season offers visitors an opportunity to sample traditional celebrations and customs that are deeply intertwined in the area's history.

The quiet countryside, with simple Acadian-style cottages and tenant houses clustered together in small communities, the black stretches of plowed fields, the sprouting cane, the skeletons of plantation homes, the memories and reality make a potpourri of nostalgia. Down the twisting road that follows the levee, the Manresa Retreat House, circa 1831, at Convent, was built to house Jefferson College and is now a Jesuit retreat for laymen. The Retreat House is not open to the public but can be viewed from the road. St. Michael's Catholic Church, circa 1831, on LA 44, contains a grotto constructed of bagasse, a by-product of sugar cane that is made into a type of wallboard.

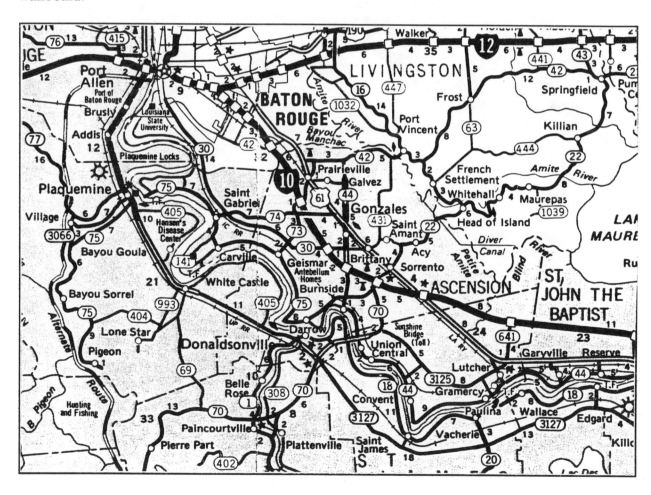

Framed by oaks, Tezcuco Plantation house, circa 1855, was built in a traditional Louisiana style. A raised cottage with Greek Revival influences, the house boasts wrought-iron trimmed galleries as well as ornate friezes and medallions to add a little architectural spice. Named for the Mexican Lake Tezcuco, an Aztec word said to mean ''resting place,'' the house was built of bricks from the plantation's kiln and cypress trees cut on the property. There's antique furniture, Newcomb Pottery, and a collection of Louisiana paintings in the house. Outside there are gardens, a gazebo, chapel, country store and other restored outbuildings. A gift and antique shop, plus overnight cottages round out Tezcuco's attractions. The complex is open daily except for major holidays. Telephone 504-562-3929. Tezcuco is located between Gramercy and Burnside.

One of the most famous mansions on the River Road is Houmas House, at Burnside. *Hush, Hush, Sweet Charlotte*, starring Bette Davis, Olivia DeHaviland and Joseph Cotten, was filmed here, as were several television dramas that capitalized on the setting. The

Tezcuco, c. 1855.

Greek Revival mansion was built in 1840 by the daughter of General Wade Hampton (who owned the place) and her husband John Preston. An earlier four-room house built on the property in the late 18th century was preserved and later attached to the big house by a carriage way. Built on land originally acquired from the Houma Indians, the house was named in their honor. In 1858 John Burnside, an Irishman, bought the house along with 12,000 acres, then expanded it to a 20,000-acre plantation. Sugar cane production dominated Mr. Burnside's interest to the extent that he became known as "the sugar prince of Louisiana."

During the Civil War when the Yankees wreaked havoc in the countryside along the river, occupying, burning or otherwise destroying any number of plantations, Mr. Burnside reminded the local Federal commanders that he was a British subject and his property was therefore under the protection of the British crown. Remarkably enough, the ploy worked. After Burnside's death in 1881, the plantation and home passed through a number of hands until it was purchased and restored by Dr. George Crozat of New Orleans in 1940.

The three-story spiral staircase inside the house, a *garçonnière* at either side of the mansion, the large collection of antiques, and the gardens surrounding the house with statuary, magnolias and live oaks make perfect settings for a hundred fantasies. And just to add a little extra atmosphere, steamboats still occasionally tie up at the plantation's riverside landing.

Houmas House is open for tours daily. An admission fee is charged. There is also a gift shop on the premises. Telephone 504-473-7841.

Take I-10 through Baton Rouge across the river to Port Allen, the port for Baton Rouge. Brides of colonial ancestry in this parish, West Baton Rouge, still receive dowries provided for them by a trust fund set up by Julien de LaLande Poydras, who in 1824 was considered to be one of the wealthiest men in the south.

Legends claim that Poydras couldn't marry the girl of his dreams back in France because her family was too poor to provide a dowry, so he shipped out with the French Navy, ending up in Louisiana as a penniless peddler who worked his way up to the presidency of the Bank of Louisiana. When he died, his bequests included a $30,000 trust fund to supply "all the girls of the parish who get the chance of being married" with dowries. The trust fund has grown over the years, with the annual interest still being shared by the brides. In the earliest years of the fund, there were only two or three weddings a year in the parish, and old records show individual dowry payments of $1000 were common. West Baton Rouge Parish brides receive

Nottoway, c. 1859.

considerably less than that today, not that the amount matters. The brides say it is the thought that counts.

LA 1 south, through Plaquemine, traverses more plantation country, the land that loved sugar cane. One of the planters who made a fortune out of the cane fields, John Randolph, took a decade (1849-59) to build Nottoway, a structure that mixes Italianate and Greek Revival styles. Many say the house is the largest in the South and refer to it an an "American castle." The surrounding community is called White Castle. Mr. Randolph had 11 children and doubtlessly needed a large home. The house's 64 rooms include a massive grand ballroom where six of his eight daughters were married.

If you are looking for a place to stay on the river, Nottoway has a room for you. There are tours, overnight accommodations, a restaurant, and a gift shop in the massive old home. And, if you are in the market for a candlelight wedding in the grand ballroom, it can be arranged. Nottoway is open daily. An admission fee is charged. Telephone 504-545-2730.

Oak Alley, Built 1837-39.

Continuing southward on LA 18 from Donaldsonville, the road passes in front of another of the grand dames of plantation architecture, Oak Alley at Vacherie. There is no more beautiful approach to a home anywhere than the arching tunnel of live oaks lined up like sentries in front of the pink-tinted classic plantation house. The house faces the river, and legend claims that once the alley of trees ran all the way to the water. Now a levee and LA 18 stand between the river and the house with its avenue of trees. Legends surrounding the house claim that in the early 1700s a French settler built a small house on the site and planted the oaks. The mansion came later, built between 1837-39 by Jacques Roman, another wealthy sugar planter. Hard times after the Civil War brought Oak Alley to the auction block. Misfortune led to the house's abandonment. But in 1925 new owners arrived to restore the place. The wide galleries waiting at the end of the quarter- mile-long alley of oaks beckon unabashedly to daydreamers.

Oak Alley is open daily. An admission fee is charged. There are overnight cabins and a restaurant on the grounds. Telephone 504-265-2151.

Cemetery Along the Mississippi.

The area along the river through St. John the Baptist and St. Charles parishes was the Côte des Allemands, the German Coast, where John Law's Company of the West settled German yeomen in the 1720s. Some of their descendants still live in the area, though their names have usually been altered by French and English spellings and translations.

On the left bank of the river back to New Orleans, the road is haunted. A thousand spirits whisper across the flat fields, whistling like the wind around the corners of the abandoned plantation houses, rustling the leaves of live oak trees. When you wrap yourself in the dream, dazzled by the blinding-white glare of the mansions, letting the subtle pink shade of the great houses tint your illusions, you can forget the other worlds that were, the places your fantasies don't want to go.

Slavery was the backbone of this real world. There's no nice name for slavery, no acceptable excuse for enslaving men. It's not just the wind you hear. It's the chilling cries of men, women and children who were denied their humanity calling out across more than a century.

This road racing through St. John the Baptist Parish, rushing on through St. Charles Parish, starting about 35 miles upriver from New Orleans, is remembered as the place runaway black slaves congregated and mounted one of the three major slave rebellions in American history. (Though there were approximately 250 revolts and conspiracies in the history of American slavery, only three—the Stono Slave Conspiracy in South Carolina, Nat Turner's Rebellion in Virginia and the insurrection here—reached the point where blacks and whites were facing each other in battle.)

In January, 1811, around 500 slaves gathered here and formed companies, each with commanding officers, then marched down the river towards New Orleans. Old reports cited by author Lyle Saxon claim the self-liberated slave army came with ''drums beating and flags flying.'' Other slaves joined them along the way.

Militia units from Baton Rouge and New Orleans met the army of primitively armed blacks and engaged them in battle. Sixty-six blacks were said to have been killed on the spot. Sixteen prisoners were taken and sent to New Orleans. Supposedly the rest of the ''army'' escaped. Records are sketchy, but we do know the 16 prisoners were tried at New Orleans and convicted of insurrection. They were beheaded, and in the grand style of ancient Rome, their heads were stuck on poles which were then placed at intervals along the River Road as a warning to other slaves dreaming of freedom. Legends say the heads of the dead slaves were first attacked and eaten by vultures, then eventually the weather tore the remaining pieces of skull from the poles.

Jean Laffite received much blame for the insurrection. Local plantation owners and officials at New Orleans were convinced that slaves he had smuggled into the country from the West Indies and sold to local planters had brought the germ of rebellion with them. The slave revolts in Haiti in the late 1700s especially worried the Louisiana plantation owners. Many white planters from Haiti sought refuge here and in New Orleans, and their tales of horror did much to influence local plantation owners.

This is history's road. History remembers both sides of the story. When men forget one, embellish the other, history sends a messenger. A faint chilly wind blows, and we think we've seen a ghost.

Baton Rouge is located 77 miles above New Orleans on the Mississippi River at the junction of I-10, US 61 and I-12.

Accommodations are available at plantation houses, as well as in Baton Rouge and New Orleans. Restaurants are plentiful. Fast food establishments are located on major highways and in the cities.

For more information and a map of the River Road Plantation Country, contact: The Louisiana Office of Tourism, P. O. Box 94291, Baton Rouge, LA 70804-9291. Telephone 800-334-8626 or in Louisiana 504-342-8119.

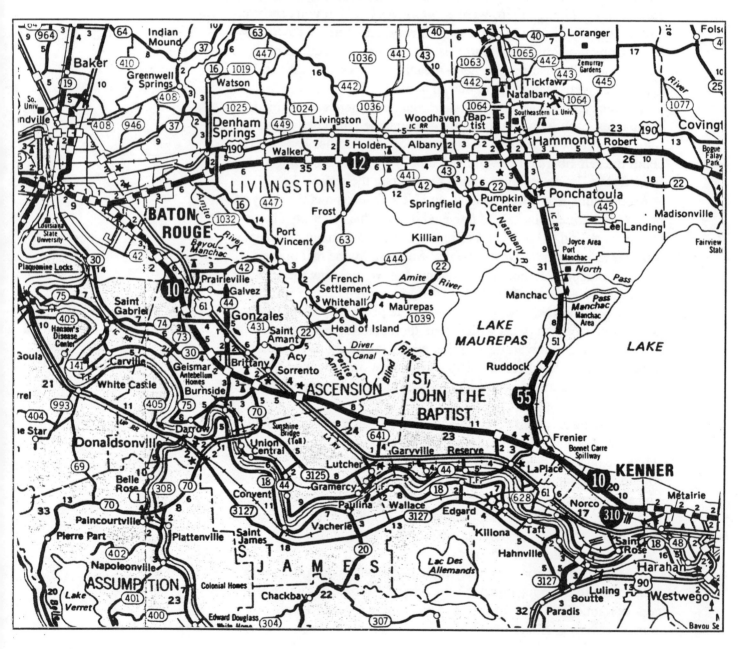

21
New Orleans

Start in the morning. Early. Down at Jackson Square. Before the sidewalk artists stretch their canvases over the wrought-iron fence, before the strolling musicians pluck their first chords, before the tourists are stirring. There is still magic in a New Orleans morning. This is the perfect time to catch a glimmer of the city's past. The square and the French Quarter are quiet now. Early morning risers hose down the sidewalks outside their shops. The air, heavy with aromas of brewing coffee and cape jasmine, wraps its cool damp arms around the city's reveries. Morning light strikes the front of St. Louis Cathedral. Up on the levee, out on the Moonwalk, you can listen to the river traffic, and watch foggy patches of river mist rise to the sun's touch. This is where it all began.

Jean Baptiste le Moyne, Sieur de Bienville, best known to us today as simply Bienville, younger brother of D'Iberville, arrived with his brother's colonizing expedition off the Mississippi Coast in 1699. In short order they were exploring the Mississippi Sound and sailing up the river past the site where the city would be located. Bienville knew a good thing, a little high ground, when he saw it and early in the 1700s declared that the site would make a good spot for a city. He finally got his chance to locate one here in 1718 and in a few years the Louisiana Colony's headquarters was moved here.

The heart of the old city was here, radiating out from Jackson Square, which was known as the Place d'Armes in the early days. It is simple enough to find the old town today, it is the French Quarter/ Vieux Carré and Jackson Square/Place d' Armes is still at its center. In its early days the town was about one mile long and about one-half mile deep, which is about the size of the quarter today.

New Orleans' history runs through a maze of personalities, governments, nationalities and events that can be confusing. The best place to begin to understand the lay of the land and the paths the city's more dramatic stories took is with the free tours offered by the National Park Service's Jean Lafitte National Historic Park French Quarter Unit.

St. Louis Cathedral. Photo by Ron Calamia.

Rangers lead walking tours every few hours daily. Tours emphasizing the basic history of the city as preserved in architecture and culture are interspersed with more specialized topics and places. The "City of the Dead" tour guides folks across the quarter, past the site of an old abandoned cemetery (now a house site), and on to St. Louis # 1, the oldest surviving cemetery in the city.

After forming at the Folklife Center, most tours start in front of Jackson Square, up on the Moonwalk, where there's an overview of the river and the heart of the quarter. Nearby is the French Market, with its outdoor cafes and colonnades, flowers and fountains, praline makers, fruit and vegetable vendors, and a flea market at the far end. The City of the Dead Tour starts at 9:30 a.m. each day just as the last vestiges of early morning quiet are evaporating.

As the park ranger begins her story, tourists cluster in close to hear the tale against the backdrop of ships' horns and street traffic. Finding a burial place was no easy task, she says. Not in this low, wet land. She says a cemetery may be under St. Louis Cathedral, but the first one she is sure of was down at St. Peter and Burgundy, which was, in the early days, "the back of town."

She talks of early sanitation methods—garbage and slops thrown in the streets, and of epidemics that wiped out thousands and thousands of city residents at a time, of the deadly menace, yellow fever, that ravaged the city more horrendously than any war or civil conflict ever did. She paints a word picture of vats filled with tar being burned around the cemetery to help purify the air and maybe even to drive the stench away. Actually, with hindsight we know, the burning tar might have helped more than the people realized because it kept the mosquitoes away.

We cross North Rampart, once the back wall of the city, and take a detour of a couple of blocks to Louis Armstrong Park. Historically, this is Congo Square, the place great throngs of African slaves congregated on Sunday, their day off. The ranger's voice set against the background of the rumble of traffic and the sporadic burst of music from the open windows of passing cars evokes the image of dancing feet raising dust, the sound of ancient songs, the practice of African rites and voodoo. This place with its locked gates, sun filtering through the live oaks, and banana trees squeezing tight between the azaleas and palmettos may well be the birth place of New Orleans-style music: jazz's garden of Eden.

St. Jude's, the old Mortuary Chapel, back on the route to St. Louis #1, dates to 1826. A sign reads, "Friday, Midnight Jazz Mass." The ranger says the first record of a jazz funeral dates from 1820. A New Orleans funeral—with a marching band and strutters—became the

Strolling Musicians, French Quarter.

custom among the slaves. Sad music accompanied the coffin to the tomb, but as soon as the tomb was sealed, the soul was free. Liberation had come. That was something to celebrate, so back from the cemetery the mourners danced to the most joyous music they could make.

St. Louis Cemetery #1, surrounded by its brick wall, has lost territory, and may be clinging precariously to what remains of its stake of damp, sinking ground. Burials here are above the ground. (Water will almost immediately seep into any hole dug in the city.) Inside the walls there are aisles of family tombs. Green ferns and moss grow from cracks in bricks. Palms and palmettos rise up when they have a chance. Individual tombs are occasionally surrounded by wrought-iron fences. Ornate wrought-iron lawn furniture got its start in places like this, the ranger says. It was originally made for cemetery lawns. She points out the grates and pits, where decomposed bodies were shoved after a time, to make room for the more recently departed. The reality of death and life's remains leaves little room for the impractical. There are society tombs where whole groups of people share space for eternity. Parts of the cemetery are in perpetual shade and its accompanying dampness.

Legends claim that this is the place of Marie Laveau's tomb. She was the voodoo queen of New Orleans. Her life lasted so long and her legends are so numerous that most local historians speculate that she was actually two people—a mother and a daughter—one carrying on the traditions and the name after the other. Marie's tomb is covered with wish marks—X's— three X's in a row, X's in a circle, all scrawled across the tomb with a piece of soft Mississippi mud brick snatched from a nearby tomb. In the past the wish marks were made with blood from the pricked fingers of the wishers. Bouquets of fresh flowers appear here everyday. Candles are burned and thank you trinkets offered for wishes granted. Coins, usually pennies wrapped in tinfoil, are tossed at the door of her tomb. In the 19th century Marie Laveau, a renowned hairdresser much sought after by the wealthy white women of the city, read fortunes and gave advice on business and affairs of the heart on the side. Two other places in town are sometimes named as the possible burial site of the voodoo queen, but St. Louis #1 is the most popular choice.

W. C. C. Claiborne, the first elected governor after Louisiana achieved statehood in 1812, has two wives buried here, one on the "American side" (protestant) of the cemetery and one on the Catholic side. Both are said to have succumbed to the yellow fever.

The ranger warns people to stay together at the cemetery, even in the early morning, and not to come back by themselves, especially after dark.

The History of New Orleans Tours start at 10:30 a.m., 1 p.m. and 3 p.m. This is the quick course, compressed with facts and figures from the days of De Soto and La Salle to the establishment of an outpost here in the early 1700s and the subsequent French, Spanish and American governments. These tours also usually begin on the Moonwalk, after the group forms at the Folklife Center. Out on the river ships bound for Baton Rouge pass those headed out for the Gulf. New Orleans is about 90 miles from the mouth of the river. The ranger says the Jackson Square area is about ten feet above sea level, making it higher than most of the city. This is mainly an architectural tour—history as seen through house styles and usages.

Among the first stops is the Ursuline Convent, one of the oldest surviving buildings in town, where the nuns took up residence in 1749. The nuns conducted the first Catholic school in the city, and ran an orphanage. The good sisters found New Orleans an area in need of much missionary work. When they first arrived in 1727, a novice wrote home that "...indeed the demon here possesses a great empire."

The convent is across the street from the Beauregard-Keyes House, circa 1827, once the residence of the notorious Confederate general and Louisiana Lottery champion P.G.T. Beauregard and later the home of the popular novelist Frances Parkinson Keyes. Lacy wrought-iron balconies garlanded around red brick buildings typify French Quarter architecture. The plant life forms an added dimension to the picture. Balconies are crowded with potted plants, and houses with gardens and courtyards can barely contain the burgeoning banana trees and willows weeping over the walls. A prime example of the Creole raised cottage, Madame John's Legacy, circa 1788-89, received its name and legends from a George Cable short story which tied it to a match made at one of the Quadroon Balls. (One of the old quadroon ballrooms is located in what is now the Bourbon Orleans Hotel. After its days as a ballroom it was enveloped by a convent which in turn has become a hotel.) One of the most common types of French Quarter structure is the Creole townhouse, with a shop on bottom, home on top, carriage way to a courtyard enclosed down the side and slave quarters in the rear.

At Pirates Alley, the tour ranger *du jour* bravely attempts to explain what a Creole is, and was, and that New Orleans is a Creole city—not to be confused with anything Cajun. He thoroughly confuses the Yankees in our midst and alarms a few southerners.

Though Creole once had a relatively simple, easily defined meaning—usually a person of Spanish or French blood born in the new world—it now means a variety of things. Creole can mean a descendant of those first "real" Creoles, or it can mean a type and style of cuisine. The word is often used as an exotic adjective to spice up commonplace nouns for commercial purposes. Webster's *New Unabridged Dictionary* offers eight definitions.

The tour ends at the statue of General Andrew Jackson, the hero of the Battle of New Orleans, on the square. The Place d'Armes was renamed for Jackson, and in 1856 the famous statue was installed largely due to the efforts of Madame Micaela Almonester de Pontalba who spruced up the whole place by building luxury apartment buildings with shops on the bottom floors on either side of the square. The Pontalba Buildings still surround two sides of the

St. Charles Avenue Street Car.

square. Next door to St. Louis Cathedral, the Cabildo, circa 1795-99, replaced an earlier structure that had served the same purpose: housing the colony's governing council. Upstairs in the Sala Capitular, the Louisiana Purchase agreement between the United States and France was finalized. Today the Cabildo, a museum, displays a death mask of Napoleon and many tangible mementoes of Louisiana's earliest days. Fire damaged the old building in 1988 but the most valuable collections were unharmed.

Fire destroyed an earlier Cabildo in 1788; in fact much of the city was destroyed twice by fire in the 18th century, in 1788 and again in 1794. The antique city that survives today, basking in its French heritage, was built in large part during Spanish rule. France ceded Louisiana to Spain secretly in 1762, just before the treaty ending the French and Indian War was signed. And though Spain returned Louisiana to France in another secret treaty in 1800, the Spanish remained in authority here until just shortly before the French sold Louisiana to the United States in 1803.

When the Americans arrived, they started their own residential section outside the old city. The Jean Lafitte Park rangers also offer a tour into the American sector. Called the Faubourg Promenade, the tour begins at 2 p.m. daily and requires reservations. The groups take the St. Charles Streetcar, which requires a modest fare, for a ride to the Garden District (and back) where the world of ''les Americains'' can be explored.

After you have enjoyed all the Jean Lafitte tours and feel well enough oriented to strike out on your own, you may want to take advantage of an offer for a free city map from the tourist and convention commission, which outlines recommended walking tours of the French Quarter and driving tours of other parts of town.

A historic tour of New Orleans can be tailored to a variety of interests. Royal Street, once the home of New Orleans' finest cabinetmakers, is now filled with antique shops offering their own perspective of the past in furniture and decorative pieces not only from New Orleans and Louisiana but all over the world. Museums are everywhere. The Historic New Orleans Collection, 533 Royal Street, telephone 504-523-4662, has an exhibition gallery as well as research facilities. The Louisiana State Museum is really eight museums sharing the umbrella title: The Mint, Jazz and Carnival Museums, housed in the old U.S. Mint, Louisiana Folk Art in the Jackson House, the Cabildo, the Presbytère, the Arsenal, the Lower Pontbala House, Madame John's Legacy, and the Creole House. For information about any of these call 504-568-6968. There's a Voodoo Museum, 637 Ann St.; Germain Wells' Mardi Gras Museum, 813 Bienville; and the Historical Museum at 130 Carondelet. Some museums charge admission fees.

Art lovers' can traipse about all over town following the paths of such artists as George Catlin, who had a studio at 78 Chartres Street in 1835; Henry Inman, who was working as an apprentice at John Wesley Jarvis' studio in the Rue Conti in 1816; John James Audubon, who visited town frequently in the 1820s and wrote in his journal about living on Dauphine Street and visiting the French Market; Edgar Degas, who came to town to visit his relatives on Esplanade in the late 19th century.

Devotees of literature can see a streetcar named Desire behind the

Corner Toulouse and Royal, French Quarter.

old U.S. Mint. Tennessee Williams, who wrote a play immortalizing the streetcar, lived at the Maison De Ville Hotel (727 Toulouse Street) in #9 for a while. Truman Capote and Lillian Hellman were born in the city. William Faulkner sojourned here as a guest of Sherwood Anderson, until Mr. Anderson pointedly suggested Mr. Faulkner rent a place of his own. Samuel Clemens spent time in the city. Walt Whitman was a tourist short of change when he became a reporter/feature writer for the *Daily Crescent* for a few months.

History lovers' can find long lists of important visitors. Abraham Lincoln came down on a keelboat. Marquis de Lafayette visited and was put up in the Cabildo, which was refurbished with living quarters for the occasion. Andrew Jackson came as a warrior and returned later for a hero's honors. His wife Rachel accompanied him on a visit and wrote a letter home that sounded remarkably like the letter the novice nun sent home a century earlier.

By the time of the Louisiana Purchase the city's prospects seemed bright, and people came to New Orleans willingly, early on that had not been the case. Though John Law easily found investors for his Mississippi Company, which acquired a monopoly on commercial privileges in Louisiana in 1717, finding settlers and colonists was another matter. When willing settlers couldn't be found for the new colony, inmates from French prisons were shackled in irons and marched across France to the seaports to be sent to Louisiana. There are reports that some of these unwilling colonists revolted along the way, preferring to be shot down in their chains on the roads of France to being sent to Louisiana. Some of the women shipped out as brides for the colonists were taken from the La Hôpital, one of the most notorious prisons in France. Country people and city dwellers of modest circumstances were shanghaied off the streets and shipped out. Louisiana was a great wilderness that swallowed up people.

A number of hardy German farmers came voluntarily, due to the salesmanship of the colony's promoters. They established the German Coast about 30 miles above New Orleans. With the possible exception of the Germans, a large number of the new colonists were ill-prepared for a life of hard work on the frontier and the colony as well as the city was ill-supplied, ill-fed, and ill-clothed until the coming of the Spanish after the secret treaty of 1762. It was several years before the folks at New Orleans learned of the treaty. When they did, they were outraged. Representatives went to France to protest. Locally they did their best to revolt against Spanish rule. When the mild-mannered Spanish governor sent to rule the province threw up his hands and quit, the Spanish crown sent in Don Alexandro O'Reilly (an Irishman in service to the Spanish crown). He arrived with several thousand soldiers and a fleet of 24 ships in July 1769. After due process he ordered several rebellious Frenchmen to be executed by a firing squad down at the corner of Decatur and Barracks Streets. In short order he had the colony running smoothly. The government now controlled the prices on basic commodities. Most historians agree that for the first time in her history, New Orleans' population was well fed. The Spanish governors were generally honest and fair in the execution of their duties, but O'Reilly is not remembered kindly by many New Orleans natives.

Other than O'Reilly, the man most hated in New Orleans in his day was General Benjamin ''Beast'' Butler, of the Federal Army. Butler's troops occupied New Orleans in April, 1862, during the Civil War and when the city's men were powerless to resist, the women of the city showed their utter contempt for the Federal troops in a number of ways. Their behavior was so demoralizing to the troops that General Butler declared that if any soldier believed a woman was treating him rudely she was to be considered a common woman of the streets, plying her trade, and treated accordingly. One of the best remembered cases is of Mrs. Philip Philips, who was brought before the general accused of teaching her children to spit at Yankee soldiers. She was released with stern warnings, but shortly thereafter Mrs. Philips was arrested for laughing out loud from a balcony when the funeral procession of a Federal officer was passing in the street. General Butler sentenced her to Ship Island off the Mississippi coast. At that time the island was a prisoner-of-war camp for captured Confederates and a Federal military prison for Union soldiers convicted of criminal acts. Mrs. Philips was the only female prisoner on the island.

General Butler feared New Orleans fevers and summers even more than he feared the women of the town. He set to work immediately after his arrival to have the sewers cleaned and repaired, an activity that New Orleans officials usually neglected. His devotion to this duty may have helped save the city from major epidemics during the war years. But his edicts, especially against the women, brought criticism even in the North, and he was removed from his command at New Orleans in December 1862.

Perhaps no city in America has a richer African heritage than New Orleans. The African cultural influences on life styles, music and food have been profound. Free people of color and slaves were thought to have enjoyed more rights under the French *Code Noir*, or Black Code, than people in similar situations elsewhere in the United States. Here in antebellum days, free people of color were brick masons, carpenters, physicians, poets and playwrights, as well as shopkeepers. Some few enjoyed great wealth. One of the best places to gain insight into the New Orleans melting pot culture with its potpourri of influences is the Jean Lafitte National Historic Park French Quarter Folklife Center.

New Orleans is often called America's most European city, and those influences can be seen; however, the city has stronger ties culturally, architecturally and ethnically to the Caribbean Isles and the West Indies.

The Folklife Center for the Jean Lafitte National Historic Park French Quarter Unit outlines the history of the city with displays and exhibits from the different peoples and cultures that come together here. Special emphasis is placed on how different people solved the same problems in different ways. The center has ongoing cooking demonstrations, storytelling sessions, and musical performances, as well as videos to entertain and acquaint visitors with the history of the area. Most activities sponsored by the park are free.

French Quarter.

New Orleans is located on I-10 and US 90 about 350 miles east of Houston, Texas, and about 70 miles west of Gulfport, Mississippi.

Accommodations are plentiful, but advance reservations may be needed for Mardi Gras, the Sugar Bowl and other times of special activities. Fast food establishments and restaurants are plentiful.

For more information contact: Greater New Orleans Tourist and Convention Commission, Inc., 1520 Sugar Bowl Drive, New Orleans, LA 70112. Telephone 504-566-5011.

For information on the Jean Lafitte National Historical Park, French Quarter Unit, the address is: U.S. Custom House, 423 Canal Street, New Orleans, LA 70130. Telephone 504-589-2636. The Folklife Center is located in the back section of the French Market at Decatur and St. Philip Streets.

*During the summer of 1990, the park headquarters and Folklife Center will move to 419 Decatur, about three blocks up river from Jackson Square.

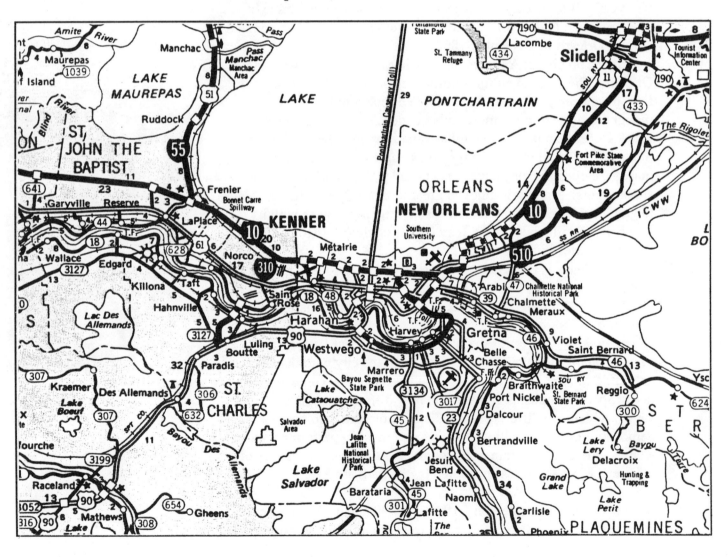

22

Chalmette, The Battle of New Orleans

Fifteen minutes by car from the French Quarter, Jackson Square, and the statue of General Andrew Jackson, hero of the Battle of New Orleans, is the battlefield where he won his laurels. Local militia units rallied forth to Chalmette while Jackson's army of volunteers and militiamen marched westward from north of Mobile to defend the city. City scenes, urban landscapes, line the road from the square. The road from the east cuts through swamps thick with willows, places where wild ferns carpet the hummocks between bogs, and the canals are fringed with palmettos. The modern skyline of the city is etched in the mist and glare on the horizon, a backdrop.

A stretch of imagination may be necessary to see the frontiersmen, Jefferson's yeoman farmers, Jackson's volunteers, crossing the marshes now blighted with patches of industrial squalor, on their way to insure American sovereignty at New Orleans in the War of 1812, but not so great a stretch as to make it impossible.

The Battle of New Orleans, one of the most important battles in early U.S. history, was won in these marshes. There are folks who claim the battle didn't matter all that much, that because it was fought after the Treaty of Ghent was signed it was meaningless. Don't believe a word of it.

Supposedly, neither the American or British forces knew that the treaty had been signed (on December 24, 1814) when the battle was fought. But the British had orders that even if they should hear of the signing of the treaty they were to proceed with the capture of New Orleans. The signed treaty would become binding only after it was ratified by both the American and British governments.

The British forces sailing towards New Orleans were planning to slip through a loophole of international law to capture and colonize the American city. Aboard their armada of ships they carried not only an invasion force of 10,000 combat troops, but a legion of bureaucrats ready to set up a British colonial government at the city which would control access to and from the Mississippi. Some of the officers even had their families and household goods on ships moored off nearby Ship Island, Mississippi, waiting for a suitable house in New Orleans to be confiscated.

Andrew Jackson took the British threat seriously as he marched here from Mobile in December 1814. Reared in the throes of the American Revolution, he never had reason to doubt British intentions. His journey to New Orleans took him across southern Mississippi near the 31st parallel, where some people claim you can still find traces of his army's corduroy roads through the marshes and swamps.

Once on the scene, Jackson and his troops set about building the meager mud rampart that has been reproduced at Chalmette National Battlefield. His frontiersmen and the local militia took an abandoned mill race (the Rodriguez Canal), a boundary between two plantations, and dug it out to make the rampart. (The Rodriguez Canal is the only remaining original manmade feature on the battlefield.) The mud wall, across the narrowest point of the only solid land between the British and New Orleans, forced the Red Coats into a bottleneck.

The American army was made up of volunteers, regular militia troops, free men of color from Louisiana, Choctaw Indians from Mississippi, other Native Americans, French privateers from south Louisiana (Laffite and his Baratarians) and enough of the other national and ethnic elements that have gone into the American melting pot to make it one of the most democratic armies ever assembled.

Many of the English troops sent to seize New Orleans were hardened from the Napoleonic wars in Europe. They brought slaves with them from the West Indies to do the manual labor necessary to move 10,000 soldiers from Lake Borgne through the swamps and marshes to New Orleans.

Actors Portray a British Officer, left, An American Volunteer, middle, and a Louisiana Pirate, right, at a Re-enactment of the Battle of New Orleans.

Chalmette Battlefield.

January in the Louisiana swamps can be chilly. January 8, 1815, American militiamen stood in knee-deep mud and bitterly cold swamp water waiting for the British. There were only about 5,000 men in the American force. Officially, the decisive battle that day lasted less than two hours. British casualties exceeded 2,000. The Americans reported only 13.

The Americans won with firepower, displaying a superior accuracy with their guns. Much of this skill has been attributed to the Baratarians, Dominique Youx in particular. Andrew Jackson's military genius, also, gets due credit for the victory, as does the devotion of the Choctaw Indians to the cause and the man. As an interesting footnote, historians remember Jackson's reluctance to accept the help of Laffite's Baratarians was overcome only at the last moment.

A vast empty space has been preserved here between the mud rampart and the National Cemetery where Civil War dead rest. At a far corner the National Park Service has marked the spot where the British general, Sir Edward Pakenham, fell. There is a Union Jack fluttering in the riverside breeze. Did the 93rd Highlanders who the

British general John Keane fed to the American cannons go to their deaths with the music of their pipers ringing in their ears? In the windswept emptiness you can imagine the haunting cry of the highland pipes being played in unending tribute to the time and place American nationalism was born.

The Chalmette Monument's cornerstone was laid in January 1840 shortly after Andrew Jackson's visit to the site on the 25th anniversary of the battle.

The Beauregard House, an example of French-Louisiana plantation architecture, was built some 18 years after the Battle of New Orleans and is named for its last private owner, Judge René Beauregard. This country house, without plantation acreage, was home to a succession of wealthy people in the 19th century. It has been restored and now serves as the park's visitors center where the importance of the battle is detailed in exhibits and a short movie. The exhibits explain that the Battle of New Orleans was the climax of about six weeks of action that included six different engagements on land and water. Chalmette preserves the site of three battles that took place between December 24, 1814, and January 8, 1815.

There is a small picnic area under mammoth oak trees near the Beauregard house. The Mississippi River levee rises high behind the house. Visitors can watch ocean going freighters and tankers pass on the river here.

Chalmette, a suburban community, has preserved the ruins of a French plantation home, de la Ronde, in the median of the St. Bernard Highway at the intersection with LA 47. The house was a British hospital during the battle. The town celebrates the heroes of both sides of the battle with street names—Pakenham, Coffee, Carroll, Gibbs, Keane, as well as Jackson.

The Chalmette Unit of the Jean Lafitte National Historic Park is located six miles east of New Orleans. From Canal Street, follow North Rampart which becomes St. Claude Avenue and then St. Bernard Highway (LA 46). From I-10 take the Chalmette/Little Woods exit (LA 47) south to St. Bernard Highway and turn right. Admission is free.

For more information contact: Jean Lafitte National Historic Park, Chalmette Unit, 8606 W. St. Bernard Highway, Chalmette, LA 70043. Telephone 504-589-4428.

23

Sunday Drives and Day Trips
(from New Orleans)

When history lovers get the urge to indulge in traditional cultural pursuits, they might consider the time-honored southern custom of the Sunday drive. Long a favored form of relaxation, a Sunday drive doesn't have to have any hard-hitting entertainment or even any predetermined destination. With a general direction in mind, you just get in your car and drive.

The area around New Orleans, east and north of Lake Pontchartrain and down river into Plaquemines Parish, offers unique opportunities for easy-going explorers. For those travelers who want some guaranteed entertainment along the way, it would be best to visit some of the towns during their annual festivals. Sunday drives can be adapted to day trips with some allowances for the loss of Sundays' special unhurried grace.

Start at New Orleans and head east for about 23 miles along US 90, one of the old Spanish trails, to the Fort Pike State Commemorative Area. The red brick fort, surrounded by a moat, sags with age in the humid breezes as the waves from the Rigolets lap at its curved back side. (Rigolets is from the French *rigole* meaning small ditch or channel.) The fort, built on Rigolets Pass, a deep water route from the Gulf of Mexico to Lake Pontchartrain and New Orleans, was begun in 1818 and completed in 1827. But the history of the site as a defensive post goes back further. During the War of 1812, Fort Petites Coquilles stood here. Carondelet is said to have built the first fort on the site in 1793.

Prior to the Battle of New Orleans, General Andrew Jackson sent orders to the fort commander to ''Defend your fort to the last extreme, and in case you should not be able to hold out, spike your guns, blow up the fort and evacuate to Post Chef Menteur.''

Even though the United States won the Battle of New Orleans, and the War of 1812 was settled by treaty, President James Monroe believed the British assault on the U.S. and their burning of the national capital should be a warning to beef up defensive fortifications around the nation's shorelines. Fort Pike was one of six Louisiana forts that came into being as a result. Named for General Zebulon Pike, the

fort was designed to repel attacks from sea or land. The fort originally had two moats crossed by bridges.

To enter the fort, cross the drawbridge over the remaining moat.
The fort is a maze of tunnel-like chambers and small rooms with
vaulted ceilings and supports encircling a parade ground. The citadel
stands inside the parade ground. Originally a one-story building, the
citadel was meant to serve as a last ditch stronghold in case enemy
troops stormed the walls. In the 1850s a second story was added.
The upper level housed enlisted men, and the lower level served as a
mess hall. During the Civil War, when Confederate troops had to
abandon the fort, they burned the citadel. It burned again in 1887.
Today the middle section of the old citadel houses a museum of
artifacts, relics and uniforms related to the fort's history, but it has
been closed due to economic cutbacks.

Signs, arrows and a map dispensed with tickets at the front gate
(there is an admission fee) guide visitors to the powder magazine,

Fort Pike, Rigolets Pass.

commissary, sutler's store, cistern, blacksmith shop, kitchen, hot shot furnace, casemates, gun positions and officers' quarters starting at the sallyport and guardroom.

Fort Pike's armament originally consisted of 24 thirty-two-pounder cannons, 15 twenty-four-pounder cannons, four thirteen-inch mortars and two ten-inch mortars. In wartime as many as 400 men were stationed here, but according to legend not a single cannon ball was ever fired from the fort.

During the second of the Seminole Wars (1835—1842), the fort served as a staging area for troops on their way to Florida, and also as a collection point for Seminole prisoners, their families and slaves who were being transported to Oklahoma. Cannons were removed from several of the casemates so the space could be used as a prison. In the Mexican War (1846—1848), the fort was again used as a staging area for troops enroute to battle. At the outbreak of the Civil War, the Louisiana Militia captured the fort and held it until Federal troops occupied New Orleans in the spring of 1862. Though Federal troops used the fort as an outpost after 1862, it was obsolete by that time due to advancements in artillery technology.

There are sheltered picnic tables, restrooms and a boat launch at the Fort Pike State Commemorative Area.

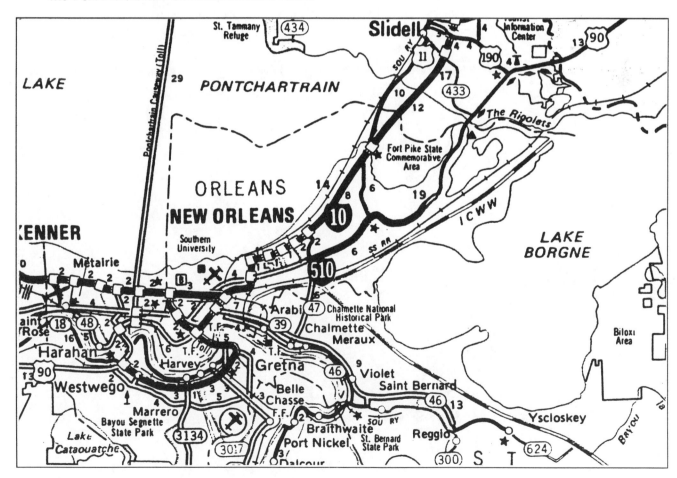

Continue eastward on US 90, crossing the narrow drawbrige over the Rigolets, and just before you reach the intersection with US 190 you'll see a historic marker telling the story of a Choctaw chief remembered as *Chef Menteur*—French for "lying chief." Supposedly, the fellow lied to such an extent that his tribe banished him. The sign offers just enough information to tease the imagination.

Take US 190 to Slidell, a town chartered in 1888. The community which had previously been known as Robert's Landing blossomed with the coming of the railroad in 1881. Some of the best times to visit Slidell are during the Pirogue Races held the first Sunday in June on Bayou Liberty; the Slidell Antique Dealers Association Street Fair usually held twice a year, in April and October; and the Ozone Camellia Club's Camellia Show (one of the largest camellia shows in the country) held the first weekend in December. Nearly a dozen antique shops call Slidell home. Many are clustered together in and around First and Eplanger streets, but only a few are open on Sundays. Slidell is in the historic Ozone Belt, the area north of Lake Pontchartrain considered especially healthy in the 19th century because it was believed that the pine forests purified the air. "Ozone" was slang for pure air.

From Slidell, continue on US 190 to Lacombe. Vast, dense pine forests covered this area when the first Europeans arrived. Old reports claim that the floor beneath the lofty trees was clear of vege-

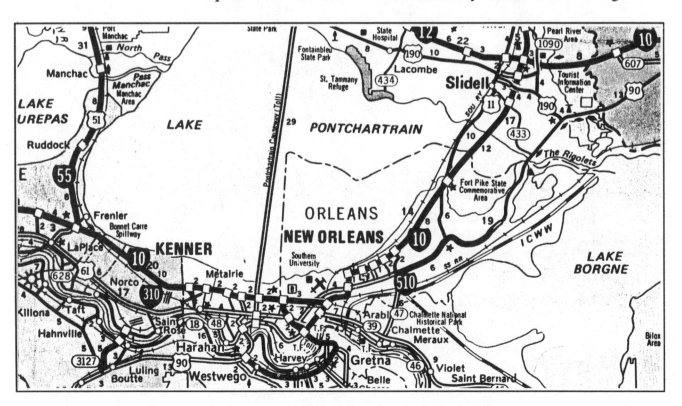

tation, and travelers believed they could see for miles. Choctaw
Indians were at home here when the Creole missionary priest Adrien
Rouquette came to live with them in 1859. Rouquette, one of the
most romantic figures in Louisiana lore, was born to a prominent
New Orleans family in 1813. His family sent him to France to study
law, but he considered himself a poet. He eventually entered the
Catholic priesthood. Legends claim he chose the priesthood after
falling in love with a Choctaw maiden who died tragically. For
whatever reason, he moved to the deep forest, established several
missions, and became so beloved by the Choctaw that they renamed
him *Chata-Ima* which means ''like a Choctaw.'' He died at the
Hotel Dieu in New Orleans in 1887 within a circle of Choctaw
warriors. The story of the silent warriors following his funeral
procession through the city is often repeated. Today, there is a
monument to Rouquette at Lacombe just off US 190.

The next town up the highway is Mandeville, a popular summer
retreat for New Orleans' affluent citizens in the early 1800s. Fon-
tainebleau State Park, US 190, offers visitors a view of the ruins of a
sugar plantation owned by Bernard de Marigny de Mandeville, one
of the wealthiest men in America in the early 1800s. The town of
pleasant, unhurried lifestyles, interesting restaurants (Bechac's on
Lake Street started life as a gambling casino in the 19th century),
massive oaks, a lingering resort atmosphere and the 24-mile-long

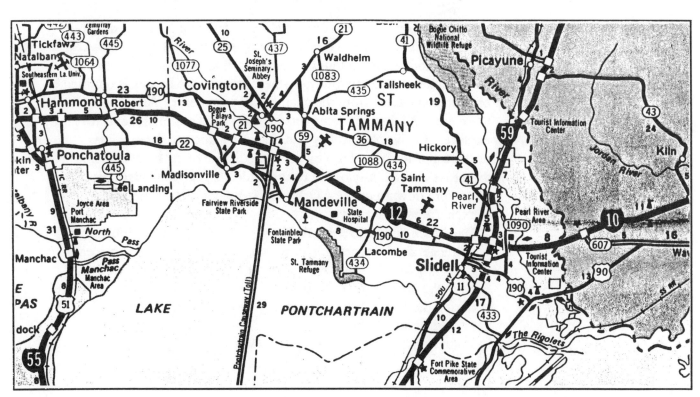

bridge called the Lake Pontchartrain Causeway make Mandeville an inviting retreat from the city.

From Mandeville, take LA 59 north to Abita Springs deep in the heart of the Ozone Belt. The Abita Springs Pavilion, a renowned health spa and resort, opened here on the site of an Indian medicinal spring in 1888. The resort site, at the intersection of LA 59 and 36, now has a tap on the grounds that provides free water from the ancient spring source. During the latter days of the last century, the air of the pine forest was considered especially beneficial for those suffering from respiratory problems, so the spa, resort and the entire area thrived on the trade of the fashionably ill as well as that of regular vacationers. The restful calm of the tree-lined streets and the cottages on their deeply recessed lots nestled in landscapes of thick, sheltering green, offer travelers a memory of what people of the last century considered a good vacation setting.

Take LA 36 to US 190 and Covington. European settlers of British origin began arriving here around 1769. The town was founded in 1812. The oldest public building still in use here is Christ Episcopal Church, circa 1846, located on New Hampshire Street. During the last weekend in March each year, the Spring Home and Garden Tour features private homes in the Covington-Mandeville area where visitors are given an opportunity to look beyond the facades into the private world of local history. Admission fees are charged.

Covington prides itself on being a country town. Sunday shoppers might especially enjoy the wide variety of antique shops here. A thirteen-block walking tour of a neighborhood containing 19th century, Victorian and other turn-of-the-century style homes is outlined on a map available from the chamber of commerce. After the walk there are a number of restaurants and fast food establishments to explore. St. Joseph's Abbey and Seminary, located three miles northeast of town, and run by the Benedictine monks, underscores the peace and serenity of the countryside. Covington is less than an hour from downtown New Orleans, if you come over the Lake Pontchartrain Causeway.

Backtrack on US 190 to LA 22, go west and discover Ponchatoula, which legends claim gets its name from an Indian expression meaning "falling hair." Supposedly, Spanish moss hanging from the trees in the area inspired the name. One of the best times to visit here is during the Ponchatoula Strawberry Festival held in April each year. Admission is free.

From Ponchatoula, take US 51 to Hammond. The Tally-Ho Railroad Museum is along the way. Railroad buffs might want to stop and explore the vintage train cars and railroad memorabilia.

Once the strawberry-growing capital of Louisiana, Hammond boasts much turn-of-the-century style architecture in the downtown area. The Queen Anne-style Illinois Central Railroad Depot, the Saik Hotel with its ornate brickwork, Fagan's Drugs with a pressed tin facade, the Boos Building with its illusion of a castle with towers and gables, and Himel's Auto Parts with its cast-iron front, added with other equally intriguing buildings have been factors in getting the downtown area declared a National Register Historic District.

Hammond's Heritage Day Festival, the first Sunday in May, gives visitors an opportunity to get a close-up look at the town's history and traditions.

Independence, a short drive (about 10 miles) up US 51 from Hammond at the intersection with LA 40, celebrates its history and heritage with the Independence Italian Festival the last Saturday in April. A parade, costumes, carnival, Italian food and street dances during this festival, as well as the Independence Italian Museum fully explain how this small city became known as "the Italian Capital of Louisiana."

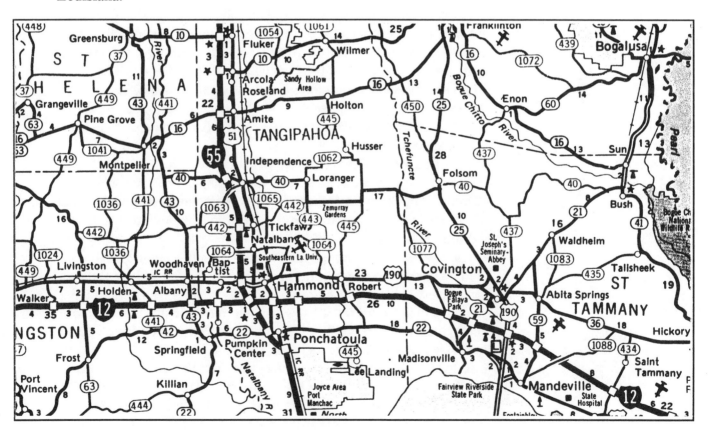

Take your choice of roads westward, then to the south. Let whim guide you. Denham Springs (LA 16 at US 190) is the home of the National Association of Louisiana Catahoulas, Inc.   The official dog of Louisiana by proclamation of the legislature, the Catahoula has ''distinctive blue eyes, leopard-like spots, short hair and a rangy build.'' Legends claim the breed was developed by the local Indians and early white settlers. The NALC maintains a museum with videos, artifacts and a kennel on LA 65 which is open occasionally by appointment and during dog shows. The NALC holds three dog shows a year: the Spring Dog Show and Craft Sale, the last Sunday in March; the Fall Dog Show, Labor Day; and the Louisiana Cow Dog Trials, the last weekend in September.

If you wander down LA 16, you will skirt along the Amite River into the out-of-the-way places that seem to be perpetual vacation homes. If the third Sunday in July finds you around French Settlement, you might want to linger for the Louisiana Sauce Patate Festival. The Creole House Museum is open during the festival. There's a carnival atmosphere, dancing and Creole foods—especially sauce patate—a potato stew.

LA 16 runs into LA 22 at Head of the Island; follow it to US 61 and then head north a few miles to Gonzales. The Tee-Joe Gonzales Museum houses collections of furniture, tools and memorabilia that depict the lifestyles of early settlers. Tee-Joe operated a general store at the present town site in 1887, so when a post office was established and installed in his store, it naturally carried his name. Gonzales modestly calls itself the Jambalaya Capital of the World, and at the Jambalaya Festival, the second full weekend of June every year, visitors can learn why.

Gonzales is 60 miles from New Orleans via I-10.

Back in New Orleans, Barataria, once Jean Laffite's stronghold, is 45 minutes by car from Jackson Square. Directions are simple. Take US 90 west out of town, turn left on Barataria Boulevard (LA 45) and follow the signs.

The road wanders through the swamps of myths and legends. From the bridge over the Intracoastal Waterway you can see the sky-line of New Orleans to the north/northeast. This is Barataria's high point, the place to view the hazy maze of marshy paths that lead to Kenta, Dupre Cutoff and Priest's canals, the Pen. Bayou Rigolettes, the villages named Lafitte and Jean Lafitte.

A detour through the public library can fill in some of the more tantalizing blanks of Laffite's life and career. His autobiography, *The Journal of Jean Laffite*, and Stanley Clisby Arthur's *Jean Laffite, Gentlemen Rover*, tell a poignant story of the Creole from Port-au-

Prince operating under letters of marque from the Republic of Cartagena. In his book Laffite laments that all the sins of those named Lafitte (a common New Orleans name in his day) were attributed to him and his brother Pierre, due to the American practice of mispelling their last name.

Jean Laffite came to New Orleans around the time of the Louisiana Purchase, moved to Barataria about 1810 and built himself a house on Grand Terre in 1811. His Baratarians helped make possible the U. S. victory at the Battle of New Orleans.

Barataria is thick with the descendants of Jean Laffite's crews, which at various times numbered as many as 1,000 men. (The number of ships in the privateers' fleet changed frequently.) Today the close-knit communities cluster around bayous and canals stuffed with shrimp boats and trawlers. This world of dusty streets and bare necessities, grocery store/bars and inquisitive stares is punctuated with small cottages nesting under rusting tin roofs. Occasionally a lavish modern house, with a trawler at a backdoor dock, has squeezed in.

On a January day, under the protective canopy of a live oak grove, several men are building a shrimp boat. Nets hang from oak branches waiting to be mended. A net maker sits in a straight-back chair knitting repairs without looking up. Barking dogs are chained

Barataria Cemetery at Indian Mound.

in grassless yards. Children peer from a mobile home doorway while images from a color TV flash behind them.

Some say Jean Laffite is buried in a remote corner of Jean Lafitte village, but others claim that his grave is in the Yucatan or that he was buried at sea. His family says he is buried in Illinois. But there is no disputing this was the privateers' gathering place, or that the commune headquarters were down at the mouth of Barataria Bay on Grand Terre. Area warehouses brimmed with captured treasure. Booty was auctioned at the Temple, a large shell mound reputed to have been the site of a Native American ceremonial center in earlier times. Hordes of respectable New Orleans businessmen came for the Baratarians' sales. Today, the Temple can only be reached by boat. Other shell mounds, used as cemeteries by Europeans, are visible from the roads which run up and down the waterways.

The Barataria Unit of the Jean Lafitte National Historical Park is a preserve of the dwindling natural world Lafitte and his men knew. Spanish moss hangs from trees, black water bayous skirt cypress knees and acres of palmettos cluster under the forest's canopy. The visitors center sits on piers over the swamp surrounded by evergreen youpons. Walkways stretch over expanses of wild irises and ferns on the Palmetto Trail from the visitors center to Bayou Coquille. Inside the center are a bookshop, movie theatre, and maps, as well as museum exhibits and displays exploring the natural wonders of the area. Exhibits, also, highlight bayou activities from trapping and fishing to moss gathering. A 25-minute movie, *Jambalaya: A Delta Almanac,* explores the culture of the region.

The Barataria Unit includes 8,600 acres of coastal wetlands including freshwater marshes, swamps and hardwood forests that are the breeding grounds for birds, fish and plants as well as the reptiles, amphibians, and mammals who roam the wetlands here. Some 200 species of birds may be observed. Shell middens, relics of Native American habitation in the area, date to 300 B. C.

Park rangers conduct a free one-mile walking tour along Bayou Coquille daily, as well as Sunday morning canoe treks. Contact the visitors center for more information.

Back in New Orleans take LA 46 past Chalmette, then down in St. Bernard Parish at Toca, just east of the village of St. Bernard, you'll find the Ducros Museum where displays and exhibits celebrate the area's past. Next door *El Museo de Los Isleños*, a unit of the Jean Lafitte National Historical Park, exhibits arts, crafts, photographs and detailed memorabilia from the culture and history of the Louisiana *Isleños*, the descendants of settlers from the Canary Islands. During the Spanish rule of Louisiana, Canary Islanders were sent here as

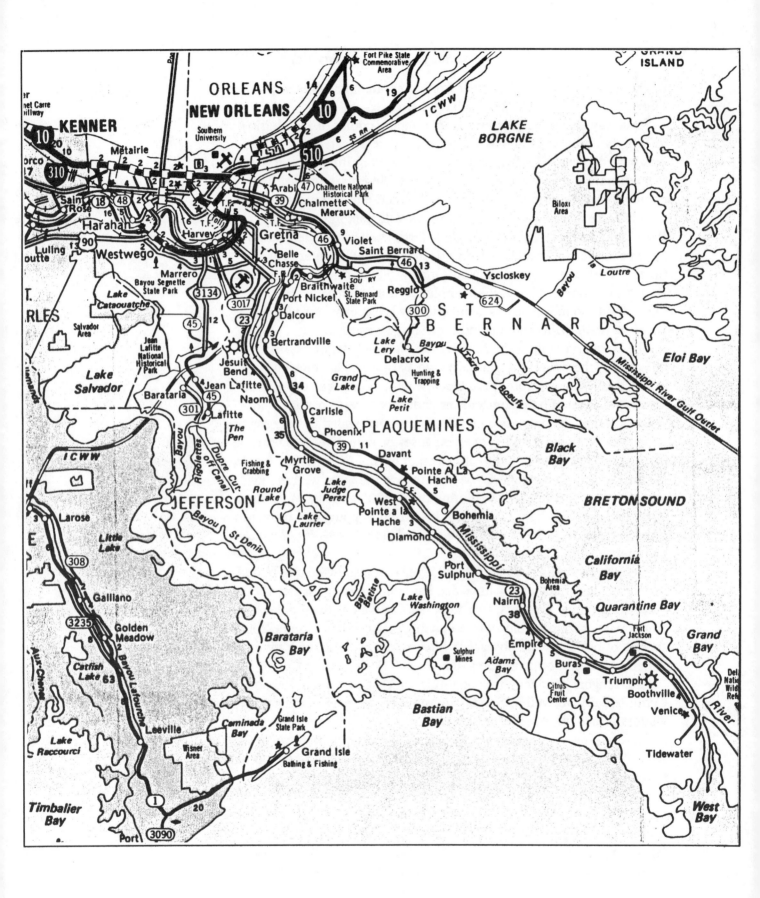

colonists. Picnic facilities are on the site, but the museum is not always open on a regular schedule. Telephone 504-682-0862 before visiting. Admission is free.

Over in Plaquemines Parish, LA 39 down the east bank and LA 23 down the west bank, visitors are offered a view of the Mississippi similar to that seen by some of the first European colonists. English Turn, a bend in the river between Belle Chasse and Braithwaite, supposedly earned its name when in 1699 Bienville and a small group of French colonists newly arrived in the area encountered a British ship here and were able to convince the captain that the French claim to the area was well established and that a larger French force nearby was ready to protect that claim. The British ship turned around and headed back downstream.

There are free ferries at Belle Chasse and Pointe a la Hache. A ferry crossing, especially at Pointe a la Hache, offers a perspective of river traffic drama you shouldn't miss.

The Judah P. Benjamin Monument at Belle Chasse memorializes one of the more intriguing Confederate leaders. Born in the West Indies, he came to New Orleans in 1828 and was elected to the U.S. Senate in the 1850s. Jefferson Davis's chief adviser, Benjamin advocated arming slaves and emancipating those who fought for the South. Later as the Confederacy's Secretary of State, he proposed emancipation of all slaves to the French and English governments in return for recognition and aid to the Confederate cause. After the Civil War he escaped to London where he became a successful lawyer.

Also at Belle Chasse, the Judge Leander H. Perez Memorial Park contains a museum as well as historic markers relating the history of Plaquemines Parish.

Myrtle Grove, LA 23, south of Belle Chasse, is the home of Woodland Plantation, circa 1823, the home idealized on the label of Southern Comfort Blended Whiskey.

At Port Sulphur mounds of sulphur wait to be loaded aboard ships at the river docks. The best view of the docks and the colorful piles of sulphur is from the levee.

Deep-sea fishing and charter boats, plus shrimp boats of all sorts make their homeport at Empire. Buras' orange groves defiantly stand along the river. Louisiana navels, Louisiana sweets, tangerines and satsumas fill the fruit baskets here during the October to January season. Orange wine is a popular local drink. The Plaquemines Parish Fair and Orange Festival, the first weekend in December at Fort Jackson, celebrates the crop and the parish's history.

Below Buras, still on LA 23, Fort Jackson, a defensive sister to

Fort Pike, rests inside its star-shaped masonry walls, retired from its early duty of defending the river approaches to New Orleans. Fort Jackson, along with Fort Philip, just across the river, were thought to be defense enough to stop Admiral David Farragut's Federal flotilla of gunboats and mortar schooners during the Civil War, but after a battle of several days, Farragut's fleet was able to pass the forts and proceed with the capture of New Orleans in late April, 1862.

Fort Jackson shares a 82-acre site with picnic facilities, a museum, historic markers and a monument to the Cavalier La Salle. The monument is said to be near the place where La Salle claimed Louisiana for France in 1682.

LA 23 continues to Venice, where the mouth of the Mississippi swallows up any tangible evidence of man's history.

For more information contact: Fort Pike State Commemorative Area, Route 6, Box 194, New Orleans, LA 70129. Telephone 504-662-5703.

St. Tammany Parish Tourist and Convention Commission, P.O. Box 432, Slidell, LA 70459. Telephone 504-649-0730. (For information on Slidell, Lacombe, Mandeville, Abita Springs and Covington.)

Tangipahoa Parish Tourist Commission, 1535 Hwy. 51 Bypass, Hammond, LA 70401. Telephone 504-542-7520. (For Ponchatoula, Hammond, Independence, etc.)

Jambalaya Festival Association, P.O. Box 1243, Gonzales, LA 70737.

Plaquemines Parish Tourist Commission, Courthouse, Pointe a la Hache, LA 70082. Telephone 504-333-4343.

The Barataria Unit, The Superintendent, Jean Lafitte National Historical Park, U. S. Custom House, 423 Canal Street, New Orleans, LA 70130. Telephone 504-689-2002.

*In the summer of 1990 the address of the Superintendent will change to 419 Decatur Street, New Orleans, LA 70130.

Louisiana Office of Tourism, Box 94291, Baton Rouge, LA 70804-9291. Telephone 800-334-8626 or in Louisiana 504-342-8119.

24

Baton Rouge

The Louisiana winter loosens her light grip on the land early. The grey, sullen skies of late January and early February often give way to some of the year's bluest skies and most pleasant temperatures. It was just this time of year in 1700 when André Pénicaut first saw Baton Rouge.

A newly arrived ship's carpenter with the D'Iberville expedition which had established its headquarters at Biloxi the year before, Pénicaut recalled the occasion in his *Narrative of French Adventure in Louisiana* which he completed in 1723, two years after his return to France.

Five leagues above Bayou Manchac, Pénicaut and his fellow explorers, who were traveling with D'Iberville, came to a series of high bluffs called *Istrouma* which Pénicaut translated as red stick (baton rouge). He explained that there was literally a wooden pole painted red here marking the boundary between the Bayagoula and the Houma nations' hunting grounds.

He wrote of visiting Baton Rouge again in 1704. This time a group of ten men, himself included, went hunting while the other men in the party stayed with the boats and made a camp. The poetic carpenter paints a word picture of a prairie, just beyond the forest, crowded with buffalo and deer. The Frenchmen were so comfortable that they lingered at Baton Rouge for ten days. But it was not until 1719 that the French colonial government established a post here.

The Red Stick Monument in Riverfront Park, River Road, is the most poignant place to begin a historic exploration of the modern city. Riverfront Park is home to the USS Kidd, a restored World War II destroyer, and the adjacent Nautical Historic Center. A Veterans Memorial Wall, coffee shop and gift shop round out the nautical attractions. An admission fee is charged to the USS Kidd.

The I-10 river bridge is the backdrop for the Riverfront Park walkway along the levee and the elevated walkways over and around the park and the city's Centroplex. Reflecting pools, cascading fountains, oleanders, willows, Confederate jasmine, banana trees, purple martin houses and flocks of mockingbirds, sparrows and cardinals

USS Kidd.

issue invitations to linger. Also in the park is the red brick Yazoo and Mississippi Valley Railroad Company Depot, which now houses the Louisiana Arts and Science Center. Here changing exhibits explore art, history and science. An admission fee is charged. A complete passenger train of another era is beside the LASC. Further down the levee, at the foot of Florida Street, is the Samuel Clemens Riverboat which offers one-hour river cruises daily for a fee. The boat also offers dinner cruises by reservation.

Back up the street, directly across the street from the LASC, is the old state capitol which Mark Twain, himself, called "Pathetic...an architectural falsehood...a sham castle...a sustainer of maudlin middle-age romanticism..." He also complained of the overpoweringly sweet smell of the magnolias. Maybe he was having a bad day. The old capitol, looking a great deal like a white castle, is delightful, a pleasant departure from the more popular antebellum styles.

The white Gothic Revival building crowns a grassy terraced mound much like the sites favored by ancient Native Americans for their temples. A people's public architecture offers none-too-subtle clues about their culture, traditions and aspirations. In Baton Rouge you can peer into the public psyche from antebellum days through Reconstruction at the old capitol. Gothic arches, a cast-iron spiral staircase, cast-iron columns, a domed skylight lined with stained glass and a multitude of flourishes once framed the world of Louisiana's political decisions. New Orleans had been the state capital until the constitutional convention of 1845 dictated that the seat of government be moved to a distance of more than sixty miles from that city. Baton Rouge was chosen as the site of the new capital the next year and plans were made for the capitol building. Completed in 1849, the capitol became the first public building in town to have a gas lighting system.

In January 1861 the legislature voted to secede from the Union and shortly thereafter joined the Confederacy. In the summer of 1862, Federal forces captured Baton Rouge. The Confederate state government moved to Opelousas. Federal troops used the capitol as a prison for captured Confederates and then as a barracks. While the Federal soldiers were making supper one night, towards the end of 1862, a grease fire got out of control and the building burned. The

Old State Capitol.

three-foot-thick walls stood around the ashes. Twenty years after the war a legislative session was held in the reconstructed capitol.

Enclosed by an elegant iron fence, the old building's grounds are quiet and park-like. Lazy stone lions rest near the front door and in a back corner of the grounds is a French railroad car of the type used by American troops in France during World War I.

The River Road runs north to the Pentagon Barracks just a few blocks away. There is limited visitor parking in front of the barracks. A small museum inside the barracks does not charge an admission fee. These barracks are not only one of the most historic sets of buildings in town, they are in the area of some of the most historic sites.

Zachary Taylor lived in a nearby cottage when he was elected president of the United States in 1848. It was the same cottage that had been the home of the Spanish *comandante* of Fort San Carlos. (The Spanish Fort San Carlos was in the area.) Nearby the British built their New Richmond fort. The area is studded with historic markers. The Pentagon Barracks built for the U.S. Army were begun in 1819 and completed in 1824 after the immediate area went through the turmoil of being ruled by France, Britain, Spain, and the West Florida Republic. The Pentagon Barracks originally consisted of five main buildings, but the fifth building (the one closest to the river) was demolished and never replaced. The brick buildings are adorned with stout Tuscan columns in front and back. Shaded by

The Samuel Clemens.

Pentagon Barracks.

Louisiana State Capitol
Faced by Statue of Huey P. Long.

massive oaks, the back courtyard offers an idealized aspect of early American military life. Zachary Taylor commanded the post at Baton Rouge several times. Visitors here included the Marquis de Lafayette, Henry Clay and Andrew Jackson. According to legends, the famous American soldiers quartered here at one time or another included: Robert E. Lee, Thomas "Stonewall" Jackson, Braxton Bragg, Wade Hampton, Jefferson Davis and Philip Sheridan.

The Pentagon Barracks are within the Capitol Complex, a 27-acre expanse of gardens and buildings. Parking is very limited when the legislature is in session, but well worth searching out. A walking tour could begin at the Pentagon Barracks Museum, where exhibits chronicle the construction of the present capitol (completed in 1932), as well as the sojourn of Zachary "Rough and Ready" Taylor and the days of Huey P. Long.

On the 27th-floor of the capitol is an observation deck which offers overall views of the river, the complex of petro-chemical plants along its banks, Louisiana State University and Huey P. Long's grave and memorial. Long was gunned down as he entered the capitol shortly after the building was completed. Memories of the politician and his dreams are still embodied in this 34-story building, the tallest state capitol in the nation. There are regular free tours of the building. The tall yellowish-grey tower rises in the gardens, jutting through the haze like a modern version of a red stick, marking the boundary between the people and the government.

Long's statue and grave are in the formal gardens, as is a commemorative to Zachary Taylor. The Old Arsenal Museum, circa 1835, celebrates the area's history under the rule of France, Spain, Britain, Republic of West Florida, United States, and the Confederate States of America. Weapons, uniforms and documents enhance the displays. Graffiti written by soldiers in the powder magazine's early days has been preserved on the inside walls. Cannons used in the Battle of Baton Rouge are just outside the building. Local historians say this was one of the few military engagements of the American Revolution fought outside the original 13 colonies. The Battle of Baton Rouge was won by the Spanish governor of Louisiana, Bernardo de Galvez, his Louisiana militia and American allies. With the surrender of the British commander here, Spain regained control over the area. An Indian mound, believed to have been part of an ancient ceremonial complex, is nearby. Visitors might want to plan their walking tours of the area in the cooler months. The months from October through April usually have the most tolerable temperatures. As early as May the steamy Louisiana heat wilts magnolia blossoms.

Louisiana State University, said to have been a pet project of Huey

P. Long, enjoys an idyllic lakeside setting in the city and is home to a number of museums open to the public during school sessions. But one of the university's best museums is located off campus on the Burden Research Plantation, at I-10 and Essen Road.

The Rural Life Museum tells the story of an earlier rural Louisiana primarily through architecture. Many different styles of rural buildings have been moved onto the five-acre site within the plantation compound to create a village where dusty streets are lined with oaks and plantings that were popular in earlier times. A commissary (plantation-style general store), overseer's house, a separate kitchen, sick house (a plantation dispensary/infirmary), schoolhouse, blacksmith shop, slave cabins, cane grinder and sugarhouse, grist mill, country church and cemetery, pioneer's cabin and corncrib, dogtrot house, Acadian house, and shotgun house make up the village buildings. Cypress fences with laundry speared on the pickets, sugar pots, bells, pirogues, fallen marble columns, a four-seater outhouse and a hundred other small touches in decorations and furnishings give the

LSU Rural Life Museum.

village a ghostly air—everything is here but the people. In the main building, there is a museum with exhibits utilizing numerous collections of lifestyle pieces and displays demonstrating work methods from early rural Louisiana. The Rural Life Museum is open from 8:30 a.m. to 4 p.m. Monday through Friday, except for university holidays. An admission fee is charged.

Baton Rouge is located on I-10 at US 61 and 190 about 77 miles up river from New Orleans.

For more information contact: Baton Rouge Area Convention and Visitors Bureau, P.O. Drawer 4149, Baton Rouge, LA 70821. Telephone 504-383-1825.

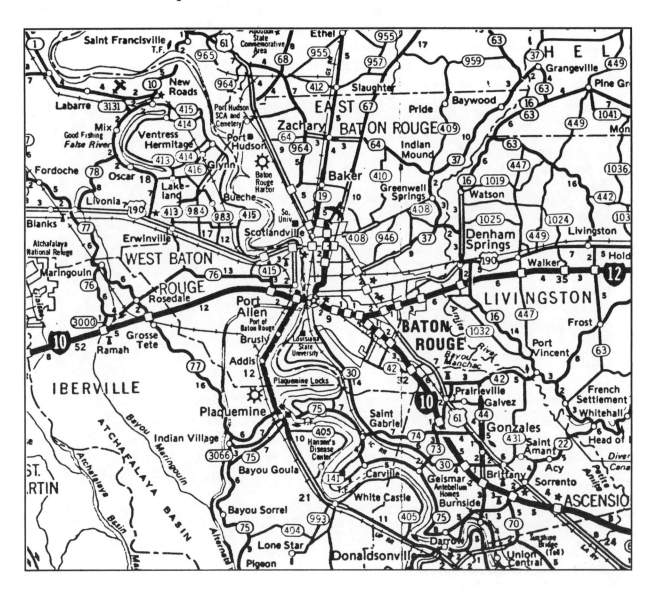

25

St. Francisville

Fog horns moan on the Mississippi as the sun burns through the
thick morning mist at St. Francisville. After the mist has lifted on
the river, it still lingers in the live oak groves, caught between the
wisps of Spanish moss veiling white-columned mansions and the
long, wrought-iron trimmed verandas of planters' houses. This
setting could conjure up visions of antebellum days, of hoop-skirted
belles and gallant Confederates, but local folks prefer a different time
frame, and cast of characters, for their dalliances with the past. This
small Louisiana community of about 2,000 souls, 110 miles north of
New Orleans, has chosen the period of the 1820s as its golden era.
The ladies' official costume is an ankle-clinging dress with an empire
waistline and the town's ultimate hero is a frontier naturalist.

In 1821 John James Audubon stepped off a river boat onto Bayou
Sara Landing here—straight into legendary dimensions. With his 13-
year-old apprentice in tow, he climbed Ferdinand Street and walked
to Oakley Plantation three miles beyond town. He came to tutor a
wealthy planter's 15-year-old daughter in drawing, music, dancing
and arithmetic for the generous sum of $60 per month, plus room and
board for himself and his apprentice. His contract called for half his
time to be free so he could pursue his pioneering study of birds.
Of his arrival, he wrote in his journal, "The magnolias covered with
fragrant blossoms, the holly, the beech, the tall yellow poplar, the
hilly ground and even the red clay, all excited my admiration. Such
an entire change in the fall of nature...seems almost supernatural..."

He called his new-found home "my beloved Happyland." Was it
love at first sight or *déjà vu*? St. Francisville's similarity to the sultry
Haitian world where Audubon was born and spent the early years of
his life, before his seafaring father took him to France, must have
comforted the vagabond's soul.

The tutor grew fond of his student, Miss Eliza Pirrie, and she was
flattered by his attention. But her mother became convinced his
behavior was improper and dismissed the artist four months after his
arrival. Audubon protested to his journal that when he arrived at the
plantation he was called a good man but now he was suspect. He
swallowed his pride, requested and was granted ten extra days to

finish up several projects before leaving Oakley. During his four-month stay he had completed 32 paintings for his *Birds of America* series.

In New Orleans he waited for his wife, Lucy, to come down from Cincinnati and join him. He was determined that Lucy, a Quaker, should go to St. Francisville and just by her presence restore his reputation. Lucy did find a position as a teacher at Beech Woods, another West Feliciana Parish plantation, just outside St. Francisville. The school, with living quarters in the same cottage, became the closest thing to a home the Audubons would have for the next eight years. Lucy supported her husband's work as he ranged hundreds of miles from their "Happyland" home in an obsessive attempt to paint and catalog the birds of North America and later to seek a publisher for his collection of paintings—a search that eventually took him to Europe. When he was in the area he often taught in her Beech Woods school and, later, at Beech Grove plantation. But the birds demanded most of his time. More than 80, and maybe as many as 100 of the 435 *Birds of America* were painted here.

The lazy, easy world of inspiration Audubon knew is still here. To gain entrance all you need do is take a leisurely walk through the town. Strollers are rewarded with more than an ethereal link to the naturalist's spirit. The supernatural atmosphere Audubon recognized here also stirred other creative souls. From 1800 to 1900 several generations of master carpenters armed with copy books of architectural drawings and a pragmatic understanding of local materials and conditions built a community of homes, stores, offices and churches that today compose an idyllic townscape, a storybook world—a nostalgic place that you might think exists only in romanticized paintings and antique photographs. An array of freely interpreted building styles—Spanish-French Colonial, Federalist, Greek Revival, Gothic and Victorian—are eclectic verses in an epic folk poem of wood and brick, design and function that touch a vulnerable place in the heart.

Bankrolled in turn by sugar cane, cotton, sweet potatoes and soybeans, the town now depends on commuters to the high tech hustle of Baton Rouge, 35 miles to the south, and workers at a nearby nuclear power plant and paper mill for its economic livelihood.

Without zoning laws, modern housing developments voluntarily confine themselves to the pine woods on the far side of US 61, the main road through the region. And most commercial establishments restrict themselves to the approaches of the old town, now called the Historic District in honor of its inclusion on the National Register of Historic Places.

A depression-era Federal Writer's Project reported, "The town is one mile long and one yard wide,'' which is still close enough to the truth to reassure even the easily disoriented that there is no danger of becoming lost.

Starting across the street from the St. Francisville Inn (a Carpenter-Gothic cottage skirted with lacy wooden eaves trim, nestling under giant oaks festooned with Spanish moss), Ferdinand Street runs straight through the heart of the Historic District.

Antique shops, in turn-of-the-century storefronts and Cajun-style cottages, stand sentinel on either side of the street. Further down, behind the hedges, through transparent lace curtains and rippled, century-old window glass a close-up view of the lingering good life in Audubon's Happyland nearly comes into focus.

White picket fences scarcely contain color-splashed gardens wild with azaleas, camellias and wisteria. Glossy green magnolias are playgrounds for flocks of cardinals, blue jays and mockingbirds. The southern forest that captivated Audubon's imagination and supplied the carpenters' materials lies lush and rampant at the back gates and garden fences, sending out leafy feelers and green warnings. One season of neglect and the wilderness will spill over the perimeters, creep back and reclaim terrain lost to civilization two centuries ago.

Flags from the area's six different national governments flutter above the West Feliciana Historical Society's home in a Greek Revival-style hardware store, circa 1895. Inside, exhibits celebrate the town founders, ranging from entrepreneural British planters to refugees from the American Whiskey Rebellion seeking a safe haven in Spanish territory, as well as the imaginative carpenters and Audubon. Two blocks down, on the right, The Widow Ross's House crowns an eroded loess bluff. Steep brick steps from the street lead to the large railed front gallery. The house was here when Audubon passed back and forth on journeys to the riverboat landing, though the Widow Ross herself came later. She gained infamy during the Civil War when after her first husband died, and her second one disappeared, she opened a dining room for Union gunboat officers.

In the next block, the fat-columned portico of the Episcopal Church's Jackson Hall squares off with the tall, lean white frame Masonic Lodge across the street, each offering an early 19th century interpretation of Greek Revival styling.

Next door to Jackson Hall, Grace Episcopal Church, circa 1858, was built to replace a church which stood here in Audubon's day. An immigrant carpenter's memories of the English country churches of his childhood inspired the red brick, restrained Gothic design. Inside, music to summon the angels slowly rises from the ancient throat of the massive Pilcher organ, a manual two-tracker installed in

Grace Episcopal Church.

1858. Gravestones, some predating the church by more than a quarter century, dot the church yard which is shaded by live oaks, adorned with azaleas and carefully hemmed in by an ornate wrought-iron fence.

Directly across the street from the church is the yellow brick parish court house, circa 1903, built to replace the original, which was heavily damaged in the Civil War. Its copper-roofed bell tower and monumental statuary are eclipsed by the first building's well-house, circa 1852. Looking like a gazebo offering a cool respite on a summer's day, the well-house is considered one of the finest examples of Greek Revival architecture in the area.

One block down from the Episcopal church, the Mt. Carmel Catholic Cemetery was established by Capuchin monks in the 1700s.

The legacy of these religious men is the town's name in honor of their patron saint, Francis of Assisi.

Continue on down the street to the driveway of Mount Carmel Catholic Church, circa 1871. From its hilltop perch overlooking a swampy stretch of willows between town and the river, you might see the steamboat sisters *Mississippi* and *Delta Queen* tie up on one of their regular visits. The disembarking passengers saunter towards town up the same road Audubon and his apprentice walked in 1821.

Back down the hill, go straight across Ferdinand to Royal Street. About a half block up the street on the right, Hillcroft (there's a name plate in almost every yard) is a tall, haughty, Neoclassical-style house of heart-pine and cypress with a widow's walk for river watching.

Next door Motley Hall hides its skeleton of heavy timber and solid infill of mud and Spanish moss under prim, white clapboards in the type of early Louisiana construction called *bousillage*. Motley Hall also has a Greek Revival-style well-house, circa 1810.

At the end of the block, the green and white Printer's Cottage, circa 1790, is one of the oldest houses in town. The core was built by the Capuchin monks and used as a holding place for bodies transported from the western side of the river for burial on higher ground. About 1812 a printer moved in and expanded the house. After the Civil War another owner founded *The Democrat*, a newspaper, which is still functioning in the red brick building at the end of the lane beside the house.

Across the lane on the steep side of the street is the Spanish Colonial house Propinquity, circa 1809, but you need to cross the narrow street to the Barrow House, a circa 1809 New England-style salt box, for the best view. From the Barrow House's raised sidewalks you can look out on the red brick house where Audubon and his wife Lucy often visited.

The Barrow House is the only bed and breakfast/private residence in the Historic District and is furnished with such authentic antiques as a traditional Louisiana Spanish moss-stuffed mattress. Fresh cut flowers in every room and a warm weather lounge/screened porch, well-appointed with white wicker, encourage guests to prolong visits.

Recross Royal Street and continue to the corner. The plain box-like stucco building on the right was built in 1809 as a hotel and in 1810 became the capitol of the Republic of West Florida when locals declared their independence from Spain and governed themselves for 74 days before being annexed by the United States. (This section of the state was not included in the Louisiana Purchase.)

Directly across the street on the right is the Bank of Commerce, circa 1905. The Renaissance Revival exterior houses a stained glass window where the Louisiana sun shines through the varied colors of a tribute to Audubon.

Behind the bank is a dogtrot, circa 1870, of rough-cut cypress with a center breezeway and an ell in the rear. Next door to the dogtrot is the white-hutched frame of the Presbyterian Church, which began life as a Jewish synagogue at the turn of the century.

Return to the bank and make a right. The next house on the right is Virginia. Its stark white magnificence is trimmed with elaborate wrought-iron railings and a classic pediment which hide its origins. Virginia began in 1817 as a one-room store and grew and grew until it became an elegant townhouse in 1855.

Directly across the street, the Judge Golsan House is a Victorian cottage, circa 1885, in the Eastlake style with gingerbread trim and fish scale shingles on the gables.

One block up the street is the Methodist church, circa 1899. The Methodists were in the area as early as 1806 and the belfry here came from one of their earlier buildings.

Across the street on the corner is Seabrook, circa 1807, which incorporates Spanish and French Colonial influences as well as decorations from the Federalist period.

Back on the right side of the street, on the bend, the brown-hued Audubon Hall, circa 1819, began as an open-air marketplace. The arches at either end of the hall were originally for the passage of wagons. After serving as town hall for years, the building has reverted to a market place today under the auspices of the Historical Society.

Next door, White's Cottage, with rocking chairs and children's toys crowding the porch, is a yellowish pen-and-passage Georgian-style house. When the passage or hall between the two sides was left open in this style, the house became a dogtrot. Continue up Royal Street; in less than a block it loops back onto Ferdinand Street.

Your walking tour can meander back to the St. Francisville Inn and maybe a lunch of crawfish pie or jambalaya. There are ample opportunities along the way to browse in antique and gift shops, or to stop and watch the birds.

After a rest break, resume your tour of the area by car. Three miles out of town, Oakley, a West Indies-style house, circa 1799, hides in a wild tangle of oaks inside a Louisiana State Commemorative Area. Scarcely changed since Audubon's sojourn, the plantation grounds still contain outbuildings, the most notable of which are the barn and the kitchen, as well as the house with its jalousied galleries that let the breezes through the rooms while keeping out rain and direct sunlight. Adam mantels, understated decoration of exterior

Oakley, c. 1799

gallery stairs, and a simple cornice frieze are Oakley's only ornaments.

Oakley's furnishings and decorations have been restored to the
functional and austere styles of the Federalist Period (1790-1830),
which reflect the way the house was decorated when Audubon
resided here.

Upstairs off the main parlor, a tiny closet of a room was
Audubon's quarters. Now a simple daybed fills one corner, and two
small tables hold eyeglasses, quill pens, drawing material, a snake's
shed skin, a bird's nest and other bits and pieces that the restorers
believe would have caught the artist/naturalist's attention. Audubon
shared the tiny space with his apprentice.

Visitors may let their imaginations roam around the possibilities
for Audubon's dismissal as they tour the frontier museum set up in
the old detached kitchen and peruse the antiquated farm implements
in the barn museum. Gravel and brick paths meander through 100
acres of grounds, twisting behind camellia bushes and thick clumps
of azaleas, bringing the guest suddenly upon a turn in the path,

perhaps the same path where Mrs. Pirrie came unexpectedly upon the artist walking with her daughter? Gossip still circulating after all these years claims he "paid too much attention" to his teenage pupil and not enough to Mrs. Pirrie. Other bits of ancient gossip say the French gentleman's habit was to frequently, and innocently, kiss the ladies in his presence but that he kissed his student once too often as far as her mother was concerned.

After an interlude at Oakley, visit the Cottage, a working plantation, five miles from town, where another view of life during the early 19th century comes into focus. Here you can explore a self-contained plantation kingdom, much like Oakley during Audubon's stay.

The long, lean main house, circa 1795, buttressed by full-length verandas and stories of a visit from Andrew Jackson, is also a rural bed and breakfast inn. Slave quarters, a school house similar to Lucy Audubon's, barns, smokehouses, kitchen cabin, family cemetery, woodland park and a rustic wooden bridge across Thompson Creek complete the centuries-old picture of plantation life.

At the neighboring plantation, Catalpa, "Miss Mamie" Fort Thompson displays a set of china decorated with wildflowers. "Tradition says Audubon painted it," Miss Mamie says, "but there's no proof."

Ancient oaks line the elliptical drive leading to the Victorian cottage built to replace an antebellum palace that burned in the last century. Salvaged family treasures include portraits of ancestors by

The Cottage.

Rosedown.

Thomas Sully and Charles Willson Peale. Antiques and memories fill visits so completely you may imagine for a moment that you are visiting a long-lost great-aunt.

Related to the parish's leading families, Miss Mamie even counts Miss Eliza Pirrie among her kin. A copy of Audubon's portrait of Miss Pirrie is in the front bedroom.

Two copper printing plates from the first edition of *Birds of America* are on display at Rosedown, an opulent, white-columned mansion, circa 1835, that Miss Mamie and her relatives inherited and then sold to a private developer who in turn converted it into a museum.

Prints of all 435 of Audubon's *Birds of America* are on display at the St. Francis Hotel On The Lake, a rare exhibit for its completeness. Installed in a maze-like gallery, the birds' flapping wings, mating cries and puffed-up feathers suspended in color become an intimate encounter.

The publication of Audubon's works brought him immediate and enduring renown for artistic endeavors and scientific observations. The long years of single-minded dedication to his birds paid off, and in 1830 he took Lucy away from his beloved Happyland to an easier life than that of a plantation school teacher.

But he left part of his soul behind, the part that bonded with the earth and air, the wildwoods and plantation society. The supernatural atmosphere here will always whisper of his ethereal link with "The magnolias covered with fragrant blossoms, the holly, the beech, the tall yellow poplar, the hilly ground and even the red clay..."

St. Francisville is located on US 61 at LA 10 on the Mississippi River 110 miles upstream from New Orleans and 35 miles north of Baton Rouge.

Accommodations, restaurants and fast food establishments are available in town.

Plantations and houses that are open for tours charge admission fees. Admission to both the West Feliciana Historical Society Museum and the *Birds of America* exhibit at the St. Francis Hotel on the Lake is free. The museum also serves as a tourist information center.

For more information contact: The West Feliciana Historical Society, P.O. Box 338, St. Francisville, LA 70775. Telephone 504-635-6330.

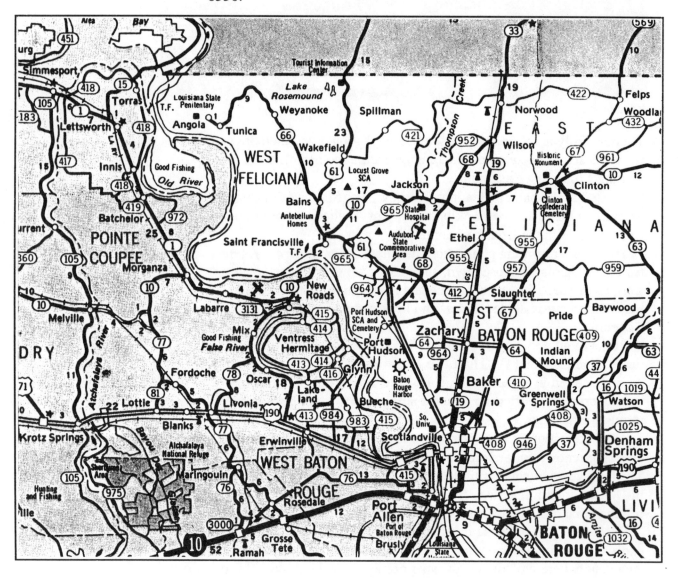

26

The Myrtles, St. Francisville's Most Haunted House

"The most haunted house in America" hides from public view behind a wall of trees and lush tropical undergrowth along US 61 on the edge of this Mississippi River town.

Visitors must turn into the drive, enter the gate, start up the lane and slip into the ghostly realm before they can get a good view of The Myrtles, a nearly 200-year-old plantation house. Spanish moss hangs from the live oak trees as they crowd together, conspiring against the sun, to perpetually shroud the house front in shade. If you have ever wanted to meet a ghost, this is the perfect setting.

There is testimony, from perfectly staid people—college professors, computer programmers, bank presidents and the like—that ghosts roam The Myrtles' nights, playing ethereal music, dancing in the ladies' parlor, laughing across the void of time. Long-departed souls have been seen walking down the lane, cavorting in the side yard, peeking in the windows, escaping to the woods behind the house.

Legends claim that the planter's saddleback-style, 22-room mansion was built on an ancient Indian burial ground. Supposedly, Indian maidens have been seen wandering about the small island in the pond behind the house. The area around the pond was a well-known buffalo wallow when the first European settlers built homes in the area.

General David Bradford of Pennsylvania, a leader of the Whiskey Rebellion, built The Myrtles after fleeing George Washington's troops and seeking refuge in Spanish West Florida in 1794. General Bradford prospered growing tobacco and indigo. He died in 1809 and one of his daughters and her husband, Judge Clark Woodruff, moved in around 1817. Then came the first of the many murders that would continue to occur over several generations and leave spirits so restless that The Myrtles would be declared the most haunted house in America by Richard Winer in his book, *Houses of Horror*.

A costumed hostess guides visitors through the house and recounts some of the more spectacular stories, explaining that more than ten murders have taken place at the house. One version of the first murder story claims that Judge Woodruff's slave mistress lost favor with her master for some now-forgotten offense, and he had her ear cut off in punishment. In retaliation she made a poison of oleanders and baked it in a birthday cake for one of the judge's daughters. The judge's wife and two of his daughters died after eating the cake. The vengeful ex-mistress was soon lynched by a local mob who learned of her alleged deed. The little girls are often seen reflected in the house's windows, and the ex-mistress, wearing a green turban, is often encountered wandering down the lane and has been known to turn down the bedcovers for overnight guests.

During the Civil War, Yankee soldiers gunned down the plantation's tutor in the gentleman's parlor. ''For no good reason,'' the hostess says. She points out the scarred spots where the stray bullets bounced off the marble mantle.

The ladies of the house took a fancy to a Confederate army deserter and hid him in a secret room until the local vigilantes discovered him, dragged him out to the nearest tree and strung him up. Some people think they have heard the deserter's restless spirit pacing about his old hiding place.

The hostess' stories go on. One afternoon, a few years after the

A Stone Lady in the Garden Has Seen Murderers and Lynching Parties Ride Through the Myrtles' Grounds.

war, the house's owner, a Mr. William Winter, who had gained a
reputation as a lawyer and a ruthless businessman, was summoned to
the side veranda by a man on horseback shouting, "Gentleman to see
the lawyer."

No sooner did Lawyer Winter step on to the veranda than he was
shot down in a hail of bullets. The horseman swiftly rode away and
was never found. Mr. Winter struggled across the veranda into the
house and started up the stairs. His wife met him on the 17th stair,
and he died in her arms. At night, in the heavy stillness of the thick
humid Louisiana darkness, steps can be heard coming up the stairs.
But they never reach the top. Seventeen steps are all that are ever
heard. When the rains come, bloodstains trail across the veranda
following Winter's route to the stairs.

Now a bed and breakfast inn, The Myrtles, named for the crepe
myrtle trees hugging the back of the house, shares its memories with
overnight guests. Many say they never hear anything other than the
old house creaking in the night and they never see anything more
than an easily explained shadow moving across the veranda.

For those guests who want a guaranteed encounter, five or six

Eerie Shadows on the Myrtles' Veranda.

times a year Mystery Weekends are held. Costumed guests are invited to participate in an antebellum-style wedding, attend a ball, a banquet and other appropriate recreations that climax in a re-enactment of William Winter's murder. The directors take some liberties with the time and activities surrounding the murder. The weekend takes a mystery writer's twist as the guests attempt to figure out who the murderer is.

In the meantime, everybody assumes that the lady in the green turban is a kitchen employee dressed to add a little spice to the house's tales, that the two little girls peering in the rippled glass windows have been carefully instructed by the management, and that the 17 steps on the stairs in the deepest hours of the night have been orchestrated to heighten the drama.

The Myrtles, on US 61 at St. Francisville, is open daily for tours. Admission fees are charged. Overnight accommodations are available. Mystery Weekend fees include accommodations and meals.

For more information contact: The Myrtles, P.O. Box 1100, St. Francisville, LA 70775. Telephone 504-635-6277.

27

LA 10 and Detours
Jackson, Port Hudson, Clinton,
Franklinton and Bogalusa

LA 10 comes across the northern toe of the Louisiana boot, from St. Francisville through Jackson, Clinton, Greensburg, Franklinton and Bogalusa to the Mississippi state border. Along the way it cuts through a different Louisiana, a Louisiana without a French accent, a Louisiana with firm roots in British and Anglo-American culture and traditions.

A free ferry crosses the Mississippi River between New Roads, Point Coupee Parish, on the west side and St. Francisville, West Feliciana Parish, on the east. The highway picks up at the St. Francisville ferry landing. Travelers to the town have been disembarking near this site for a couple of centuries. Loess hills, the river bluffs, make a brief buffer behind the town and the river.

Even a brief automobile ride from the ferry landing through town is enthralling. The romance of the place hangs heavy in the humid air. The essence of the historic community spills over into the countryside. Plantations' gatehouses front along the road out of town.

Jackson, a little more than a dozen miles away, began as Bear Corners, a name memorialized by a downtown restaurant, in a circa 1832 building. For a while the town was called Buncombe, after a county in South Carolina, but after the Battle of New Orleans, it was renamed in honor of Andrew Jackson. In 1816 Jackson became the seat of Feliciana Parish. In 1844 the parish was divided into two separate parishes, East and West Feliciana.

The town hall, an isolated architectural jewel, was a silver-domed bank in earlier days. Today the city clerks work behind the teller's wooden cage. In 1847 an insane asylum was located in the town. In 1854 the state legislature authorized the building of an asylum that "did not look like a prison." The air of dignity in architecture still surviving on the grounds of the East Louisiana State Hospital has its roots in that legislation.

Centrally located downtown, Milbank, circa 1836, appears to be an antebellum private home, but the pinkish mansion with its thick

Doric columns served as a bank when it was first built. Over the years the house did serve as a private residence, as well as barracks for Federal troops during the Civil War, a public assembly hall, apothecary shop, a millinery shop, a small hotel and ballroom, and a newspaper office. Located just around the corner from the Bear Corners Restaurant, LA 10 at Bank Street, the house is open for tours (an admission fee is charged) and for bed and breakfast by reservation. Telephone 504-634-5901.

Around the corner from Milbank is another antebellum mansion, Roseneath, circa 1830. Across the street from Milbank, on the opposite corner of LA 10 and Bank, the Charter Street Market sports a large mural/map of the area on its outside walls. If you need directions to any of the town's 41 historic buildings, this is the place to come. The town is packed with ''early American''-style houses. The small, red brick old Feliciana Courthouse, on Glenmora Street, is a museum.

Detour down LA 68 south. The woods are thick with memories of the antebellum era. Asphodel Plantation hides in the dense forest

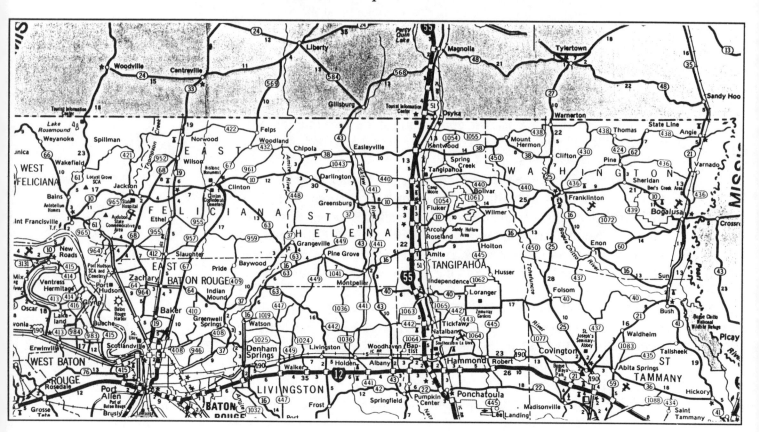

Roseneath, c. 1830, Jackson.

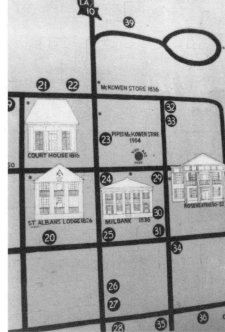

Map at Charter Street Market, Jackson.

along the narrow road. The main house, circa 1820, has been the setting for several movies, including a version of *The Long Hot Summer* starring Joanne Woodward and Paul Newman. The house is open for tours daily. There is an admission fee. Surrounding the house is Asphodel Village, which squeezes together several antebellum buildings moved onto the place, as well as a turn-of-the-century train depot. Overnight accommodations are also available here. Telephone 504-654-6868.

On US 61, just south of LA 68, the antebellum era exploded in the fury of the Civil War at Port Hudson. Here Confederate forces tried to retain control of the Mississippi River after the fall of Baton Rouge in August 1862. They constructed a series of batteries along the bluff as well as a four-and-one-half-mile long earthworks in front of the batteries for additional protection.

An attack by Federal forces was repelled in March 1863. Then in May, General U. S. Grant began the siege of Vicksburg, and General Nathaniel Banks with about 13,000 troops under his command laid siege to Port Hudson. Three major attacks against the Confederate stronghold were repulsed. By early July food supplies for the 6,000 Confederates had dwindled, and they were running low on ammunition. With no hope of relief, the Confederates surrendered on July 9, 1863, ending the siege. Port Hudson fell five days after the surrender at Vicksburg. With its fall, Federal forces gained full control of the Mississippi River.

Many casualties on both side were attributed to disease and sunstroke. Photographs made after the battle show the devastation—cannons blown from their mounts, remnants of the timber defenses scattered about in the mud, as well as the defeated soldiers of both sides. There is some unnamed magic in old photographs, some conjuring ability in the cool, clear gaze of a young soldier's eyes looking out across the time gap forever focusing on the ache war brings.

Today, the Port Hudson State Commemorative Area, a 643-acre site, is best recommended to history-loving hikers. Six miles of trails take hikers over the highly contested ground. An elevated boardwalk is over the breastworks in the Fort Desperate area. There are three observation towers in different areas of the park for an overall view of the battle ground, as well as a woodland picnic area and restrooms. There is a museum in the visitors center which sits in an open field surrounded by breastworks.

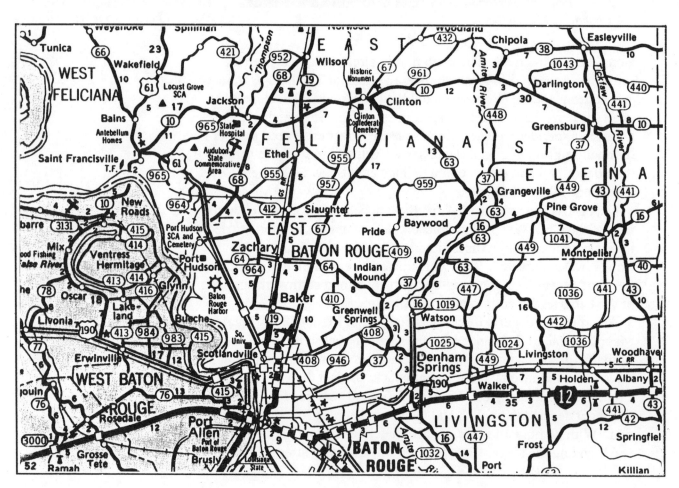

Ravines run through the park. Stands of hardwoods with green moss growing on their damp, shaded sides reverberate with cardinals' songs. Mockingbirds call from the tulip trees. In the lonely woods the wind rustles the leaves. The quiet tries to drown out the rumbling traffic from the nearby highway.

On a late April day, caterpillars cover the rails of the walkway at Fort Desperate. They are everywhere, literally falling out of the trees. One small swarm of lovebugs is a harbinger of things to come. Trumpet vines and blackberry briars compete for space on the woodland floor. Wild Carolina jasmine scents the air. Tarzan-style vines dangle from tall trees. The walkway crosses a wilderness of ferns. Sights and aromas change. The smell of green and damp, of fallen leaves and decaying plants evolving to earth wafts up. Mysterious clicking sounds, rabbit holes, opossum retreats, the sun-dappled woods, all make it easy to forget this was death's arena. This was war's chosen spot.

Further down the raised walkway a still life emerges: mushrooms, palmettos and a few sprigs of blooming wild mustard. A butterfly disrupts the stillness, making its way past youpons and huckleberry bushes to a log fallen over a ravine.

History lovers must come armed with imagination to keep the troops in mind, to keep their thoughts from becoming ensnared in the muscadine vines with clusters of blossoms yearning to be fruit.

An admission fee is charged to the Port Hudson State Commemorative Area.

When you leave Port Hudson, take LA 68 back to Jackson, back down the narrow, winding road, past the Asphodel Baptist Church, blinding white, tiny, unadorned, waiting for Sunday down its lane of pines. Then on the opposite side of the road, Asphodel with its house, village, shops, roses, and magnolias appears again. On down the road there's a stretch of pristine, white board fence and a yellow sign warning that this is a prison area: "Don't pickup hitch hikers," it says.

In Jackson take LA 10 on to Clinton. Here the streets are lanes to places created in another time by people assured by their culture that they lived in the best of all possible worlds.

Clinton, Courthouse.

Sillman Institute, on Bank Street, was Sillman College. The three brick buildings with their Doric columns and double galleries connected by breezeways were built between 1850 and 1894. Today, Sillman is a private school. On the same street as the school are buildings from the antebellum era with mammoth columns as well as Victorian and turn-of-the-century country houses. Though in town, these graceful houses are surrounded with idyllic flower-filled yards stretching to meadows in the back.

Sunlight strokes shadows and softly graduated shading around the columns of the antebellum parish courthouse, circa 1841. Behind the courthouse, Lawyer's Row, a line of small Greek Revival buildings, has served as law offices since 1826. One of the buildings now houses the Audubon Library, open weekdays from 8 a.m. to 12 p.m. and from 1 p.m. to 5 p.m. Admission is free. Afternoon light hits the front of the buildings, making a white-on-white composition, as the tiny temple-looking structures squeeze together in their straight line. For a non-antebellum vision, there's St. Andrews Episcopal Church, circa 1871. Victorian Gothic in style, the church has made appearances in several films.

LA 10 continues over the gently rolling hills, through the woods to Greensburg. The St. Helena Parish Heritage Museum, in the old parish jail, circa 1855, displays memorabilia from the area's early days. Open daily. Admission is free. The Land Office Building, circa 1820, served as a clearinghouse for all public lands between the Mississippi and Pearl rivers north of New Orleans. Open weekdays. Located on the courthouse square.

La 10 crosses I-55 at Fluker. A short detour north to Tangipahoa, US 51, will take visitors to the Camp Moore Commemorative Area. The Confederate Museum and Visitor's Center here has been temporarily closed. Camp Moore boasts islands of trees in its wide-open field.

Camp Moore
between Fluker and Tangipahoa.

This was the site of one of the largest training camps for the Confederate army. A minor engagement was fought with Federal troops nearby from October 5 to October 9, 1861. The men buried in the cemetery here died of disease, mostly measles. Concrete benches are scattered under the oaks in the shade of the tree islands. The wooden bridge leading to the cemetery is deep in pine straw. One stone soldier, on a pedestal, watches over the tiny white markers. A fence around the graveyard keeps out the forest. Magnolia trees stand in the open spaces of the cemetery, guarding the outer edges. The smell of spring is cool and green, clean with scents of pine and jasmine. But outside the cool shade of the trees, the April sun is already relentless.

A railroad runs across the front entrance to the camp. It is easy to imagine the recruits from neighboring southern states disembarking as the trained soldiers left. No echoes of the training ground commands drown out the cardinals' songs or the rustling sound of unknown animals scurrying through the brush.

Back on LA 10, Franklinton nestles at a crossroads on the Bogue Chitto River. One of the best times of year to visit Franklinton is during the Washington Parish Fair in late October. The fairgrounds include a pioneer village with log cabins, syrup mill, blacksmith shop, church and general store.

Between Franklinton and Bogalusa, LA 10 crosses the Old Choctaw Trail, the "only official state road in Washington Parish until 1843," according to the historic marker at the intersection. The marker also claims that the Choctaw Indians cut the trail for trade with tribes in Baton Rouge, New Orleans, Biloxi and Mobile, and that white men are believed to have used the trails as early as the 16th century. The road north from the intersection, goes to Pine, passing dairy farms and country homes along the way. South from Pine, LA 62 takes travelers to LA 10 at Sheridan.

Traffic between Franklinton and Bogalusa often backs up behind log trucks with no chance of passing for miles. Easily frustrated motorists might not appreciate the unpretentious beauty of the countryside under such circumstances. All of LA 10 can be considered off the beaten track. It is a winding, narrow road for the most part, through empty country, farmlands, small towns. Tight schedules will have to be abandoned here.

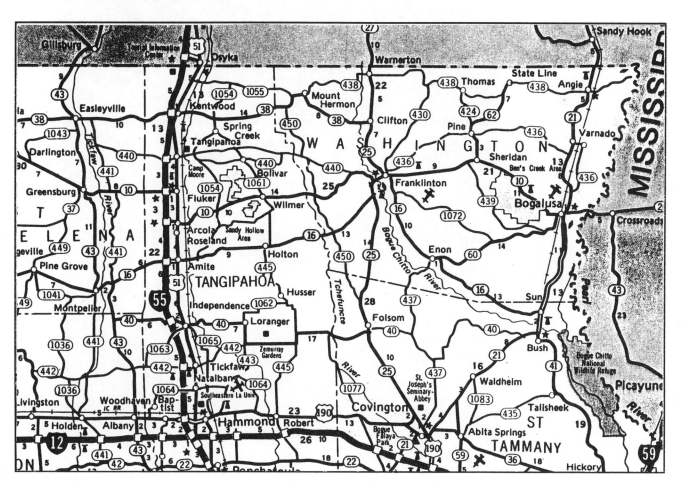

Bogalusa is pine country. Timber feeds the local economy. The tree-lined streets foretell the importance of summer shade while wrapping the town in a green blanket year round. Situated along the Pearl River, the area is popular with fishermen. Travelers passing through might want to stop at the Lake Vista Nature Preserve. A trail one mile long through the piney woods and around a cypress swamp are the major attractions. Picnicking is a perfect activity for the area. Spread your blanket on the ground by the glassy-surfaced lake, surrounded by willow, sweetgum and pine, and listen to a dozen different birds join in a lunchtime chorus. Huckleberry bushes are

Bogalusa, Road to the Pearl.

loaded with wild fruit in the summertime. If your timing is right, you might enjoy nature's bounty as dessert.

On down the road, at the Pearl's edge, a blue heron wades in the water. Boaters sit quietly, waiting, their motor turned off, their fishing rods extended. There's a sudden plop in the brown stained water.

LA 10 runs from St. Francisville, 110 miles from New Orleans on US 61, east to Bogalusa at the junction of LA 10 and LA 21. Bogalusa is about 73 miles north of New Orleans and about 100 miles northeast of Baton Rouge.

Overnight accommodations are available at Baton Rouge and St. Francisville, as well as at bed and breakfast establishments scattered about the area. Restaurants and fast food establishments are located in most towns.

For more information contact: Port Hudson Commemorative Area, P. O. Box 453, Zachary, LA 70791. Telephone 504-654-3775. (Port Hudson is located about 15 miles north of Baton Rouge on US 61.)

Baton Rouge Convention and Visitors Bureau, P.O. Drawer 4149, Baton Rouge, LA 70821. Telephone 504-383-1825. (Request information for plantation country north of Baton Rouge.)

Louisiana Office of Tourism, Box 94291, Baton Rouge, LA 70804-9291. Telephone 800-334-8626 or in Louisiana 504-342-8119.

28

Louisiana Postscript:
Fairs and Festivals

Louisiana residents celebrate their heritage and history in a variety of fairs and festivals each year. Visitors will find these occasions offer easy access to events and traditions that might otherwise be out of reach.

The Louisiana Association of Fairs and Festivals publishes an annual list of events, dates and contact addresses that are registered with their office. For a copy write Secretary, LAFF, Route 3, Box 174, DeRidder, LA 70634-9540. For information about other fairs and festivals contact the Louisiana Office of Tourism, Box 94291, Baton Rouge, LA 70804-9291. Telephone 800-334-8626 or in Louisiana 504-342-8119.

The most notorious Louisiana festival, Mardi Gras or carnival, has a host of satellite activities and celebrations. The dates for carnival change yearly. Mardi Gras Day is always the day before Ash Wednesday. In New Orleans the carnival season officially starts January 6, Twelfth Night, with the Twelfth Night Revelers Ball, the appearance of king cake and various frolics. The festivities don't let up until the beginning of Lent. Usually the two weeks preceding Ash Wednesday see the most intense partying and parading. Most of Louisiana celebrates Mardi Gras. Contact individual towns' chambers of commerce or tourist bureaus for specifics.

The following list of fairs and festivals are of events that usually are held at or around the same time each year. For the current status of a fair or festival contact the state department of tourism.

JANUARY
Cameron—Louisiana Fur and Wildlife Festival, second weekend.

FEBRUARY
Baton Rouge—LSU Jr. Livestock Show and Rodeo; LSU Open Live stock Show and Rodeo.
Broussard—Louisiana Boudin Festival, second weekend.
Delhi—Northeast Louisiana Livestock Show.

Logansport—Frontier Days.

New Orleans—Black Heritage Festival.

Opelousas—Bayou Ramble Tour of Homes, last full weekend.

MARCH

Amite—Tangipahoa Parish Fair; Amite Oyster Day.

Bogalusa—Dogwood Festival.

Covington—Spring Home and Garden Tour, last weekend.

Denham Springs—Spring Dog Show and Craft Sale, last Sunday.

Franklin—Annual Tour of Homes, last Sunday.

Grant Parish—Dogwood Trail and Festival, March/April.

Harrisonburg—Catahoula Dogwood Trail, late March/early April.

Houma—Southdown Sunday, March or April.

Iowa—Iowa Rabbit Festival.

Jackson—Assembly Antique Show and Sale, last weekend.

Lafayette—Azalea Trail, late March/early April.

New Orleans—Tennessee Williams Literary Festival; St. Patrick's Day parades and festivities; St. Joseph's Day parades and festivities.

St. Francisville—Audubon Pilgrimage, third week.

Sulphur—West Calcasieu Old Spanish Trail Association Festival.

Ville Platte—Boggy Bayou Festival.

APRIL

Abbeville—French Acadian Music Festival, second Saturday after Easter.

Covington—Chef Soirée.

DeQuincy—Louisiana Railroad Days Festival.

Folsom—The Country Market Arts and Crafts Show.

Gonzales—East Ascension Strawberry Festival.

Houma—Blessing of the Shrimp Fleet; Praline Festival.

Independence—Italian Festival, last Saturday.

Lafayette—Festival International de Louisiane.

Lake Charles—Contraband Days, late April/early May.

Napoleonville—Madewood Plantation Arts Festival, first weekend.

New Orleans—French Quarter Festival (celebrates history of the quarter); Spring Fiesta, first Friday after Easter; New Orleans Jazz and Heritage Festival, late April/early May; Easter Parade through the French Quarter.

Olla—Trade Days, first week.

Pleasant Hill—Battle of Pleasant Hill Re-enactment.

Ponchatoua—Strawberry Festival.

St. Bernard—Louisiana Crawfish Festival.

Shreveport—Holiday in Dixie (celebrates Louisiana Purchase), ten-day festival.

Slidell—Street Fair.
Thibodaux—Fireman's Parade & Festival, last week.
Walker—Louisiana Pine Festival.
Washington—Pilgrimage & Steamboat Festival, last week.
Winnfield—Louisiana Forest Festival.

MAY
Alexandria—Cenlabration, late May/early June.
Bastrop—ARK-LA-MISS Timberfest.
Baton Rouge—Flavour of Louisiana Plantation Weekend; River City
    Blues Festival; Fest for All.

THE FLAVOUR OF LOUISIANA

Blanchard—Poke Salad Festival, second weekend.
Breaux Bridge—Crawfish Festival, first weekend.
Chalmette—Tomato Festival, first weekend.
Cheneyville—Historic Tour and Arts & Crafts Festival, third Satur-
    day.
Coushatta—Olde Time Country Festival.
Covington—Art At The Park Festival.
Denham Springs—Great Amite River Catfish Festival.
Fisher—Sawmill Days Festival, fourth week.
Hammond—Louisiana Balloon Festival and Air Show, first full week-
    end; Heritage Day Festival, first Sunday; Southeast Louisiana Dairy
    Festival and Livestock Show.
Homer—Claiborne Parish Jubilee.
Houma—Cajun Country Opry, third weekend.
Logansport—River City Fest, first weekend.
Marion—Mayhaw Festival.
Mount Lebanon—Homecoming & Tour of Homes, first Sunday.
Shreveport—Rose Festival.
West Monroe—Ole Susannah's Bluegrass Festival.

JUNE
Baton Rouge—Bon Marche Arts and Crafts Show; United American
    Indian Pow-wow.
Galliano—South Laforche Cajun Festival, third weekend.
Gonzales—Jambalaya Festival, second full weekend.

Kenner—Okra Festival.

Lacombe—Bayou Lacombe Crab Fest.

Lafitte—World Championship Pirogue Races.

Mamou—Cajun Festival.

Mansfield—Louisiana Blueberry Festival; De Soto Fly-in.

Natchitoches—Melrose Arts and Crafts Festival, second weekend.

New Orleans—Cajun Fest; Popeye's Offshore Grand Prix; La Fete, late June/early July.

Ruston—Louisiana Peach Festival, third week.

Shreveport—Good Time Festival.

Slidell—Bayou Liberty Pirogue Race.

Sulphur—Louisiana Championship High School Rodeo.

JULY

Bogalusa—Louisiana Paper Festival.

Charenton—Chitamacha Indian Fair.

Church Point—Buggy Festival.

Des Allemands—Louisiana Catfish Festival, second weekend.

Erath—Fourth of July.

Farmerville—Watermelon Festival, last week.

Franklin—De Barbue Festival.

Franklinton—Washington Parish Watermelon Festival.

French Settlement—Louisiana Sauce Patate Festival, third Sunday.

Galliano—Louisiana Oyster Festival.

Grand Isle—International Grand Isle Tarpon Rodeo, third week.

Jennings—Bastille Day.

Kaplan—Bastille Day Celebration.

Natchitoches—Natchitoches/NSU Folk Festival, third weekend.

New Orleans—Food Festival; Bastille Day.

Slidell—Freedom Fest, Fourth of July.

West Monroe—Arts and Crafts Folk Festival, third weekend; Louisiana Legend Heritage Festival.

AUGUST

Delcambre—Shrimp Festival and Blessing of the Fleet, third weekend.

Empire—Southpass Tarpon Rodeo, second weekend.

Galliano—Cajun Heritage Festival.

Henderson—Cajun Crab Festival.

Hodges Gardens—Arts and Crafts Show, second weekend.

Lafayette—Acadian Village, Fete Des Acadiens; Bal De Maison; Louisiana Honey Festival.

Lafitte—Seafood Festival, second weekend.

Mandeville—Greater Mandeville Seafood Festival.

Star Hill (St. Francisville)—Bopotamus Festival.

SEPTEMBER
Abbeville—Tarpon Fishing Rodeo, Labor Day weekend.
Bastrop—North Louisiana Cotton Festival and Fair.
Denham Springs—Fall Dog Show, Labor Day; Louisiana Cow Dog
    Trials, last weekend.
DeRidder—Beauregard Parish Fair.
Gueydan—Duck Festival.
Houma—Pirogue Festival, Labor Day weekend; Southdown Market
    Place.
Jonesville—Louisiana Soybean Festival.
Lafayette—Festivals Acadiens, third weekend.
Lake Charles—Southwest Louisiana State Fair.
Luling—Alligator Festival.
Many—Sabine Fair Festival.
Monroe—Ouachita Riverfest.
Morgan City—Louisiana Shrimp and Petroleum Festival, Labor Day
    weekend.
New Iberia—Louisiana Sugar Cane Festival, last weekend.
Plaisance—Zydeco Festival, Saturday before Labor Day.
St. Francisville—Heritage Festival Salutes the Arts.
Thibodaux—Bayou Laforche Antique Show and Sale.
Vidalia—Chamberee.

OCTOBER
Abbeville—Cattle Festival and Fair, first weekend.
Angola—Louisiana State Prison Rodeo, Sunday afternoons all month.
Baton Rouge—Greater Baton Rouge State Fair, late October/early No-
    vember; Falls Crafts Festival.
Bridge City—Gumbo Festival, second weekend.
Chauvin—Lagniappe on the Bayou, second weekend.
Columbia—Art and Folk Festival, second weekend.
Covington—St. Tammany Parish Fair.
Crowley—International Rice Festival.
Franklin—International Alligator Festival.
Franklinton—Washington Parish Fair.
Houma—Cajun Country Opry, third weekend.
Keatchie—Heritage Day Festival, late October.
Lafayette—Louisiana Gulf Coast Oil Exposition, third week of Octo-
    ber in odd numbered years.
Laplace—Andouille Festival.
Larose—French Food Festival, last full weekend.

Livingston—Parish Fair.

Marthaville—Rebel State Commemorative Area Bluegrass Fest.

Metairie—Great Southern Louisiana State Fair.

Natchitoches—Annual Pilgrimage, second weekend.

New Orleans—Swamp Festival; Halloween.

New Roads—Pointe Coupee Fair and Festival, fourth week.

Opelousas—Louisiana Yambilee, last full weekend.

Plaquemine—International Acadian Festival.

Raceland—Sauce Piquante Festival, first weekend; La Vie La Fourchaise Festival.

Shreveport—Red River Revel; Festa Italiana; Louisiana State Fair, last ten days of month.

Sulphur—Calcasieu-Cameron Free Fair, first full week.

Ville Platte—Louisiana Cotton Festival, second week.

Youngsville—Festival of Beauties, first full weekend.

Zwolle—Tamale Fiesta, second weekend.

NOVEMBER

Basile—Louisiana Swine Festival, first weekend.

Bastrop—Morehouse Arts and Crafts Day, first Saturday.

Clinton—Louisiana Cycling Jambalaya Tours, Thanksgiving weekend.

Destrahan—Autumn Festival, second weekend.

Florien—Sabine Free State Festival, second weekend.

Grand Coteau—Festival de Grand Coteau.

Gretna—Mississippi River Fair & Trade Expo, first week.

Mamou—Armstice Day Celebration, November 11.

Ville Platte—All Saints' Day, November 1.

DECEMBER

Elizabeth—Christmas in the Country Festival.

Fort Jackson—Plaquemines Parish Fair & Orange Festival.

Franklin—Plantation Christmas Tour, first Sunday.

Gramercy—Bonfires on the Levee, Christmas Eve.

Hodges Gardens—Christmas Celebration, first Friday through 23rd.

Houma—Houma-Terrebonne Christmas Festival, first Saturday.

Jennings—Christmas Celebration, first two weeks.

Lafayette—A Cajun Christmas, all month.

Many—Christmas parade, second Saturday.

Monroe—Christmas Madrigal Dinners, first week.

Napoleonville—Madewood Plantation Christmas Heritage.

Natchitoches—Christmas Festival/Festival of Lights, first Saturday.

New Orleans—A Creole Christmas, all month.

St. Francisville—Christmas in the Country, first weekend.

Shreveport—Christmas in Roseland, day after Thanksgiving until New Year's Day.

Sulphur—Christmas parade, mid-month.

Vacherie—Oak Alley Plantation, Christmas Bonfire Party, second Saturday.

Index

NOTES